China's Securities M

MW01232702

This book provides an analysis of the development of the Chinese securities market, with special reference to the information disclosure regimes in Mainland China, UK and Hong Kong. It examines the listed companies, stock exchanges, securities companies, financial intermediaries, financial regulators and investor protection of the system in China, the UK and Hong Kong. The book looks at the role and functions of the securities regulatory commission, and highlights the details and insights that generally reveal the past and current status of the information disclosure regime in the Chinese securities market. By identifying problems and their reasons, the book forms an approach to further develop securities regulation.

Jing Bian teaches in the Faculty of Law and Social Sciences at SOAS, University of London, UK.

Routledge economic growth and development series

Series Editor Linda Yueh

Fellow by Special Election in Economics at St Edmund Hall and Director of the China Growth Centre, University of Oxford, UK

The aim of the series is to publish a series of books that applies rigorous economic analysis to the field of economic growth and development. The scope includes regional and country-specific studies, as well as cross-country comparisons, to examine the evidence surrounding the pressing and interesting questions on the growth prospects of developed and developing countries.

China's Securities Market

Towards efficient regulation

Jing Bian

LONDON AND NEW YORK

First published 2014 by Routledge

2 Park Square, Milton Park, Abingdon, Oxon OX14 4RN
711 Third Avenue, New York, NY 10017, USA

Routledge is an imprint of the Taylor & Francis Group, an informa business

First issued in paperback 2016

British Library Cataloguing in Publication Data
A catalogue record for this book is available from the British Library

Library of Congress Cataloging in Publication Data
Bian, Jing, 1976–
China's securities market : towards efficient regulation / Jing Bian.
    pages cm. – (Routledge economic growth and development series ; 2)
    Includes bibliographical references and index.
    1. Capital market–China. 2. Securities–China. 3. Stock exchanges–
    China. 4. Finance–China. I. Title.
    HG5782.B43 2014
    332'.04150951–dc23   2013030990

ISBN: 978-0-415-82277-0 (hbk)
ISBN: 978-1-138-20590-1 (pbk)

Typeset in Times
by Wearset Ltd, Boldon, Tyne and Wear

To those who love me for nothing and to those whom I have lost forever.

Contents

.

Figures

Tables

Preface

The Chinese securities market has been established and remarkably improved in a relatively short period. However, it still remains at an early stage with a developing supervision mechanism on information disclosure. It has been adversely affected by malpractices of violations of the information disclosure regulations: many incidents and scandals have caused significant negative impacts to the market.

The book provides a critical and comparative legal analysis of the development of the Chinese securities market, with special reference to the information disclosure regimes in Mainland China, UK and Hong Kong. It aims to examine the supervision mechanism of information disclosure, the transparency of the securities market and the legislative techniques of information disclosure in the Chinese securities market. In this book, legislative and case studies have been carried out. In addition, relevant theories are reviewed, including information asymmetry, Efficient Market Hypothesis and corporate governance theory. Further issues, for instance listed companies and stock exchanges, have been examined. Moreover, the following topics have been covered: how to evaluate the performance of the securities companies, in particular, in the aspect of information disclosure? How to further enhance the regulatory regime for the Chinese intermediaries? Is the China Securities Regulatory Commission efficient? Has the Chinese legal system provided the investor with a strong legal protection framework?

The book generally reveals the past and current status of the information disclosure regime in the Chinese securities market. Although much has been achieved, there is still a long way to go. With the identification of problems and the causes, an approach to further develop the securities regulation can be identified, in particular with regards to the information disclosure system in China. Reforms are needed both to the current legislation and to the practices and procedures of regulation.

Acknowledgements

This book is based on my original PhD research. In preparing the book, special appreciation is owed to my research panel: Dr Richard Alexander, Professor Laixiang Sun and Dr Sanzhu Zhu. In the company of their encouragement, inspiration and guidance, I have completed my book. Without their continuing help over the years, the research would have remained fruitless. In particular, with their continuing support, I brought myself into the academic world. I would also like to give my special thanks to those who directed, advised and motivated me.

In conducting my PhD research, funding was received from the Central Research Fund (University of London), Great Britain–China Centre, SOAS Additional Fieldwork Award, SOAS Conference Grant and AHRC Generic Training Fund. I am grateful for the generous support from them.

Additional thanks are given to my mother and brother, who generously support me all the time. Appreciations are given to Mr John Gears and Mrs Shirley Gears, who made England my second home during my study. I am also grateful to the editors.

This book is especially for those who love me for nothing and for those whom I have lost forever.

Abbreviations

AIM	Alternative Investment Market
BCBS	Basel Committee on Banking Supervision
CBRC	China Banking Regulatory Commission
CEO	Chief Executive Officer
CIRC	China Insurance Regulatory Commission
CGSDTC	China Government Securities Depository Trust & Clearing Co. Ltd
CRAs	Credit Rating Agencies
CSDCC	China Securities Depository and Clearing Corporation Limited
CSRC	China Securities Regulatory Commission
DTR	Disclosure Rules and Transparency Rules
ESMA	European Securities and Markets Authority
EU	European Union
FCA	Financial Conduct Authority
FSA	Financial Services Authority
FSCS	Financial Services Compensation Scheme
FSMA2000	Financial Services and Markets Act 2000
GEB	Growth Enterprise Board
GFCI	Global Financial Centres Index
HKCC	Hong Kong Clearing Corporation Limited
HKEx	Hong Kong Exchanges and Clearing Limited
HKFE	Hong Kong Futures Exchange Limited
HKSE	Hong Kong Stock Exchange
IAIS	International Association of Insurance Supervisors
IASB	International Accounting Standards Board
IAS	International Accounting Standards
IASC	International Accounting Standards Committee
ICBC	Industrial and Commercial Bank of China
ICC	Investor Compensation Company Limited
IOSCO	International Organization of Securities Commissions
IPO	initial public offering
LR	Listing Rules
LSE	London Stock Exchange
M&A	merger and acquisition

MiFID	Markets in Financial Instruments Directive
MOFCOM	Ministry of Commerce
MOU	Memorandum of Understanding
NDRC	National Development and Reform Commission
NPC	National People's Congress
OECD	Organization for Economic Cooperation and Development
OTC	over-the-counter
PBOC	People's Bank of China
PRA	Prudential Regulation Authority
PRC	People's Republic of China
QDIIs	Qualified Domestic Institutional Investors
QFIIs	Qualified Foreign Institutional Investors
RNS	Regulatory News Service
RMB	Renminbi (Chinese currency)
RMBS	Residential Mortgage-backed Securities
SAC	Securities Association of China
SAIC	State Administration for Industry and Commerce
SARs	Special Administrative Regions
SASAC	State-owned Assets Supervision and Administration Commission
SCSC	State Council Securities Committee
SDIC	State Development & Investment Corporation
SEC	Securities and Exchange Commission
SFC	Securities and Futures Commission
SFCO	Securities and Futures Commission Ordinance
SFO	Securities and Futures Ordinance
SIPF	China Securities Investor Protection Fund Companies Limited
SMEs	Small and Medium-sized Enterprises
SSE	Shanghai Stock Exchange
SOE	State-owned enterprise
SPC	Supreme People's Court
SZSE	Shenzhen Stock Exchange
UK	United Kingdom
UKLA	UK Listing Authority
UNCTAD	United Nations Conference on Trade and Development

List of legislation and international agreements

People's Republic of China

Central Committee of the Chinese Communist Party

Decision of the Central Committee of the Chinese Communist Party on Several Issues Concerning the Reform of Economic System (adopted at the Third Plenary Session of the 12th CPC Central Committee on 20 October 1984)

1993 Decision of Central Committee of CPC on Several Issues Concerning the Establishing the Socialist Market Economy Structure (issued by the Central Committee of CPC on 14 November 1993)

The National People's Congress and its Standing Committee

1985 Accounting Law of the People's Republic of China (adopted by the Ninth Session of the Standing Committee of the Sixth National People's Congress on 21 January 1985, and amended in 1993 and 1999 respectively, then came into force on 1 July 2000)

1986 General Principles of Civil Law (adopted at the Fourth Session of the Sixth National People's Congress on 12 April 1986 and promulgated by Order No. 37 of the President of the People's Republic of China on 12 April 1986)

1993 Company Law of the People's Republic of China (adopted by the Fifth Session of the Standing Committee of the Eighth National People's Congress on 29 December 1993, revised 25 December 1999 and further amended on 28 August 2004 and 27 October 2005, and came into force on 1 January 2006)

1995 Commercial Bank Law of the People's Republic of China (adopted at the 13th Session of the Standing Committee of the Eighth National People's Congress on 10 May 1995, and amended according to the Decision on Modifying the Law of the People's Republic of China on Commercial Banks as adopted by the Sixth Session of the Standing Committee of the Tenth National People's Congress on 27 December 2003, and came into force on 1 February 2004)

1995 Law of the People's Bank of China of the People's Republic of China (adopted at the Third Session of the Eighth National People's Congress on 18 March 1995, and amended according to the Decisions on Revising the 'Law of the People's Republic of China on the People's Bank of China' at the Sixth Session of the Standing Committee of the Tenth National People's Congress on 27 December 2003)

1997 Criminal Law of the People's Republic of China (adopted by the Second Session of the Fifth National People's Congress on 1 July 1979, then amended by the Fifth Session of the Eighth National People's Congress on 14 March 1997 and came into force on 1 October 1997)

1998 Securities Law of the People's Republic of China (adopted by the Sixth Session of the Standing Committee of the Ninth National People's Congress on 29 December 1998, amended 27 October 2005, and came into force on1 January 2006)

1999 Accounting Law of the People's Republic of China (adopted by the Ninth Session of the Standing Committee of the Sixth National People's Congress on 21 January 1985; amended in 1993, 1999. The amendment came into force on 1 July 2000)

2003 Securities Investment Fund Law of the People's Republic of China (adopted by the Fifth Session of the Standing Committee of the Tenth National People's Congress on 28 October 2003 and came into force on 1 June 2004, replacing 1997 Tentative Rules of Securities Investment Funds)

2006 Amendment (VI) to the Criminal Law of the People's Republic of China (adopted at the 22nd meeting of the Standing Committee of the Tenth National People's Congress on 29 June 2006, and came into force as of the date of promulgation)

2007 Lawyer's Law of the People's Republic of China (adopted at the 19th Session of the Standing Committee of the Eighth National People's Congress on 15 May 1996; amended according to the Decision on Amending the Law on Lawyers of the People's Republic of China at the 25th Session of the Standing Committee of the Ninth National People's Congress on 29 December 2001; and revised at the 30th Session of the Tenth National People's Congress on 28 October 2007, 2nd revision on 26 October 2012)

2007 Property Law of the People's Republic of China (adopted at the Fifth Session of the Tenth National People's Congress on 16 March 2007, came into force on 1 October 2007)

2009 Amendment (VII) to the Criminal Law of the People's Republic of China (adopted at the Seventh Session of the Standing Committee of the 11th National People's Congress of the People's Republic of China on 28 February 2009, came into force on 28 February 2009.)

Amendment (VIII) to the Criminal Law of the People's Republic of China (adopted at the 19th meeting of the Standing Committee of the 11th National People's Congress of the People's Republic of China on 25 February 2011, came into force on 1 May 2011)

The State Council and its Ministries and Commissions

1987 Interim Regulation on Administration of Corporate Bond (issued by the State Council on 27 March 1987)

1988 Opinions (I) of the Supreme People's Court on Several Issues concerning the Implementation of the General Principles of the Civil Law of the People's Republic of China (For Trial Implementation) (promulgated on 26 January 1988, came into force on 26 January 1988)

1993 Provisional Regulation of the Qualification for Provision of Securities Legal Services by Lawyers and Law Firms (issued by the Ministry of Justice and the CSRC and on 12 January 1993)

1993 Interim Provisions on the Management of the Issuing and Trading of Stocks (issued by the State Council and came into force on 22 April 1993)

1993 Regulation on Administration of Corporate Bond (issued by the State Council on 2 August 1993 and came into force on 2 August 1993)

1993 Standard Rules on Enterprise Accounting (issued by the Ministry of Finance on 30 November 1992 came into effect on 1 July 1993)

2001 Accounting Systems for Business Enterprises (issued by the Ministry of Finance on 29 December 2000 and came into force on 1 January 2001, replacing the 1998 Accounting System for Joint Stock Limited Enterprises)

2001 Notice of the Supreme People's Court on Temporary Refusal of Filings of Securities Related Civil Compensation Cases (No. 406 [2001] of the Supreme People's Court 21 September 2001)

2002 Notice of the Supreme People's Court on Relevant Issues of Filing of Civil Tort Dispute Cases Arising From False Statement in the Securities Market (No. 43 [2002] of the Supreme People's Court 15 January 2002)

2003 Several Provisions of the Supreme People's Court on Hearing Civil Compensation Cases Arising from False Statement in Securities Market (No. 2 [2003] of the Supreme People's Court 9 January 2003)

2004 Several Opinions on Promoting the Reform and Opening-up and the Stable Development of the Capital Market (issued by the State Council and came into force on 31 January 2004)

2005 Guiding Opinions on Share-trading Reform of Listed Companies (issued by the Ministry of Finance, the Ministry of Commerce, People's Bank of China, State-owned Assets Supervision and Administration Commission, and the CSRC on 23 August 2005 and came into force on 23 August 2005)

2006 Circular of the General Office of the State Council on Several Issues about Rigorously Cracking Down on Illegal Issuance of Stocks and Illegal Operation of Securities Business (No. 99 [2006] of the General Office of the State Council) (issued by the General Office of the State Council and came into force on 12 December 2006)

2006 Provisions of the Supreme People's Court on Several Issues concerning the Application of the PRC Company Law (1) (issued by the Supreme People's Court on 28 April 2006 and came into force on 9 May 2006)

2007 Measures for the Administration of the Provision of Securities Legal

Services by Law Firms (adopted at the chairmen's meeting of China Securities Regulatory Commission and the executive meeting of the Ministry of Justice on 09 March 2007 and came into force on 1 May 2007)

2008 Provisions of the Supreme People's Court on Several Issues concerning the Application of the PRC Company Law (2) (issued by the Supreme People's Court on 12 May 2008 and came into force 19 May 2008)

2008 Circular of Relevant Issues concerning Suppression of Illegal Securities Activities (issued jointly by the Supreme People's Court, the Supreme People's Procuratorate, the Ministry of Public Security and the CSRC and came into force on 2 January 2008)

2008 Regulation on the Supervision and Administration of Securities Companies (adopted by the 6th Executive Meeting of the State Council on 23 April 2008 and came into force on 1 June 2008)

2009 Issues on Opinions of the State Council on Promoting the Development of Shanghai's Modern Service Industry and Advanced Manufacturing Industry, and Promoting the Construction of Shanghai International Financial Centre and International Shipping Centre (issued by State Council on 29 April 2009)

2010 Rules for the Securities Legal Practices of Law Firms (for Trial Implementation) (issued by Ministry of Justice and CSRC on 20 October 2010 and came into force on 1 January 2011)

2010 Detailed Practicing Rules for the Legal Services of Law Firms for Securities Investment Funds (for Trial Implementation) (issued by Ministry of Justice and CSRC on 20 October 2010 and came into force on 1 January 2011)

Securities and Banking Regulatory Authorities

1990 Provisional Regulations on Securities Firms (issued by the People's Bank of China on 12 October 1990, came into force on 12 October 1990)

1993 Standards for Disclosure by Companies Issuing Shares to General Public: No. 1: Content and Format of Prospectus (for trial use) (issued by CSRC and came into force on 8 July 1993)

1993 Interim Administrative Measures for the Issuing and Transaction of Securities (issued by the SCSC on 22 April 1993, came into force on 22 April 1993)

1993 Interim Measures for the Prohibition of Issuing Securities by Fraudulence Means (issued by the SCSC on 2 September 1993, came into force on 2 September 1993)

2001 Code of Corporate Governance for Listed Companies (issued by the CSRC and State Economic and Trade Commission and came into force on 7 January 2001)

2001 Measures on the Management of Clients' Transaction and Settlement Funds (issued by the CSRC on 16 May 2001 and came into force on 1 January 2002)

2001 Administrative Measures on Stock Exchange (issued by the CSRC and came into force 12 December 2001)

2003 Rules of Corporate Governance of Securities Companies (Trial) (issued by the CSRC on 15 December 2003 and came into force on 15 January 2004)

2003 Rules for Credit Rating Agencies on Issuing Rating Report of Bond of Securities Companies (issued by the CSRC on 29 August 2003 and came into force on 8 October 2003)

2003 Guidance on Internal Control for Securities Companies (issued by the CSRC on 15 December 2003 and came into force on 15 December 2003)

2004 Interim Measures for the Administration of Bonds of Securities Companies (issued by the CSRC on 29 August 2003, revised on 15 October 2004)

2004 Circular of the China Securities Regulatory Commission on Several Issues Concerning the Promotion of Innovation Activities in Securities Industry (issued by the CSRC on 12 August 2004 and came into force on 12 August 2004, repealed on 10 April 2009)

2004 Circular on Several Issues concerning the Book-building Procedure for IPOs (issued by the CSRC on 7 December 2004 and came into force on 1 January 2005)

2005 Administrative Measures of Securities Investor Protection Fund (issued by the CSRC on 30 June 2005 and came into force on 1 July 2005)

2005 Rules of the CSRC on Complaint Letters and Visits Work (Trial) (issued by the CSRC on 14 July 2005)

2005 Measures on Administration of Split Share Structure Reform of Listed Companies (issued by the CSRC and came into force on 4 September 2005)

2005 Measures of Freezing and Sealing up Account (issued by the CSRC on 30 December 2005 and came into force on 1 January 2006, revised on 23 May 2011, and came into force on 1 October 2011)

2006 Measures for Applying for the Use of Securities Investor Protection Fund (Trial) (issued by the CSRC on 7 March 2006 and came into force on 7 March 2006)

2006 Guidelines for the Articles of Association of Listed Companies (issued by the CSRC and came into force on 16 March 2006)

2006 Measures on Administration of the Initial Public Offering and Listing of Shares (issued by the CSRC on 17 May 2006 and came into force on 18 May 2006)

2006 Measures for the Administration of the Takeover of Listed Companies (issued by the CSRC on 31 July 2006 and came into force 1 September 2006, then amended on 27 August 2008)

2006 Measures on Administration of the Offering of Securities by Listed Companies (issued by the CSRC on 6 May 2006 and came into force on 8 May 2006)

2006 Criteria No. 1 on the Content and Format of Information Disclosure by Companies Conducting Public Offer of Securities – Prospectus (issued by the CSRC and came into force on 18 May 2006)

2006 Administrative Measures for the Risk Control Indexes of Securities Companies (issued by the CSRC on 5 July 2006 and came into force on 5 July 2006, revised on 24 June 2008)

2006 Regulation on Domestic Securities Investment by Qualified Foreign Institutional Investors (issued jointly by the CSRC, People's Bank of China and

State Administration of Foreign Exchange on 24 August 2006 and came into force on 1 September 2006, replacing the 2002 Temporary Regulation on Domestic Securities Investment by Qualified Foreign Institutional Investors)

2007 Administration Measures for the Disclosure of Information of Listed Companies (issued by the CSRC and came into force on 30 January 2007)

2007 Implementation Measures for the Payment of Securities Investor Protection Funds by Securities Companies (Trial) (issued by the CSRC on 28 March 2007 and came into force on 1 January 2007)

2007 Provisional Regulation on Overseas Securities Investment by Qualified Domestic Institutional Investors (issued by the CSRC on 18 June 2007 and came into force on 5 July 2007)

2007 The Interim Measures for the Administration of the Credit Rating Business Regarding the Securities Market (issued by the CSRC on 24 August 2007 and came into force on 1 September 2007)

2008 Standards on the Contents and Format of an Annual Report of a Securities Company (issued by the CSRC on 19 November 1999, revised on 4 February 2002 and 14 January 2008)

2008 Guiding Opinions on the Listed Companies' Transfer of Original Shares Released from Trading Restrictions (issued by the CSRC on 20 April 2008 and came into force on 20 April 2008)

2008 The Compilation Rules for Information Disclosure by Companies that Offer Securities to the Public: Special Provisions for Information Disclosure of Commercial Banks (issued by the CSRC on 25 July 2008, and came into force on 1 September 2008)

2009 Provisions on Strengthening the Supervision and Administration of Listed Securities Companies (issued by the CSRC on 3 April 2009 and came into force on 3 April 2009, revised on 30 June 2010)

2009 Tentative Measures for the Administration of the Initial Public Offering of Shares and the Listing thereof on the Growth Enterprise Board (issued by the CSRC on 31 March 2009 and came into force on 1 May 2009)

2009 Provisions on the Classified Supervision and Administration of Securities Companies (issued by the CSRC on 26 May 2009and came into force on 26 May 2009, revised on 14 May 2010)

2009 Interim Provisions on the Eligibility Management of Investors in the Growth Enterprise Market (issued by the CSRC on 30 June 2009 and came into force on 15 July 2009)

2012 Contents and Formats of Information Disclosure by Companies Offering Securities to the Public No. 2 – Contents and Format of an Annual Report (latest revision date 19 September 2012 and came into force 1 January 2013)

2012 Rules for Governance of Securities Companies (issued by the CSRC on 11 December 2012 and came into force on 1 January 2013)

Local Authorities

1992 Provisional Regulations of Shanghai Municipality on Companies Limited by Shares (issued by Shanghai Municipal People's Government on18 May 1992 and came into force on 1 June 1992)

1993 Regulations of Shenzhen Special Economic Zone on Companies Limited by Shares (adopted at the Fifth Session of the First Shenzhen Municipal People's Congress on 26 April 1993, and came into force on 1 October 1993)

2009 Draft Regulations of Shanghai Municipality on Promoting the Building of International Financial Centre (adopted by the 12th Session of the Standing Committee of the 13th Shanghai People's Congress on 25 June 2009 and came into force on 1 August 2009)

2012 Rules Governing the Listing of Stocks on Shanghai Stock Exchange (promulgated by the SSE on 8 June 2001 and amended 25 February and further amendment on 29 November 2004 and came into force on 10 December 2004, the seventh revision in July 2012)

2012 Rules Governing the Listing of Stocks on Shenzhen Stock Exchange (promulgated by the SZSE on 7 June 2001 and amended 24 February 2002 and further amendment on 29 November 2004, and came into force on 10 December 2004, the seventh revision in July 2012)

EU

Directive 2004/39/EC of the European Parliament and of the Council on Markets in Financial Instruments Directive

2008 Proposal for a Regulation of the European Parliament and of the Council on Credit Rating Agencies

2009 Regulation (EC) No. 1060/2009 of the European Parliament and of the Council on Credit Rating Agencies

The United Kingdom

Legislation

Companies Act 1985
Financial Services Act 1986
Company Directors Disqualification Act 1986
Criminal Justice Act 1993
Financial Services and Markets Act 2000
Companies Act 2006
The Credit Rating Agencies Regulations 2010
Financial Services Act 2012

Regulations

FSA Handbook
Listing Rules
Prospectus Rules
Disclosure Rules and Transparency Rule
Conduct of Business Sourcebook
FCA Disclosure and Transparency Rules
FCA Listing Rules
FCA Prospectus Rules

Hong Kong SAR

1974 Securities Ordinance
2002 Securities and Futures Ordinance
2004 Code on Corporate Governance Practices
2004 Companies Ordinance
2005 Code on Takeovers and Mergers and Shares Repurchase
2006 Circular to Intermediaries Licensed or Registered for Type 6 Regulated Activity
2010 Rules Governing the Listing of Securities on the Stock Exchange of Hong Kong Limited
2010 Code on Unlisted Structured Investment Products
2011 Code of Conduct for Persons providing Credit Rating Services

United States

Public Company Accounting Reform and Investor Protection Act 2002 (Sarbanes–Oxley Act)

International

1886 Berne Convention for the Protection of Literacy and Art Works

UNCTAD

2006 International Standards of Accounting and Reporting

IOSCO

2002 Principles for Ongoing Disclosure and Material Development Reporting by Listed Entities
2002 Investor Disclosure and Informed Decisions: Use of Simplified Prospectuses by Collective Investment Schemes
2003 Objectives and Principles of Securities Regulation

2004 Financial Disclosure in the Banking, Insurance and Securities Sectors: Issues and Analysis, Joint Forum (by IOSCO, BCBS and IAIS)

2004 Code of Conduct Fundamentals for Credit Rating Agencies

2007 International Disclosure Principles for Cross-Border Offerings and Listings of Debt Securities by Foreign Issuers – Final Report

2007 Final Report of International Disclosure Principles for Cross-border Offerings and Listings of Debt Securities by Foreign Issuers

2008 Code of Conduct Fundamentals for Credit Rating Agencies

OECD

1999 OECD Principles of Corporate Governance

2004 OECD Principles of Corporate Governance

IASB

1989 International Financial Reporting Standards

Introduction

The Chinese securities market has gained significant developments in the last few years. Information disclosure, as one of the central issues in the securities market, has been established gradually. It directly influences the trading price of securities and subsequently imposes an impact on the distribution of profits. At the same time, it is also one of the principal approaches for the effective regulation and supervision of the securities market. Moreover, the global financial market is in the forefront of evolution. Whilst the creation and application of complex financial products and new technology are more frequent, the occurrence of cross border financial activity is increasing. Many financial crimes, such as insider dealing and market manipulation, are related to the failure to disclose information. Much has been said, much has been written and much has been researched regarding transparency and disclosure in the recent financial crisis, all of these comments suggest an enhanced regulatory regime for information disclosure.

China's securities market has been established and remarkably improved in a relatively short period since the economic reforms. However, the Chinese securities market still remains at an early stage with a supervisory mechanism on information disclosure which needs to be further enhanced. The securities market in China has been affected by malpractices of violation of the information disclosure regulations. Many incidents, such as the Guangxia (Yinchuan) Industrial Co., Ltd case and the Zhejiang Hangxiao Steel Structure Co., Ltd case have caused significantly negative impacts on the market.[1] Facing the challenges internationally and nationally, the quality of information disclosure and its regulatory structure need to be improved. Therefore, the study of the nature and effectiveness of the information disclosure regime will have both theoretical and practical resonance for China. This book, taking the information disclosure regime as an example, examines the development of the Chinese securities market, transparency of the securities market, and the legislative techniques of information disclosure.

Since the establishment of the Chinese securities market, the introduction of best practices into the domestic market has been sought. This book conducts a comparative study between Mainland China, the United Kingdom and the Hong Kong Special Administrative Region (SAR).[2] To examine the regulatory approaches in the developed markets and find suitable models for China this book seeks to further improve the structure of the Chinese regulatory framework. Relatively comprehensive information disclosure regimes have been established in the mature markets. Although some scandals happened in the UK, the legal control of corporate disclosure can still be seen as one of the effective models in the world. Hong Kong, as one of the major financial centres in the world, is well-known for its sophisticated financial regulatory environment. Also, as the 'gateway' for inward and outward investments in China, Hong Kong has significant interaction with Mainland China. There were 148 Mainland companies listed on the Hong Kong stock exchanges (Main Board) at the end of April 2013.[3] Moreover, the dual listing has enabled a number of Hong Kong listed companies to announce their intention to raise funds via the Chinese markets. One explanation for the lack of effective control may be the inadequacy of international cooperation. Facing the challenges from the global financial crisis, it is important for China to adopt disclosure requirements in line with international standards.

Primarily, this book focuses on the study of legislation. Regulating the securities market is a complex issue; therefore, the study is based on detailed discussion and analysis of the law, regulation and rules. It must be accepted that the Chinese securities market is undergoing continuing reform. Hence, the regulating system for corporate disclosure is improving constantly. In this book, only the most important and relevant legal documents have been chosen for examination. The following laws and regulations, particularly with special regard to information disclosure, form part of the examples discussed in this book: relevant parts of Chinese Company Law, Securities Law, General Principle of Civil Law and Criminal Law; from the UK perspective, Companies Act 2006, Financial Services and Markets Act 2000, Financial Services Authority (FSA) Regulatory Handbook, Financial Conduct Authority (FCA) Regulatory Handbook; from the Hong Kong jurisdiction Company Ordinance, Securities and Futures Ordinance, Securities and Future Commission (SFC) Regulatory Handbook. Another important aspect is the international public law and 'soft' law, such as the international and regional treaties and agreements, for instance: International Organization of Securities Commissions (IOSCO) documents; International Financial Reporting Standard; Organization for Economic Cooperation and Development (OECD) Principles of Corporate Governance; United Nations Conference on Trade and Development (UNCTAD) International Standards of Accounting and Reporting.

Case study is an essential approach in this research. Civil litigation arising from false or misleading statements made by Chinese listed companies on the securities market has affected a large number of shareholders and investors. A series of cases have been analysed with the aim of finding how to improve the regulation of information disclosure and thereby reduce market malpractice. This book includes typical cases which have had tremendous impacts on the securities market, for instance: Guangxia (Yinchuan) Industrial Co., Ltd case, Zhejiang Hangxiao Steel Structure Co., Ltd case and Securities & Futures Commission v Cheung, Yeung,

Li, Chan and Styland Holdings.[4] On the basis of the examination and discussion on these cases, further possible improvements have been suggested.

Due to the comparative approach of this book, the sources are both Chinese and English. As for the discussion about China, the materials are mainly in Chinese, including books, articles, news reports, newspapers and commentaries from Chinese officials, scholars and practitioners. Furthermore, the websites of the regulatory bodies, stock exchanges and listed companies have provided essential contents. English sources are important components. In particular, the arguments of Chinese and western scholars have been analysed. The literature in English is the source for the UK and Hong Kong perspectives, and at the international or EU level.

Data collected through field work in Mainland China, UK and Hong Kong has been included in the book. I have interviewed government officials, financial regulators, legal scholars, practitioners and the senior management of listed companies. Furthermore, my own working experience in Mainland China, UK and Hong Kong enabled me to re-think and re-examine the topic from a more practical approach.

Libraries in China, UK and Hong Kong were visited in order to collect data and information from relevant materials. The libraries of the School of Oriental and African Studies (University of London), Institute of Advanced Legal Studies (University of London) and University of Hong Kong were particularly helpful. Lastly, personal visits to the stock exchanges and securities companies in Mainland China and Hong Kong enabled me to understand the securities markets on a new level. Moreover, some of the English translations of Chinese law are referenced from bilingual websites.[5]

Discussion and analysis of the law and regulations, and their inclusion in this book, is mainly addressed in chronological order. The current situation can be seen as tightly linked to problems in the past; therefore, conducting an investigation into the past regulatory regime may help to examine present issues. Based on the study of the emerging stage, earlier regulatory phases, the current situation of the disclosure regime has been analysed in sequence. However, while the key focus of this book is financial regulation, less attention has been given to theoretical issues. Notably, the information disclosure regime itself contains vast detailed legal requirements. The process is mainly being illustrated in a mode which combines the concepts, overview, theory review, problem investigation, factor analysis, consequence exploration and comparative study. More particularly this book is not only focusing on the disclosure requirements, but observes the regime as a whole. Systemically, it examines the theoretical and practical issues, listed companies and stock exchanges, securities companies, financial intermediaries, financial regulators and investor protection regarding information disclosure.

Being one of the world's fastest and largest growing economies, China obviously deserves great attention. However, the risks and challenges faced by the Chinese economy, and particularly for the purpose of this book, the Chinese securities market, cannot be overlooked. A rising China will find the environment more resistant if she is not able to discover and subsequently correct the existing and potential problems ahead. The global market is putting more stress on the financial and economic aspects of the Chinese financial system regardless of their political backgrounds; for instance, the appreciation of the Chinese currency, the degree that the securities market is being opened up and the extent of the foreign exchange control. The pressure is inhibiting global economic recovery after the economic crisis, as well as the healthy growth of the Chinese securities market.

As for the problems of the information disclosure system, existing literature has examined the conflicts of the fast growing economic phenomenon and obstacles inside China from several different perspectives, for instance, motivation, firm performance, share structure and corporate governance. But more often, the literature is restricted to the corporate level and ignores the overall influences of the historic background, legal framework, financial intermediaries, financial regulator and investor education as a whole; in particular, under a globalized and cross-border business environment. The Chinese securities market is complicated by the high degree of socio-political and socio-economic pressure. Therefore, this book tries to look at the securities markets by means of a systemic study.

This book will address the issue from the following aspects:

1   The reliability of disclosure, historical problems and the current situation
2   The dissemination of financial information by companies
3   The processing of information by financial intermediaries
4   The overseeing of the disclosure regime by the financial regulators
5   What are the consequences of information asymmetry, and in particular, how can investor protection be improved?
6   The effectiveness of the laws and regulations concerning disclosure in the light of promoting a modern securities market

The theory and practice

What are the basic theories in the aspect of information disclosure? To examine the questions addressed in this book, an understanding of the various methodological mechanisms historically and currently employed in the research of the information disclosure regime is needed. The hypotheses and methods provided by the earlier researchers are particularly helpful. Furthermore, to what extent do these hypotheses and theories apply to the Chinese securities market? What are the real reasons for the problems inside the Chinese securities market? An extra question arising is, what is the contribution of these hypotheses and theories to the development of the Chinese securities market?

To address the above issues in this book, the past and present structure of the information disclosure regime in China has been examined. First of all the definition of information disclosure is examined. Relevant theories are introduced from both an international and national level; for instance, the information asymmetry, and Efficient Market Hypothesis. Moreover, based on the literature reviewed, the actuality of the Chinese information disclosure regime has been analysed. Following this the regulatory regime in the UK, Hong Kong and some selected international standards are discussed.

The listed companies and stock exchanges

In respect of information disclosure, are Chinese listed companies well regulated, and are the stock exchanges in China functioning well? The legal, cultural, political and economic conditions inevitably influence the information disclosure regime. To a certain extent, malpractices that relate to corporate disclosure are not new in Mainland China. To a degree imperfect information disclosure has assisted law breaking behaviour. In exploring the causations, the key considerations are whether the Chinese disclosure regime has been well designed and whether the channel for dissemination of information is efficient enough. Also, are the stock exchanges performing as the 'front line' regulators?

This book analyses the internal and external relationship between information disclosure rules, listed companies and stock exchanges in order to suggest an effective regulatory regime. Basic information on listed companies has been studied. Moreover, the detailed disclosure requirements have been examined. Beyond this, a comparative study between Mainland China, UK and Hong Kong has been carried out. Studies on the function of the stock exchanges have been made. This book suggests that the information disclosure regime is an efficient approach to preventing and controlling the offences and crimes conducted by listed companies; and the stock exchanges can perform a unique role in this aspect.

The securities companies

As for the securities companies, how to evaluate the performance of them, in particular in the aspect of information disclosure? Whether the corporate disclosure regime can serve as a valuable means to enhance the regulation and supervision of Chinese companies? The approach of market development itself (particularly in an emerging and transitional one, which has experienced many difficulties such as the ownership problem, weak governance and insufficient investor protection) may not be able to settle all these dilemmas. With respect to these questions, taking securities companies as an example, the book investigates the inter-relationship between regulatory behaviour and the information disclosure systems.

Currently, the Chinese securities markets' emerging and transitional nature has determined that securities companies are still in the process of development. Typical problems have been concentrated on: lack of transparency; misappropriation of clients' funds; misleading and false disclosure; or even non-disclosure. Information disclosure is essentially important to the regulatory regime of securities companies. Considering the nature of the business, securities companies are in a more advantaged position than the general public. They are responsible for huge amounts of funds.[6] Furthermore, the mixed operation system (which means the business involves the banking, securities and insurance sectors) has emerged in Mainland China. Therefore, when the securities companies are dealing with clients, the prevention and control of conflict of interest must be considered. It has been illustrated in the western system that a conflict of interest is likely to occur due to the close linkage between different departments within a comprehensive financial institution. A Chinese wall or Firewall mechanism that aims to separate the different branches, and further prevent the leaks of information inside an institution, is required to be established and further enhanced. All these factors are called on to improve information disclosure in an effective and practical manner.

The financial intermediaries

How to further enhance the regulatory regime for Chinese intermediaries in an emerging market, without sufficient and efficient legal control? Even when the professional standards or self-regulatory system have been short of probity for some time, the processing of information is an issue in question. While initial compliance with the law and regulation is important, in the developing period, the legal framework continues to play a crucial role in monitoring financial intermediaries. To combat market misconduct, such as insider dealing and market manipulation, an enhanced and completed regulation system is needed.

This book also analyses the influence on financial disclosure from the perspective of financial intermediaries. It analyses the relationship between the information disclosure regime and the independence, professionalism and regulation of intermediaries. The research shows that, on one hand, securities professionals constitute an essential part of the market and help to establish a healthy and active securities market; on the other hand, some of the existing scandals have illustrated that they may perform opposite roles. In these scandals, it was a common theme that the professionals took advantage of information which they obtained directly from their employment. As examples, the historical and current regulatory approaches of the Credit Rating Agencies are examined. International initiatives have also been introduced; for instance, the IOSCO, US and EU have played a leading function in establishing new standards.[7]

In this book, securities lawyers have been examined as another typical example of financial intermediaries. Considering the importance of their responsibilities in the securities market, an effective regulatory regime must be established. Chinese securities lawyers are moving towards a more open and fair approach in dealing with securities business. However, some problems remain, in particular, in facing the new challenge from financial globalization. How the Chinese securities lawyers will meet the demand remains to be studied.[8]

The role and function of the China Securities Regulatory Commission

Is the China Securities Regulatory Commission (hereafter the CSRC) efficient enough? A weak regulatory and supervisory framework for information disclosure may result in a market failure. Scandals and the current financial crisis amplify this point. One interesting point is that the improvements in the securities regulatory structure are often made in a direct response to a scandal or crisis. Similarly, China's capital market has developed substantially in the past decades. In China, regulatory measures are continuously being enhanced. Without doubt, the essential regulatory influence of the Chinese securities regulator needs to be addressed.

The CSRC has been playing an important role in the regulation and supervision of China's newly emerging capital market. However, there are questions that need to be raised, among other issues, as to whether the CSRC has the powers required to supervise and regulate the information disclosure regime, with regard to the effectiveness of supervision and regulation of information disclosure in China. As a comparison study of the function and role of the regulators in the UK and the Securities and Futures Commission of Hong Kong, this research offers an analysis of the regulatory behaviour of the CSRC and further discusses the way in which the information disclosure regime in China could be improved more effectively.

The importance of investor protection

Has the Chinese legal system provided the investor with a strong legal framework? Confidence and trust from the investors is the basic requirement to ensure the healthy development of a securities market. When attempting to achieve the objective of completely harmonized and sustainable development of the economy and society, investor protection cannot be ignored. This requires great transparency and effective financial supervision. Chinese investors, in particular retail investors, have been in a weak position for a while. The protection provided to them was limited and subjected to various restrictions. To some extent, the quality of investor protection determines the quality of a market. Therefore the application of a complete legal protection system is needed immediately.

This book examines the protection methods for investors, in particular when retail investors suffer losses arising from imperfect information disclosure. Civil compensation for investors has always been an issue in China. This research analyses necessity and the current situation of the civil compensation system in the securities market. Starting from an introduction of the Chinese investors, the basic legal method for investor protection has been examined. The Securities Investor Protection Fund is analysed in detail.

China is growing globally, with remarkable growth and increasing liberalization of the national economy, and in recent years more Chinese enterprises have been seeking listing on foreign stock exchanges. However, without a full understanding of the different regulatory regimes, particularly corporate disclosure requirements, those seeking overseas listing will face many challenges. Moreover, domestically, information disclosure is not good enough. It should be accepted that realizing the achievements and understanding the shortages are equally important.

This book aims to examine the development of the Chinese securities market. It focuses on the problems and drawbacks of the information disclosure regime, examines theories and methods of corporate disclosure and takes the securities companies as an example to illustrate the role and function of financial disclosure in the light of the processing of information. The results and findings obtained from this book contribute to the understanding of the past and current status of the information disclosure regime. With the identification of problems and the reasons behind them, the book investigates an approach to develop securities regulation, in particular with the regards to the information disclosure system in China. Furthermore, the findings also help to understand the importance of maintaining a fair, open and transparent disclosure regime in the securities market. Moreover, it also provides an understanding of the differences between legal systems. I am grateful to the following for permission to use material in which they hold copyright: Sweet & Maxwell for material incorporated into Chapter 4, Prof. Francis Snyder for material incorporated into Chapter 3.

The law is stated as of 1 May 2013.

Notes

1 Details of the cases can be found in Chapter 1.
2 In this book, Mainland China will sometimes be shortened to China, Hong Kong SAR will be shortened to Hong Kong, and the United Kingdom will be shortened to the UK. Details of the regimes of the UK and Hong Kong can be found throughout the main part of the book. The key aim of the book, as titled, is to analyse the information disclosure regime in Mainland China. Therefore, the UK and Hong Kong experiences, though compared in different chapters, do not occupy equal portions with the Mainland China part. Differing from traditional comparative legal study, the comparing and contrasting incorporated in this book serves as a means to illustrate the development approaches in different jurisdictions. The function of conducting the comparative research employed in this book is to introduce the best or better practices, then further conclude what aspects in Mainland China can be improved; in particular, when facing similar problems and constraints.
3 The data was collected from the Hong Kong Exchanges and Clearing Limited.
4 The details of the cases can be found in Chapters 1, 3 and 6.
5 For example, www.lawinfochina.com/ and www.westlawchina.com/index_en.html.
6 Details can be found in Chapter 3.
7 For details, see Chapter 4.
8 For details, see Chapter 4.

1 The Chinese securities market and information disclosure

Introduction

To further improve the regulation of the securities market, information disclosure is one of the central issues. The regime itself has been changed with the reform of securities markets. In this chapter, the past and present structure of the securities market, law and regulation, particularly the information disclosure regime in China, will be examined. First, in order to define the scope of the book, the chapter introduces the Chinese securities market and regulation. Second, definition of the information disclosure and relevant theories will be summarized from both international and national levels. Moreover, based on the literature reviewed, the realities of the Chinese securities market will be analysed. Furthermore, the regime in the UK, Hong Kong and some selected international standards will be introduced. Based on this comparative study, conclusions will be drawn for the evolution of Chinese procedures.

The development of Chinese securities market and regulation

It is foreseeable that the development of national macro economy and industries will significantly and profoundly influence the prosperity of the Chinese securities market. As a main force among developing countries, the Chinese securities market has attracted a lot of attention in the world. Subsequently, the regulatory regime has also been placed in an important position. In this section, the general scope of the regime will be examined.

The economic reform has boosted the development of China's modern securities market. The Third Plenary Session of the 11th Central Committee of the Communist Party of China which was held in 1978, drove the rural economic system reform. Having witnessed the positive result of the rural economic reform, the importance of urban economic reform attracted great interest. One of the major steps of the urban economic reform was the modernization of the state owned enterprises (SOEs). In October1984, the Decision of the Central Committee of the Chinese Communist Party on Several Issues Concerning the Reform of Economic System,[1] identified the significance and urgency of deepening the economic restructuring and gave recognition to the importance of the vitality of enterprises as a central part of economic reform.

At the early stage, the Chinese securities market was tightly associated with the reform of SOEs. The transformation of some of these enterprises into joint stock company played a important role in this process. Beijing Tianqiao Department Store Company was the first joint stock company in China. It faced a three-fold risk at that time; namely, political, policy and operational risks.[2] Shanghai Feilo Acoustics Joint stock Company, also formed in 1984, became the first listed joint stock company in China.[3] In 1998, the number of joint stock companies in China reached more than 8,000.[4] With the deepening of the reform on the national economy, the need for a well organized securities market become increasingly necessary.

The formal establishment of Shanghai Stock Exchange (hereafter the SSE) and the Shenzhen Stock Exchange (hereafter the SZSE) indicated the formation of the securities market in the People's Republic of China. The SSE was founded on 26 November 1990 with the aim to develop on the principles of 'legislation, supervision, self-regulation and standardization' to create a transparent, open, safe and efficient marketplace.[5] Since created in 1990, the SZSE has blossomed into a market of great competitiveness in the country, with a market capitalization around RMB1 trillion (US$122 billion); adhering to the principles of 'Regulation, Innovation, Cultivation and Service', the SZSE will continue to maintain its focus on developing the Small and Medium Enterprises Board, while seeking for a multi-tier market.[6] Notably, the SZSE was founded ten years after the creation of Shenzhen as one of the Chinese Special Economic Zones, therefore, it plays a unique role. Moreover, the reform of Chinese securities market is still continuing.

In every jurisdiction, the regulatory system for a certain degree could not be separated from the whole social background. Being a country with a long history, China has a unique character on almost all issues. The combination of traditional form and new emerging trends pervade all aspects of social areas in China. Shares in China at an early stage in their development were based on a classification of the nature and holder, and were categorized as: legal person owned shares, state owned shares, individual owned shares, internal employee shares, public shares and foreign owned shares. These divisions associate with another two distinctions, between the tradable and non-tradable shares, and between the A shares and B shares.[7]

Securities regulation in China

Securities regulation in China can be headed by 'Legislation (Fazhi), Supervision (Jianguan), Self-regulation (Zilü) and Criterion (Guifan)'.[8] These can be viewed as the general principles of the regulatory regime for the Chinese securities market. It has far reaching impacts on China. Furthermore, these principles promoted the development of a positive, reliable and comprehensive regime. For a clearer picture, the regulation of securities can be divided into different periods; the pre-securities law period, the 1998 Securities Law and the current stage.

Before the Securities Law was enacted, there was no uniform legislation for the securities market. During this period, there were some national and regional regulations which governed the securities market; for instance, the following legislation and rules can be seen as typical examples: Company Law,[9] Accounting Law,[10] Commercial Bank law,[11] Law of People's Bank.[12] As for the regulations, typically: Provisional Regulations on Securities Firms,[13] Standard Rules on Enterprise Accounting,[14] Standards for Disclosure by Companies Issuing Shares to General Public: No. 1: Content and Format of Prospectus (For Trial Use).[15] Other rules that need to be noticed: Shanghai Securities Trading Regulations[16]; Provisional Regulations of Shanghai Municipality on Companies Limited by Shares[17]; Regulations of Shenzhen Special Economic Zone on Companies Limited by Shares.[18]

General Principles of Civil Law (GPCL) can be regarded as one of the most important laws in this aspect.[19] Scholarly arguments towards whether China should have a civil code have never stopped in China. Though there is not an actual law named the 'Civil Law', the GPCL has served as a civil code.[20] The general content of GPCL covers citizen (natural person), legal person, civil juristic acts and agency, civil rights, civil liability, limitation of action, the application of law in civil relations with foreigners and sets up the most fundamental principles of the civil and commercial law. Article 3 emphasizes the equal status between the parties to a civil activity.[21] Article 4 established the principles of voluntariness, fairness, making compensation for equal value, honesty and credibility in the civil activities.[22] Furthermore, Article 5 states that lawful civil rights and interests of citizens and legal persons shall be protected by law; no organization or individual may infringe upon them.[23] Importantly, Article 6 promulgates that, where there are no relevant provisions in the law, the civil activities shall be in compliance with state policies.[24] Thus, in the absence of a centralized national securities law, the GPCL played a fundamental role in regulating the relevant behaviours.

The second period started with the coming into force of the 1998 Securities Law.[25] It indicated that a centralized regulatory regime would be primarily established. From that time, CSRC has taken the main regulatory function. During this period, the securities transactions have been mainly regulated by the Company Law and Securities Law.[26]

After the first Securities Law came into force, the situation in the international and national economy changed gradually. With the development of global and regional financial markets, the financial products diversify. Furthermore, the requirements of the World Trade Organization (hereafter WTO), which China joined in December 2001, as well as other international agreements, also required the Chinese financial system to make active responses. Hence, securities regulation needed to be adjusted for the purpose of embodying more flexibility. Under these contexts, the amendment of Securities Law was presented to the National People's Congress on 26 April 2005. After discussion, the revised Securities Law has been published. At the same time, the revised Company Law has also been published. These two laws became the main legislation governing the transaction of Chinese securities and the regulation of the securities market entered into the current stage.

Compared to the previous law, there are some significant improvements in the revised regime. The following can be seen as typical examples of these improvements; first, the revised Securities Law allowed more flexibility for globalized trends in financial evolution; for example the applicability of new law is broadened. It has been mentioned in the Article 2 that the regulation of securities derivatives should be in accordance with the present law,[27] while in the 1998 version derivatives were not mentioned.

Another important improvement is that the new law has prearranged the space for mixed management in the future. This can be seen in Article 6: the securities companies and the business organs of banks, trusts and insurance shall be established separately, unless otherwise provided for by the state.[28] The words and expressions of 'unless otherwise provided for by the state' indicated the flexible attitude. Beside this, Article 81 stated that the channel for capital to go into the stock market shall be broadened according to law.[29] The word 'broadened' expressed an encouraging approach toward the legal fund to be allowed to be involved in the securities market.[30]

From the above sample articles, it can be seen that the attitude towards the securities market became more open. One of the main reasons behind this change was the transforming nature of the Chinese securities market. As an emerging market which is under transition, new issues, new products, new problems may emerge frequently. On the other hand, the balance between risk and financial innovation should be considered carefully; in particular, whether such an innovation is suitable for the Chinese financial market at the present time and situation. Rashness will result in negative effects. For this reason, it is quite necessary for the legislative and regulatory body to be the 'forecaster' in order to avoid the radical changes in law and regulation.

Second, this new regime has strengthened the regulation of the securities market. The new law does not just focus on opening up the market but also showed determination in enhancing regulation and supervision; for instance the information disclosure issue. The enhancement of the disclosure system is one of the central points and will be analysed in the later part of this chapter. In addition, the revised regime is also aimed at the protection of investors.[31] Furthermore, the function of the CSRC should be examined carefully under the new law. As the centralized regulatory authority, the CSRC should have the sufficient regulatory tools to maintain an effective supervision. For instance, the power of carrying out an on-the-spot examination of a securities issuer, listed company, securities company, securities investment fund management company, securities trading service company, stock exchange or securities registration and clearing institution; the power of making investigation and collecting evidence; the power of consulting the capital account, security account or bank account of any relevant party concerned in or any entity or individual relating to a case under investigation.[32] The CSRC should also be able to formulate rules and codes of conduct, and execute administrative penalties, such as fines.

These provisions give legal status to the CSRC and facilitate the prevention and control of financial crime. The Chinese securities market is under transformation, and the law and regulation are not yet complete. Besides the potential gains for pursuing financial crime, the so called 'low costs', meaning the light punishment compared with the potential proceeds of crime, may also lead to financial crime. Under this context, the administrative measures, such as imposing significant amounts of fines, 'naming and shaming' and being banned from market practice, will facilitate the control and prevention of illegal behaviour. More importantly, the efficiency of the regulatory body is a core element that needs to be considered. During its daily operation, the CSRC has more direct resources concerning the securities market, therefore it may be able to react to and better control securities crimes.

On the other hand, the work of CSRC must also be monitored. When performing its functions and duties of supervision, examination or investigation, the personnel shall be no less than two and must show their legitimate certificates and the notice of supervision, examination and investigation; if failing to do so, the entity under examination and investigation has the right to refuse such regulatory action.[33] Moreover, the regulations, rules, the working system of supervision and administration, and punishment decision issued by the CSRC must be published to the general public.[34] From a comparative perspective, the UK and Hong Kong financial regulators issue press releases containing details of all cases in which they impose penalties, which is seen as a deterrent against breaking the rules as well as providing useful information to the market. The CSRC also publishes similar information on its website, and the 'naming and shaming' is seen as an effective approach for the regulatory regime.

Last but not least, the remedial system has also been set down systemically by revised law. When the prospectus, measures for financing through issuance of corporate bonds, financial statement, listing report, annual report, midterm report, temporary report or any information as disclosed that has been announced by an issuer or a listed company has any false record, misleading statement or major omission, and thus incurs losses to investors in the process of securities trading, the issuer or the listed company shall be liable for compensation; any director, supervisor, senior manager or any other person of the issuer or the listed company directly responsible shall be subject to joint and several liability for compensation, except for anyone who is able to prove his exemption of any fault; when any shareholder or actual controller of an issuer or a listed company has any fault, he shall be subject to joint and several liability for compensation together with the relevant issuer or listed company.[35]

As can be seen from the above Articles, the revised legal framework has clearly stated the different kinds of liabilities and compensation in the circumstances that arise from false records, misleading statements or major omissions. Similar provisions can be found in other articles; for instance, Article 76 (about insider dealing), Article 77 (about market manipulation) and Article 79 (about enticing customers to buy securities by fraudulent means). It is not difficult to understand that every amendment of a single concept will have far reaching impacts on the Chinese securities market. Furthermore, it must be borne in mind that the reforming and restructuring of the legal framework is still continuing.

Definition and theories of information disclosure

It is necessary to define the meaning of 'information' before embarking on the research. The meaning, according to the Longman Dictionary of Contemporary English is: 'information' is 'facts or details that tell you something about a situation, person, event etc.'.[36] As a general term, the above definition may not meet the requirements of legal research, but the basic function of the information has been clearly pointed out, meaning 'to notify something', and the receiver can obtain certain knowledge from it.

More specifically from the aspect of economics, 'information' could be described as 'what the market relies on to determine the price of whatever commodity is the subject of the market'.[37] Hereby, the relationship between 'information' and 'price' has been identified. In the commercial world the former may decide the latter. In the modern market system, information can be seen as one of the central elements that may influence the formation of commodity prices, whether the commodity is good or has other modalities. This has also been reflected in the securities market. According to the Efficient Market Hypothesis, all available information about a company's financial prospects may fully and virtually instantaneously be reflected in the market price of the company's securities.[38]

Since information is vitally important to the securities market, the disclosure issue may be seen as the keystone of securities regulation. Early research has already pointed out the importance of corporate disclosure. It is not easy to find a uniform definition of information disclosure. But generally speaking, information disclosure is that listed companies publish the information or data which describes their business position, management situation and the audit report to supervisory bodies, stock exchanges and the general public. It may be done according to legislation, regulatory rules or voluntarily. This book will mainly focus on the mandatory disclosure system, since the mandatory disclosure system constitutes one of the most important parts of supervisory regulation in most of the important jurisdictions. It emphasizes openness, fairness and justice, and facilitates the establishment of a modern financial regulatory structure.

Furthermore, it should be borne in mind that the primary purpose of information disclosure is to give investors the opportunity to understand the basic financial condition of listed companies. The investors require sufficient data before forming their rational investment decisions. As a result, it is not enough for the listed companies to only publish a prospectus in order to give the potential investors an initial impression. The listed companies are also required to maintain an adequate disclosure in the future. Based on information available, the investors can assess the companies continually, and further make their investment decisions. Under the above conditions, the disclosure system is mainly comprised of two types of disclosure, namely, before listing (prospectus), and after listing (annual report or midterm report, temporary report, etc.).[39]

Other concepts need to be further identified: financial markets; capital markets; securities markets and stock markets, etc. There are various views about the differences in the above terms. From the view of economics, a financial market is a mechanism that allows people to buy and sell (trade) financial securities (for example, stocks and bonds), commodities (for example, precious metals or agricultural goods), and other fungible items of value at low transaction costs and at prices that reflect the efficient market hypothesis. Furthermore, the financial markets can be divided into different subtypes: capital markets which consist of stock markets (which provide financing through the issuance of shares or common stock and enable subsequent trading) and bond markets (which provide financing through the issuance of bonds, and enable subsequent trading). Other markets include: commodity markets, money markets, derivatives markets, insurance markets and foreign exchange markets.

In general, the capital market can be seen as the market for securities, where companies and governments raise long-term funds. Here, securities refer to the paper certificates (definitive securities) or electronic records (book-entry securities) evidencing ownership of equity (stocks) or debt obligations (bonds). The capital market includes the stock market and the bond market. The stock market (called the equity market) is the market for trading equities. The bond market (also known as the debt, credit or fixed income market) is a financial market where participants buy and sell debt securities, usually in the form of bonds.[40] This book covers both equity and bond markets. In the Chinese financial market, stock trading occupies the majority of the market; therefore, the differences between the securities market and stock and bond market will not be explored in depth in this book.

The information disclosure regime is developed based on various theories. Information asymmetry is one of the leading examples. George A. Akerlof discussed the issue of information asymmetry, which occurs when the seller has more information about a product than the buyer.[41] Akerlof took the market of used cars as a model to illustrate the problem of quality uncertainty. It suggested that owners of good cars will not place their cars on the used car market. This phenomenon can be summarized as 'the bad driving out the good', in the market this is called 'adverse selection'. Consequently, this theory means that typically in a market where there is asymmetrical information with respect to quality, the owners of moderately high quality goods will not wish to sell. So, can the same theory be applied to the securities market? The answer is affirmative. As information is a type of public goods, the investors and listed companies have different approaches towards the information. Therefore, similarly, there is an asymmetric nature in the securities market.

Comparing listed companies, under information asymmetry, the investors, in particular the retailed investors, are in an unequal position. The listed companies control relatively comprehensive information, while normally investors only have access to the information that has been published by the companies.

Therefore, due to a lack of complete information, the investors may have difficulty in making their judgement. Without sufficient information, the investors may not be reasonably able to distinguish the 'good' from the 'bad' companies. As a result, they tend to estimate the value of companies on an average basis. Thus, 'the bad driving out the good' occurs in the financial market. The long-term effect is that the securities market operates an unhealthy approach that deviates from the original purpose of the financial market: optimizing resources.

Under these conditions, it is necessary to establish a corporate disclosure mechanism, in particular, a mandatory information disclosure regime, which aims to eliminate this imbalance. However, the efficiency of this regime needs to be further examined.

Efficient Market Hypothesis (hereafter the EMH) is another leading theory in this area.[42] It claims that the financial markets are 'informationally efficient'. Based on this theory, investors cannot consistently obtain returns higher than average market returns on a risk-adjusted basis, if the information is publicly available at the time when the investment is made. There are three major varieties of the hypothesis; namely, the 'weak', 'semi-strong' and 'strong' forms. The weak EMH claims that prices on traded assets reflect all the past publicly available information. The semi-strong EMH claims that prices reflect all publicly available information, and the prices also react instantly to new changes of public information. Third, the strong EMH asserts that prices instantly reflect all the information, including publicly available and private information.

According to EMH, in an efficient capital market, the prices of securities reflect their true market value. Ideally, the market should be strong and efficient, in that the share prices reflect all information, public and private, and no one can consistently obtain excess returns. Under these conditions, the disclosure system can be seen as part of the markets basic structure, which then has less influence on the securities prices. However, a 'strong' form of efficient market is not easily established, for instance, in developing financial markets. In the Chinese securities market, earlier research has suggested that it has reached the weak form of efficiency level.[43] Under these conditions, the disclosed information could not impose a significant impact on market prices, but had to be linked with historical information. Notably, with the improvement of market infrastructure and legal environment, the Chinese capital market is developing rapidly. Therefore, in order to achieve a semi-strong form of efficiency, the information disclosure system should be well established. In the semi-strong form of efficiency, the share prices adjust to publicly available new information rapidly, so that no excess returns can be earned only by trading on the existed information. It should be noted that in such a market forum, the non-publicly available information cannot be reflected by securities prices, thus, those who have insider information may be able to earn extra profits from this knowledge. To avoid this situation, if information has been sufficiently disclosed, there will be fewer chances to get these extra benefits, and it is much more open, fair and just for the general investors.

The above analysis is the major western view on the information disclosure regime. Notably, Chinese scholars have published relevant studies. Jianying Tian and Jianfeng Hu examined a numbers of cases concerning Chinese listed companies, and analysed the reasons for false disclosure and other law breaking behaviours from the following aspects: share structures, internal control, non-rational investments and supervisory framework.[44] They argued that the share structure itself, the excessive portion of non-tradable shares and lack of risk awareness by the listed companies and a weak regulatory regime are the main reasons which led to this illegal behaviour.

Libin Tang examined the characteristics of the illegal activities of Chinese listed companies.[45] The author gave the hypothesis of the relationship between the different uniqueness of listed companies and the activities of disobeying information disseminating regulations, and then tested it by using the data of the listed companies of China. It was argued by the author that the ownership structure led to unfair and illegal disclosure. He further suggested that in order to resolve this problem, changing the ownership structure is the key issue.

Yanjun Huang examined the sample listed companies of China from February 2003 to August 2004, and included the non-condemned listed companies for the same period as partnership samples via stratified random sampling.[46] The author conducted an empirical study on the samples from the characteristics of the industry, structure of shareholders' rights, company's scale, payoff capacity and debt of listed companies. The result revealed that the characteristics of the industry, the company's size and payoff capacity were the most influential factors.

Junwei Wang claimed that the frequent violations of listed companies in China were the result of competition between different stakeholders.[47] He further argued that the games between the majority and minority shareholders were incomplete and non-cooperative. The author constructed a game model between majority shareholders, minority shareholders and regulators.[48] He discovered that the main factors that influence the probability of listed companies violating the system were violation costs and supervisory power. Finally, the author suggested that to achieve the effective governance of listed companies, it was useful to set up shareholders' co-governance, to enhance the legal framework, and to oversee the financial regulators.

Similarly, Qiguang Li examined the Chinese listed companies' violation behaviour concerning corporate disclosure.[49] After analysing the main reasons and results, the author reached a conclusion from the perspective of the legal framework. It was believed by the author that the key issue of controlling illegal disclosure is to enhance the liabilities of the law breaching activities, and further developing a 'trinity' liability system which is composed of criminal, civil and administrative punishment.

It can be seen from the above research literature, information disclosure in the securities market has been placed in an important position in China and in the western world. Earlier studies focused on system establishment, namely, the function of information and corporate disclosure. The second stage of the studies emphasized corporate governance, for instance, the causation of violation disclosure requirements by listed companies. The third stage highlighted the enforcement issue; for example, the role of financial regulators. However, the recent financial crisis calls for the re-thinking of the disclosure regime. It has been argued by numerous governments, financial regulators, commentators and analysts that the lack of transparency and proper disclosure contributed to a great extent to the current financial crisis. Globally, it is an ongoing issue. In China, the incomplete legal framework is also one of the reasons that led to unfair and illegal disclosure. Furthermore, previous research may have laid emphasis on individual factors, but has overlooked the system as a whole. In fact, the disclosure system cannot perform without general recognition from the listed companies, financial regulators, stock exchanges, financial intermediaries and investors. Therefore, based on the previous research, this book will move forward to focus on the following aspects: the development of a legal framework; the detailed disclosure regime; the securities companies and corporate disclosure; the professionals in the securities market; the function of financial regulators; and the investors' protection regime.

Information disclosure in China

Generally speaking, one of the central issues in improving the efficiency of a securities market is to resolve the various information problems. Especially those that will influence securities price formation; for example, information disclosure, diffusion and swap should be carefully taken into account, with a view to prompt an open, fair and just information disclosure regime. China has set down the basic legal control framework and has made some improvements. It has regulated Chinese securities transactions towards a legal, orderly and fair approach, but there are still some problems.

Over the last few years there have been scandals in the Chinese securities market concerning information disclosure. The results from one survey illustrated the negative impacts on the securities market.[50] Notably, conducted by the main stock exchanges and securities companies in 2001, which was around the 10th year after the Chinese securities market was formally formed, the results obtained from this survey illustrated the perception of the enforcement of the information disclosure regime.

In this survey, as for whether the individual investors would read through the prospectus, 63.26 per cent of the interviewees chose only skimming; 23.41 per cent answers stated they would read carefully; and 13.03 per cent said that they had never read it. Furthermore, 56.71 per cent of interviewees stated that they would skim the annual report; 35.13 per cent of them stated they would read it carefully; 7.71 per cent said that they had never read it. There were two major reasons for the above figures: first, information listed in the prospectus and financial reports were not easy to understand; second, there was a suspicion that the information was unreliable.

Table 1.1 shows the results regarding the reality of the listed companies' reports. It should be noticed that most of the individual and institutional investors thought that the reports were only basically or partly believable. It is quite interesting to find that there were no institutional investors who completely

Table 1.1 The reality of the listed companies reports

	Individual investors (%)	Institutional investors (%)
Completely Believable	8.45	0.00
Basically Believable	26.98	41.41
Partly Believable	45.17	54.54
Basically Unbelievable	16.10	3.03
Completely Unbelievable	3.14	1.01

Source: www.cnstock.com/ssnews/2001–9–20/shiban/200109200181.htm.[51]

believed the listed companies reports. Furthermore, for the listed companies' reports, there were more individual investors (16.10 per cent) that held the opinion of 'basically unbelievable' than institutional investors (3.03 per cent). It showed that the believed reliability of such reports was really low in the investors' minds.

The survey went further in seeking the reasons for the above results. 23.42 per cent of the individual investors and 33 per cent of institutional investors considered that the lack of good corporate governance is one of the main reasons. 26.97 per cent of individual investors and 5 per cent of institutional investors believed that accounting standards were not good enough. 22.95 per cent of individual investors and 24 per cent of institutional investors thought the information disclosure system should be improved. 12.43 per cent of individual investors and 8 per cent of institutional investors stated that the accountants did not fulfil their duties. 11.33 per cent of the individual interviewees and 27 per cent of institutional interviewees believed that the listed companies did not fulfil their obligations of disclosure. Other reasons were stated by 2.37 per cent (individual investors) and 3 per cent (institutional investors). It can be seen from the data that the individual investors were inclined to highlight regulatory problems, for instance, the information disclosure system and accounting standards. On the contrary, the institutional investors recognized that corporate governance should be improved and reformed. Another interesting point is that the most extreme responses ('completely believable' and 'completely unbelievable') were more common among individual investors than institutional investors.

This survey was carried out by the main stock exchanges and securities companies in 2001, around the tenth year after the Chinese securities market was formed; in particular, two years after the enforcement of the first Securities Law.[52] It should be noted that the information disclosure system had already been basically set down at that time. All these consequences suggest that enhancement of the information disclosure system should be undertaken immediately.

There were some scandals during the last two decades. The following are some typical cases that took place within the scope of unfair information disclosure: Zhengzhou Baiwen case (hereafter Zheng Baiwen),[53] Huoli 28 case,[54] Qiongminyuan case,[55] and Yinguangxia case. These cases demonstrate that the fake information and profits contained in the company's prospectus and financial reports seriously jeopardized the corporate disclosure regime.

The above cases breached the regulations regarding information disclosure, and had an enormously negative influence on the Chinese securities market. For instance, the share price of Guangxia (Yinchuan) Industrial Limited Company, a biochemical company, had jumped nearly 440 per cent in 2000, but investigation proved that the company fabricated profits of RMB745 million by way of simulating the purchase and sale of contracts, and fabricating exportation declaration statements, added value tax invoices, duty-free documents, financial notes and the amount of business revenue.[56] Besides the economic losses, the occurrences of such scandals also affected the confidence of investors.

Additionally, it must be borne in mind that illegal behaviour may be found in almost all aspects of securities transactions. This conduct can be summarized into three categories: information disclosure is untrue and inaccurate; information disclosure is insufficient and incomplete; information disclosure is not timely.

The problems of information disclosure are not isolated. There are various causative reasons that should be taken into account. From the economic perspective, in a profits-pursuing industrial sector, a listed company may tend to demonstrate that its business position is competitive. It may also tend to present its potential through attractive financial reports. In this situation, information disclosure may become a type of tool; for instance, it is quite often the case that the forecasted profits were high and actual profits were low; interim reports are significantly higher than in annual reports in a financial period.[57] Hongguang Shiye fabricated wonderful financial statements in order to meet the standard for listing on the Shanghai Stock Exchange. Another example is Zheng Baiwen, this company not only made fake profit reports before listing but continued to do so after listing.

On the other hand, with information that may affect the price of securities, companies often take a cautious attitude, particularly with negative news. Thus, a company may prefer to conceal poisonous information from the public. It is also one of the main reasons that listed companies create false financial information in their reports. STJinma is a typical example; under the majority shareholders' control, it disguised the business losses for more than five years from the public. Similar approaches can be found in other cases. Lantian Gufen fabricated profits in its financial report. This is not unique to China. In other jurisdictions, at a corporate level, Enron conducted the same type of charade, while, at an individual level, Nick Leeson hid his large losses from his superiors at Barings Bank.

Information disclosure may increase business costs to companies. Sometimes, to disclose a massive amount of financial information can put companies into a negative position in the market. One important issue that cannot be ignored is the effectiveness and reliability of accounting principles in China. Although, as with other emerging markets, reform regarding the accounting principles is continuing in China, it does need time to implement changes. All these economic elements contributed to the reluctance of Chinese companies to duly disclose information in the earlier stages of the Chinese securities market.

Additionally, the incomplete legal environment is one of the main reasons for lawbreaking behaviour in securities transactions. Simply relying on the Securities Law or Company Law cannot effectively regulate such a complex issue. It also needs cooperation from other legal sectors. Currently, punishments include: ordering the company to observe correct behaviour; giving a warning; confiscating illegal income; imposing fines; suspension and revocation of business licenses; revocation of post holding qualifications or securities practice qualifications; and, in the case of breach of criminal law, imprisonment. Although it is not easy to judge whether a certain kind of punishment for breaching of the law and regulations is strict enough this has been discussed time and time again, and it is still an ongoing issue.

In China there is a need for the further strengthening of legal remedies. Compared with other economic criminal offences; for instance, the crime of financial fraud, smuggling and endangered species collecting and the management of taxes, crimes in the securities market emerged in the last few decades only. The enforcement of Company Law and Securities Law has enhanced civil remedies, namely, civil compensation. However, Criminal Law still needs to be enhanced on these issues. Although there were some significant improvements in Amendment (VI) to the Criminal Law[58]; for instance, the typology of crimes, stricter penalties, and the rationalization of the linkage between the crime and the penalty; however, the harmonization of the gap between different legal sectors still needs to be considered more carefully.[59] One typical improvement was that crimes concerning public fund management institutions have been added to the legislation.[60] This indicates that the Criminal Law has enhanced the regulation of the financial system, not only focusing on the insurance or securities companies, but by extending its scope. The Amendment (VII) and (VIII) to the Criminal Law further developed the relevant areas.[61]

Due to the structure of Chinese criminal law, i.e. the coexistence of the Criminal Law and regulations, rules and judicial interpretations, there is likely to be some gaps between the different documentation. It also needs to be borne in mind, that continuing reforms, the development of the Chinese economy and social structure has led to daily changes within China. Therefore, on one hand, the conflicts of maintaining the stabilities of law and regulation and addressing the latest changes in law and regulation have created complexities. On the other hand, too frequent amendments of the contents and provisions of the law generate further problems for implementation.

A further reason for these problems is a lack of efficient supervision and social surveillance. The supervisory bodies should bring their roles into full play. It is argued that some cases have created furores in the Chinese market, but the tactics of the listed companies are hardly extraordinary in developed markets; this is because, when compared with the complexity and amount of capital involved in deals in the mature markets, the Chinese cases pale into insignificance.[62] How the regulatory bodies enhance their professional abilities is a major task for China. Furthermore, the promotion of a socially acceptable supervisory system is also necessary. The media is also expected to play a vital role.

Lack of professional moral standards instigated illegal conduct. Some of the brokers, accountants and lawyers associated with the listed companies have 'added fuel to the fire'. Zhongtianqin is one of the leading accounting firms in China; however, it became notorious after the Yinguangxia case. As the auditor of Yinguangxia, it was proved to be complicit in the fabrication of the financial reports. It is similar to the role that Arthur Andersen LLP played in the Enron scandal. The conclusions reached from similar cases in developed securities markets suggest that the development of accounting and auditing systems in China will give the information disclosure system a powerful boost.

Lack of legal awareness could be seen as a reason for failure to comply with the law or regulations. The question of how to promote legal education to practitioners, shareholders and other involved personnel has become a very important task for China. Beside this, Chinese investors have lacked an understanding of the laws and regulations. Thus, investors, and in particular, some retail investors must build up a strong legal awareness in order to protect their legal rights.

The revised Securities Law came into force in 2006.[63] It must be noted that the new Securities Law has improved the control of information disclosure. Based on previous experiences and lessons, the revised law added that the actual controller of the company should be made public in the annual report.[64] Moreover, this law clearly set out the requirements on the disclosure of major events. It states that in the event of a major event that may considerably affect the trading price of a listed company's shares and that is not yet known to the investors, the listed company shall immediately submit a temporary report regarding the said major event to the securities regulatory authority under the State Council and the stock exchange and make an announcement to the general public as well, in which the cause, present situation and possible legal consequence of the event shall be indicated.[65]

The regulation went further, listing the different circumstances of major events: a major change in the business guidelines or business scope of the company; a decision of the company on any major investment or major asset purchase; an important contract as concluded by the company, which may have an important effect on the assets, liabilities, rights, interests or business achievements of the company; the incurrence of any major debt in the company or default on any major debt that is due; the incurrence of any major deficit or a major loss in the company; a major change in the external conditions for the business operation of the company; a change concerning directors, no less than one-third of supervisors or managers of the company; a considerable change in the holdings of shareholders or actual controllers each of whom holds or controls no less than 5 per cent of the company's shares; a decision of the company on capital decrease, merger, division, dissolution or application for bankruptcy; any major litigation in which the company is involved, or where the resolution of the general assembly of shareholders or the board of directors have been cancelled or announced invalid; where the company is involved in any crime, which has been filed as a case as well as investigated by the judicial organ or where any director, supervisor or senior manager of the company is subject to compulsory measures as rendered by the judicial organ.[66] Compared with the previous version, if the company is involved in any crime which has been filed as a case as well as investigated by the judicial organ, or where any director, supervisor or senior manager of the company is subject to compulsory measures as rendered by the judicial organ that these should be disclosed is added in the revision.

The obligation of information disclosure has been strengthened in that the directors and senior managers of a listed company shall subscribe their opinions for recognition in the periodic reports of their company in written form; the board of supervisors of a listed company shall carry out an examination on the periodic report of its company as formulated by the board of directors and produce the relevant examination opinions in writing; the directors, supervisors and senior managers of a listed company shall guarantee the authenticity, accuracy and integration of the information disclosed by the company.[67]

Furthermore, compared with the previous law, Article 69 provides the liabilities in detail: when the prospectus, measures for financing through issuance of corporate bonds, financial statement, listing report, annual report, midterm report, temporary report or any information as disclosed that has been announced by an issuer or a listed company has any false record, misleading statement or major omission, and thus incurs losses to investors in the process of securities trading, the issuer or the listed company shall be subject to the liabilities of compensation; any director, supervisor, senior manager or any other person of the issuer or the listed company directly responsible shall be subject to the joint and several liabilities of compensation, except for anyone who is able to prove his exemption to any fault; when a shareholder or actual controller of an issuer or a listed company has any fault, he shall be subject to the joint and several liabilities of compensation together with the relevant issuer or listed company.[68]

The revised law shows the determination of China to enhance the management of the information disclosure system. It aims to promote the disclosure regime to be more efficient and transparent. However, there are some new challenges to meet. With the globalization of financial markets, the regulation of information disclosure also faces new international challenges. The mid-1990s has been seen as an important period for regulatory initiatives addressing the complex issues of international cooperation and cross-border transactions; for instance, the Windsor Declaration covered the issue of information sharing.[69] The Windsor Declaration is an agreement by the regulators from 16 jurisdictions, made in Windsor, England, in 1995. It aimed to improve international information sharing, customer protection, default procedures, and emergency cooperation among different regulators. The conclusions were greatly influenced by the Barings collapse. Barings Bank, established in 1762 and collapsed in 1995, was the oldest merchant bank in London. The bank's failure was due to unauthorized trading by its head derivatives trader in Singapore, Nick Leeson. Moreover, the management failure, information failure and lack of accountability, supervision and internal control were believed to be the causes. In this period, after the collapse of Barings Bank, it has been widely accepted that close international cooperation is crucial to meeting the regulatory challenges of the future.

So far as developing countries are concerned, the new emerging financial markets in East Asia have become an important issue. Considering the deeply rooted reasons such as the political motivation, economic interdependence and cultural aspects, one of the regulatory questions is focusing on 'whether regionalism is intended to replace the multilateral regulatory regime for international finance', and 'if not, how far will it go?'[70] It has been argued that regional regulatory cooperation may be the more powerful approach. However, the diversified political views may be an obstacle for reaching this aim. Given the fact that China has become the most important economy in East Asia, in particular, the aim of establishing Shanghai as the leading financial centre in Asia, even in the world, the cultural and historic barriers should not be overlooked. Furthermore, in order to promote the effective regulatory regime, the domestic legal infrastructures in the countries that have new emerging financial markets must also be reformed.[71] Concentrating on China, the challenges for Chinese securities regulation may appear as follows: liberalization of capital markets and other policy issues; foreign invested risk firms involvement in the domestic market; Chinese companies' overseas listing; cross and overseas listing issue; new technology-related securities crimes; Chinese securities firms' abilities to address these changes.

The securities market in China is facing a much more complex situation than before. The Zhejiang Hangxiao Steel Structure Co., Ltd case illustrates this point. The company had made improperly timed, inaccurate and incomplete disclosures.[72] Another important case is 'Leading Brother (Daitou Dage) 777'.[73] From January 2006, 'Leading Brother (Daitou Dage) 777', whose true name is Xiujie Wang, had opened his own Weblog on www.163.com, and illegally operated an investment consultancy business.[74] He published a large amount of stock analysis, forecasting and recommendation information. Furthermore, from January 2007, he had set up the 'QQ group', and charged the group members for stock consulting. The CSRC reached an administrative decision and delivered the case to the public security sector.[75] Eventually, Xiujie Wang was sentenced to three years imprisonment.

The CSRC had pointed out the approaches of 11 similar cases, using the internet to operate illegal securities business, in particular, to disseminate information.[76] It is not difficult to understand that such behaviour will have a massive negative influence on the Chinese financial markets. First of all, the common nature of such actions, that are easy to conceal, will bring more difficulties for the financial regulators. The operators may use fake names, business licenses and locations to defraud investors. Moreover, investigations have found that the operators even regularly change the places where they access the internet; for example, using internet cafés and hotels. Second, these behaviours expand very rapidly, and the operators may believe that they will not be seized easily. The high transmission speed of the internet will also assist these actions. It is interesting to examine the psychology of retail investors. The herd effect may also assist illegal actions. Some investors blindly believe the information from the internet website or personal Weblog, for example, the 'Leading Brother (Daitou Dage)

777' case. It can be seen from the above, that the internet related securities business may become a 'Gordian knot' for the Chinese securities market.

To sum up, with the development of the world economy, the information disclosure regime in China may face some new challenges. New issues will emerge from various avenues. Wide cooperation from different sectors is needed to 'grasp the nettle'. In fact, the main aim of the information disclosure regime should not only be concerned with the information itself. If it can go further to consider a much wider scale, which means the whole order of the Chinese financial market, the performance of such a regime may reach a higher level. The securities regulatory regime in China has to pay more attention to the latter issue.

Comparative study with other jurisdictions

The Chinese securities market has played an important role in the economic infrastructure of China and the world. Chinese legal research is continuing to focus on the disclosure issue. There have been some significant improvements. On the other hand, compared with other mature markets, there are still some problems remaining in China. For instance, it should be noted that disclosure standards primarily aim to form comprehensive regulatory systems. However, as China is in a transitional state, it is not easy to establish a constant regime. Therefore, the lack of coherence between different legal requirements can lead to listed companies taking advantage of weak regulations and laws. An integrated approach is needed.

Importantly, the wide use of computers and the internet in securities transactions also requires a comprehensive understanding of different legal systems. Observers believe that the loosening of regulatory controls, lack of oversight and enforcement will cause an increase in fraud and stock manipulation, and weaken a company's value.[77] Since many of the listed companies are transnational corporations, the need to understand a variety of global securities markets has become more urgent.

Regarding the information disclosure regime, some mature markets have already pointed out the importance of full disclosure; for example, listing particulars have been described as the 'vehicles of information for investors'.[78] The necessary elements for healthy disclosure have now been understood. Besides the comprehensive method for legal control, 'efficiency' has been given an important position in mature markets; for instance 'the obligation to give all the information that investors require is overriding' and

> the information relevant to the particular issuer must be given in a form that can be analysed and understood as easily as possible so that varying emphasis should be given to the items of information included in order to indicate their relative importance.[79]

Furthermore, the principles contained in the continuing obligations requirements in the UK, clearly affirmed that there should be timely disclosure of all relevant information, and the equal treatment of all shareholders forms the very bedrock of regulation in the area of finance law.[80]

Taking lessons and learning new measures from other jurisdictions may help to reduce risks for the Chinese securities market. So, what lessons should China take?

The UK perspective

As one of the major financial centres, the securities market in the UK has also experienced reforms. There are some benchmarks that should not be ignored. In the early years, there was no specific governmental organization to regulate the securities market. Self-regulation played an important role at that time. Some provisions which related to securities transactions can be found in the Companies Act 1985.[81] For instance, Part 16 (Account and Report) deals with detailed disclosure issues.

In the 1980s, the economic position of the UK became more prosperous. The improvement in the national economy, together with the explicit political aim of Prime Minister Margaret Thatcher to involve the general public in the securities markets, had contributed to and prompted the emergence of Financial Services Act 1986, which re-adjusted the structures of the financial market in the UK.[82] After the 'Big Bang', London's financial services industry made substantial changes to its structure, that have led to the City's elevated status as one of the largest financial centres for global business.[83]

After experiencing financial scandals – for instance, the case of Barings Bank in 1994 – it was necessary to adjust the regulation of financial services. Another reform of financial services regulation was completed in June 1998, when responsibility for banking supervision was transferred to the Financial Service Authority (hereafter the FSA) from the Bank of England. In May 2000, the FSA took over the role of the UK Listing Authority from the London Stock Exchange. The Financial Services and Markets Act 2000 (hereafter FSMA 2000)[84] transferred the responsibilities of several other organizations; for instance, the Building Societies Commission, the Friendly Societies Commission, the Investment Management Regulatory Organization, the Personal Investment Authority, the Register of Friendly Societies and the Securities and Futures Authority to the FSA.

Thus, the FSA became an independent non-governmental body, given statutory powers by the FSMA 2000. The main working objectives for the FSA focused on: market confidence, maintaining confidence in the financial system; public awareness, promoting public understanding of the financial system; securing the appropriate degree of protection of consumer protection; the reduction of financial crime, reducing the extent to which it is possible for a business to be used for a purpose connected with financial crime.[85]

Since then, the FSMA 2000 placed the securities market in the UK under the supervision of the FSA until April 2013. During this period, the information disclosure system was mainly regulated by the Companies Act and the FSA

Regulatory Handbook. Basically, the information disclosure regime can be found in the Companies Act 2006, Listing Rules (hereafter the LR), Prospectus Rules (PR), Disclosure Rules and Transparency Rule (DTR). Furthermore, apart from UK legislation, European legislation also plays an important role. For instance, the Markets in Financial Instruments Directive (hereafter the MiFID) came into effect on 1 November 2007. The act introduces new and extensive requirements to which firms will have to adapt, in particular regarding their conduct of business and internal organization.[86] The act has detailed requirements for pre-trading and post-trading transparency.

One result from the 2008 financial crisis is the restructuring of the financial regulators in the UK. The FSA has been replaced by two separate entities, the Prudential Regulation Authority (hereafter the PRA) and the Financial Conduct Authority (hereafter the FCA). Criticisms had been around the previous tripartite system, in which the Treasury, the Bank of England and the FSA shared the responsibilities. This system was blamed for a lack of systemic oversight, especially in the time of crisis. The Financial Services Act 2012 gave status of the PRA and FCA.[87] On 1 April 2013 the PRA became responsible for the prudential regulation and supervision of banks, building societies, credit unions, insurers and major investment firms.[88] The FCA regulates the financial services industry in the UK, with aims to protect consumers, ensure the financial services industry remains stable and promote healthy competition between financial services providers.[89] The FCA oversees the admission process to a Regulated Market, to assess issuers' eligibility and to ensure the relevant rules are met. More specifically, it monitors market disclosure by issuers and others under the FCA Disclosure and Transparency Rules; reviews and approves of prospectuses published by issuers and offfereors of securities under the FCA Prospectus Rules; and operates the UK listing regime under FCA Listing Rules.[90] Thus, currently, the PRA and FCA work under a twin peaks regulatory structure in the UK.

Conclusions may be drawn from the reforms of the UK's regulatory framework: the effective regulatory regime is one of the major modern approaches to the regulation of the securities market. Such an approach shall focus on both macro and micro levels, and aim to maintain systemic stability.

The Hong Kong perspective

Hong Kong, as one of the major financial centres, has played a very important role in promoting economic development in Asia. The securities market has exerted an important influence on the prosperity of the local economy in Hong Kong. It has also experienced several deeply rooted reforms, which accelerated the procedures towards a mature market.

Considering the special relationship between Mainland China and Hong Kong, it is quite helpful to examine the reforming procedures of the securities market in Hong Kong. It is well known that before China liberalized its economy, Hong Kong had taken the role of an intermediary between Mainland China and other jurisdictions. Today, although several other business centres have been established in Mainland China, for instance, Beijing, Shanghai, Shenzhen and Guangzhou, Hong Kong and its financial markets still perform an important function. Furthermore, in respect of the securities market, Hong Kong has been the one of centres for mainland companies seeking to raise funds, especially through the listing of companies and sales and subsequent trading of shares.

It may be argued that the evolution of Hong Kong's financial market has experienced three periods; namely, the non-regulatory age, the early stage and the current regime.[91] Prior to the financial market crash of 1973, there was virtually no regulatory supervision of the Hong Kong financial markets.[92] There was a lack of sufficient statutory requirements regulating the listing of securities. During this period, the securities industry was mainly regulated by Companies Ordinance,[93] and the main focuses were the general prospectus requirements for companies. However, regulatory control still remained weak. It was described as 'withholding relevant information, misrepresentation, forgery, and fraud were prevalent in the financial markets'.[94] In particular, the virulent competition between the four stock exchanges; namely, Hong Kong Stock Exchange (established in 1891), Far East Stock Exchange (established in 1969), Kam Ngan Stock Exchange (established in 1971), and Kowloon Stock Exchange (established in 1972) reduced the quality of listed companies and resulted in a series of illicit transactions.[95]

Following the financial market crash, the government started to tighten the regulatory regime for the financial market. In this period, several pieces of legislation were published. The Securities Ordinance (1974), the Protection of Investors Ordinance (1974), the Code on Takeovers and Mergers (1975) and the Securities (Stock Exchange Listing) Rules (1976) were the important legal documents.

Remarkably, the Securities Commission, in which were vested a series of regulatory powers, was established according to the Securities Ordinance. Beside this, the Protection of Investors Ordinance intended to protect investors by ensuring accurate information was provided to them.[96] It should be noted these legislations have, to a certain degree, promoted the establishment of a healthy market. During this period, there was a rapid growth in the global financial market. Moreover, financial innovation had hastened procedures towards modernization. In particular, the merger of the four stock exchanges conducted under the Stock Exchanges Unification Ordinance (1980) has enabled the securities market in Hong Kong to be regulated under a uniform system, and the Stock Exchange of Hong Kong Ltd was incorporated.[97]

However, in 1987, the deficiencies of the regulatory structure were made apparent by the October crash, and resulted in the closure of both the Hong Kong stock and stock index futures markets for four days.[98] After drawing conclusions from the worldwide stock markets chaos in 1987, the Securities and Futures Commission Ordinance (1989) came into force. At the same time, the Securities and Futures Commission (hereafter the SFC) was formed. It has been endowed with a series of powers; for instance, supervision, intervention, investigation, prosecution and adjudication, which will ensure that it fulfils its function effectively.

Since then, the securities market and regulatory regime in Hong Kong is continuing to develop towards a more comprehensive and modern structure. There are three parts to the basic regulatory system, namely, the government of Hong Kong, the SFC,[99] and the Hong Kong Exchanges and Clearing Limited (hereafter the HKEx).[100] This is called a 'three-tier system'. The SFC is an independent non-governmental statutory body outside the civil service, responsible for regulating the securities and futures markets in Hong Kong. In May 1989, following the enactment of the Securities and Futures Commission Ordinance, the SFC was established. The HKEx operates a securities market and a derivatives market in Hong Kong and is the clearing house for the markets. HKEx was listed in Hong Kong in 2000 and is now one of the world's largest exchange owners based on the market capitalization of its shares. On 6 March 2000, the Stock Exchange of Hong Kong Limited (SEHK), Hong Kong Futures Exchange Limited (HKFE) and Hong Kong Securities Clearing Company Limited (HKSCC), merged under a single holding company, HKEx. The three parts cooperate together in order to maintain a healthy securities market. The government fulfils a full scale regulatory function, while the SFC operates as the oversight regulator, and the HKEx focuses on trading operations and risk management.

There are a set of ordinances relating to securities transactions in Hong Kong. Among them, the primary legislation is the Securities and Futures Ordinance (hereafter the SFO), which has been called the largest and most detailed ordinance in the history of Hong Kong.[101] Furthermore, numerous subsidiary legislation has been enacted pursuant to the SFO; for example, Securities and Futures (Accounts and Audit) Rules (Cap. 571P), Securities and Futures (Disclosure of Interests – Securities Borrowing and Lending) Rules (Cap. 571X), and Securities and Futures (Disclosure of Interests – Exclusions) Regulation (Cap. 571AG).

The SFC Regulatory handbook plays an important role in the securities market. Key areas of the handbook cover regulatory philosophy and business standards; for instance, Licencing of Intermediaries and Continuing Obligations of Licenced Persons, Specific Requirements for Regulated Activities, Regulated Investment Products, Enforcement Related. The SFC has also issued a series of codes and guidelines; for instance, Code of Conduct for Corporate Finance Adviser in March 2003, Guidelines on Use of Offer Awareness and Summary Disclosure Materials in Offerings of Shares and Debentures under the Companies Ordinance in March 2003, and guidelines for the Exemption of Listed Corporations from part XV of SFO (Disclosure of Interests) in March 2003.

Besides the above, there are various rules of HKEx that are part of the regulatory regime. The most important are the Rules Governing the Listing of Securities on the Stock Exchange of Hong Kong Limited.[102]

It can be seen that the regulatory regime of the securities market in Hong Kong is moving towards a modern and comprehensive system intended to fall into line with international standards. The detailed information disclosure system will be discussed in a later chapter.

Retail investor survey 2003[103]

In October and November 2003, the SFC conducted research in order to explore the investment behaviour of retail investors, in dealing in stocks and funds, and to investigate what deterred non-investors from investing. Survey data were collected through telephone interviews from 15 October to 17 November 2003; a questionnaire was used to collect information from the respondents. The results showed that apart from stock code and company name nearly all stock investors were familiar with the company's nature of business (91 per cent), prospects (88.2 per cent) and risks of holding its stock (85.2 per cent). These were the three attributes that stock investors knew most about a listed company before investing in its stock. They were less aware of the company's senior management (42.6 per cent) and the treatment of minority shareholders (24.7 per cent). Moreover, 1.3 per cent of stock investors admitted that before buying a stock they only knew the company name and stock code and lacked awareness of the company's fundamentals. As for importance, financial position, prospects and nature of business of a listed company were the top three attributes in evaluating a stock.

With regard to the question, 'What did stock investors rely on to make, buy and sell decisions?', it is interesting to note that 82.5 per cent of stock investors had relied on their own analysis in making buy and sell decisions for listed stocks, followed by transaction volume (53.4 per cent) and celebrity analysts' comments (44.8 per cent). 42.2 per cent read analysis reports compiled by newspapers, televisions or financial information websites. 33.9 per cent of stock investors referred to corporate documents such as annual reports and company circulars in making trading decisions.

As for the factors that influenced fund investment decisions, the investment needs and recommendations made by salesmen were most influential in arousing investors' interest to buy funds. 56.5 per cent of the fund investors bought funds because of recommendations from the sales staff of fund houses or distribution agents. A total of 55.9 per cent acted according to their own investment needs. Friends' recommendations: 22.7 per cent, Comments in newspapers or websites: 20.8 per cent, Fund brochures: 13.3 per cent, Fund advertisements: 10.6 per cent. When making investment decisions, 62.2 per cent of fund investors had relied on both offer documents and marketing material.

To sum up, compared with Hong Kong, there are some similar aspects either in the reforms of the financial market or in the regulatory framework. However, with a detailed examination, differences can be found. Compared with the survey results in the Mainland (see the early part of this chapter), it is suggested that the Hong Kong retail investors had greater trust in the Hong Kong market during the survey period.

International cooperation

Financial globalization requires a wide international cooperation in securities regulation. There are some international agreements and organizations focusing on this issue. Among them, the IOSCO, International Financial Reporting Standards, OECD Principles and UNCTAD have played a leading role in establishing global standards.

International Organization of Securities Commissions

The International Organization of Securities Commissions (IOSCO) is one of the most important organizations in the regulatory area of securities transactions. It was established in 1983, and aims to promote high standards of regulation in order to maintain just, efficient and sound markets; to exchange information in order to promote the development of domestic markets; to unite members' efforts to establish standards and an effective surveillance of international securities transactions; to provide mutual assistance to promote the market integrity by a rigorous application of the standards and by effective enforcement against offences.[104] Furthermore, the basic objectives of IOSCO are the following: protection of investors; ensuring that markets are fair, efficient and transparent; and the reduction of systemic risks.[105]

In 2010, IOSCO revised its basic objectives. Drawing on lessons learned from the financial crisis, this revision incorporated eight new principles, which cover specific policy areas such as hedge funds, credit rating agencies and auditor independence and oversight, in addition to broader areas including monitoring, mitigating and managing systemic risk; regularly reviewing the perimeter of regulation; and requiring that conflicts of interest and misalignment of incentives are avoided, eliminated, disclosed or otherwise managed.[106] It can be seen that these newly developed principles are targeted to strengthen the global regulatory regime.

Moreover, IOSCO has set down a series of documents for the regulation of international financial markets. It is not possible to list all the documents, so the following are some typical examples that relate to information disclosure: International Disclosure Principles for Cross-Border Offerings and Listings of Debt Securities by Foreign Issuers – Final Report, Report of the Technical Committee of IOSCO (March 2007), Financial Disclosure in the Banking, Insurance and Securities Sectors: Issues and Analysis, Joint Forum (IOSCO), Basel Committee on Banking Supervision (BCBS) and International Association of Insurance Supervisors (IAIS) (April 2004), Principles for Ongoing Disclosure and Material Development Reporting by Listed Entities, Statement of the Technical Committee of IOSCO (October 2002), Investor Disclosure and Informed Decisions, Use of Simplified Prospectuses by Collective Investment Schemes, Report of the Technical Committee of IOSCO (July 2002).

IOSCO has taken some very important steps to build links between its member states, in particular regarding financial globalization. China has been a member state of IOSCO since July 1995.[107]

International Financial Reporting Standards

International Financial Reporting Standards (hereafter the IFRS) are a set of standards for accounting. Currently they have been adopted by many countries. Some of the standards forming part of IFRS are known by its original name of International Accounting Standards (hereafter the IAS). International Accounting Standards Committee (hereafter the IASC) has issued these standards.

IFRS focuses on establishing the rules but does not address the detailed operations. Its framework contains the basic accounting principles, which deal with the following issues: the objective of financial statements; the qualitative characteristics that determine the usefulness of information in financial statements; the definition, recognition and measurement of the elements from which financial statements are constructed; and concepts of capital and capital maintenance.[108]

IFRS 7 deals with the disclosure issue. It requires that entities provide disclosures in their financial statements in order to enable users to evaluate the significance of financial instruments for the entity's financial position and performance; to evaluate the nature and extent of risks arising from financial instruments to which the entity is exposed during the period and at the reporting date, and how the entity manages the risks; the qualitative disclosures describe management's objectives, policies and processes for managing those risks; the quantitative disclosures provide information about the extent to which the entity is exposed to risk, based on information provided internally to the entity's key management personnel; together, these disclosures provide an overview of the entity's use of financial instruments and the exposures to risks they create.[109]

It should be noted that the IFRS applies to all entities, including entities that have few financial instruments and those that have many financial instruments. The high standard of quality is another reason that IFRS has been adopted by different countries. At first glance, the standards have provided a comprehensive model for the financial report. Without doubt, to apply a high international standard may help the corporate body to establish its reputation. Subsequently, it can attract more investors. Indeed, in the era of financial globalization, to adopt the uniform international standard is also a requirement of overseas listing.

However, what problems will China face using such a standard in the securities market? On one hand, it can prompt Chinese listed companies to supply more accurate financial information. Moreover, it can provide a more straightforward approach to understanding the financial reports by harmonizing the differences that arise from the different accounting systems. On the other hand, the effect of adopting the IFRS also depends on how the Chinese listed companies will address it. Again, the degree of supervision from the CSRC will become an important issue.

OECD Principles of Corporate Governance

The financial crises that occurred in 1997/1998 were one of the main reasons that led to the emergence of the first international standard of corporate governance, namely, the 1999 OECD Principles of Corporate Governance (hereafter Principles). Importantly, since it focused on corporate governance, 'disclosure and transparency' as one of the main issues was explored in a separate chapter. It set down a framework for the disclosure issue; for instance, the basic contents of disclosure: the financial and operating results, the company objectives, foreseeable risk factor.[110] However, it had been argued that the follow up work to implement the principles was confined to the developing and transitional countries.[111]

After the first edition of the Principles came into force, there were some financial scandals that happened in the USA and Europe. These scandals not only resulted in the enactment of the Sarbanes–Oxley Act 2002, but also led to calls from the USA, that suggested that OECD should undertake a revision of the Principles.[112]

Compared with the 1999 edition, the Principles of 2004 have certain improvements. The Principles have been advanced by ensuring the basis for an effective corporate governance framework, the effective exercise of ownership, and dealing with conflicts of interest. It set down six basic aspects of disclosure principles: the basic contents of disclosure; information should be prepared and disclosed with high quality standards; an annual audit should be conducted by an independent, competent and qualified auditor; external auditors should be accountable to the shareholders and owe a duty to the company to exercise due professional care; disseminated information should be provided equally, promptly and be cost efficient; corporate governance framework should be complemented by an effective approach designed to ensure that there are no material conflicts of interest.

It can be seen from the above that disclosure issues have been given an important position in the Principles. Since good practices of corporate governance can promote a healthy disclosure regime, and subsequently help in attracting investors and building up their confidence in the capital markets, it is necessary to examine the Principles carefully. In fact, the important relationship between corporate governance and the disclosure regime has already been recognized by China. Focusing on the issue of corporate governance, the CSRC has published the Code of Corporate Governance for Listed Companies in China in order to promote the establishment and improvement of a modern enterprise system by listed companies.[113] Information disclosure and transparency has been put in a separate chapter in the Code.

United Nations Conference on Trade and Development and International Standards of Accounting and Reporting[114]

Intergovernmental Working Group of Experts on International Standards of Accounting and Reporting (ISAR) aims to assist developing countries and economies in transition to implement best practices in accounting and corporate transparency in order to facilitate investment flows and economic development. The Working Group not only focuses on its own standards, but also helps developing countries to master other international standards, for instance, the practical implementation issues of the International Financial Reporting Standards (IFRS) were among its main agenda items in 2006. It is serviced by the United Nations Conference on Trade and Development (hereafter UNCTAD) as one of the central features of UNCTAD's work on corporate transparency and accounting.

Besides this, UNCTAD has published Guidance on Good Practice in Corporate Governance Disclosure 2006. The guidance is a technical aid for regulators and companies; in particular, for developing countries and transition economies. The purpose of the guidance is to help those responsible for preparing company reports to produce disclosures on corporate governance that address the major concerns of investors and other stakeholders.[115] As an international guidance, the focus is on widely applicable disclosure issues that are relevant to most enterprises: financial and non-financial corporate governance disclosures; disclosure issues regarding general meetings, timing and means of disclosure and compliance with best practice.[116]

As noted before, the disclosure of corporate governance forms a major part of information disclosure in the securities market. From this point of view, studying the relevant documents of UNCTAD is helpful for China.

Summary

It can be seen from this study that the information disclosure regime in China has experienced several reforms, which promote it towards a healthy, just and transparent regime. However, with the new challenges from both external and internal aspects or national and international aspects, how the regulatory regime can play its full function should be examined carefully.

At the same time, there are some experiences from which China can learn; for instance, the regulatory regimes of the UK and Hong Kong. The evolution of these regulatory regimes may produce useful ideas for Mainland China. It is vitally important for the developing process. Addressing international standards would be another effective approach, however, the need to make steady progress also must be considered.

Notes

1 Promulgated on 20 December 1984.
2 Junrong Tian (22 July 1998), 'Building the Bridge, Crossing the Mountain – The First Stock Company Beijing Tianqiao Department Store Company (Feijia Tianqiao Du Guanshan – Diyijia GufenZhi Qiye Beijing Tianqiao Gufen Baihuo Youxian Gongsi Xunzong)', People's Daily (Renmin Ribao).
3 See Shanghai Feilo Acoustics Co., Ltd website, www.facs.com.cn/about.htm, last accessed: 22 May 2013.
4 Chengguang Ma (23 October 1998), 'Securities Law to regulate the Booming Sector', China Daily (Zhongguo Ribao).
5 SSE website, http://static.sse.com.cn/sseportal/en_us/ps/about/bi.shtml, last accessed: 21 June 2012.

6 SZSE website, www.szse.cn/main/en/aboutsse/sseoverview/, last accessed: 21 June 2012. Shenzhen is a front line city in the developing progress of the Chinese economy.
7 For details see Chapter 5.
8 See the Government Report in 10th National People's Congress, published in March 2003.
9 Company Law, promulgation date: 29 December 1993, effective date: 1 July 1994.
10 Accounting Law, promulgation date: 21 January 1985, revised on 29 December 1993 and 1999.
11 Commercial Bank Law, promulgation date: 19 May 1995, revised on 27 December 2003, effective date: 1 February 2004.
12 Law of People's Bank 1995, promulgation date: 18 March 1995, revised on 27 December 2003, effective date: 1 February 2004.
13 Provisional Regulation on Securities Firms, by the People's Bank of China, promulgation date: 12 October 1990, effective date: 12 October 1990.
14 Standard Rules on Enterprise Accounting, by the Ministry of Finance, promulgation date: 30 November 1992, effective date: 1 July 1993.
15 Standards for Disclosure by Companies Issuing Shares to General Public: No. 1: Content and Format of Prospectus (for trial use), by China Securities Regulatory Commission, promulgation date: 8 July 1993, effective date: 8 July 1993.
16 Shanghai Securities Trading Regulations, by Shanghai Municipal People's Government, promulgation date: 1 December 1990, effective date: 1 December 1990.
17 Provisional Regulations of Shanghai Municipality on Companies Limited by Shares, by Shanghai Municipal People's Government, promulgation date: 18 May 1992, effective date: 1 June 1992.
18 Regulations of Shenzhen Special Economic Zone on Companies Limited by Shares, by First Shenzhen Municipal People's Congress, promulgation date: 26 April 1993, effective date: 1 October 1993.
19 General Principles of Civil Law, promulgation date: 12 April 1986.
20 William C. Jones (ed.), Basic Principles of Civil Law in China, Armonk, New York; London: M.E. Sharpe, 1989.
21 Ibid., Article 3.
22 Ibid., Article 4.
23 Ibid., Article 5.
24 Ibid., Article 6.
25 Securities Law, promulgation date: 29 December 1998, effective date: 1 July 1999. Revised: 27 October 2005, effective date: 1 January 2006.
26 Details of the relevant provisions will be discussed in Chapters 2, 3, 4, 5 and 6.
27 Securities Law, Article 2: the present Law shall be applied to the issuance and transaction of stocks, corporate bonds as well as any other securities. Any listed trading of government bonds and share of securities investment funds shall be governed by the new law. Importantly, the measures for the administration of issuance and transaction of securities derivatives shall be prescribed by the State Council according to the principles of the present Law.
28 Ibid., Article 6.
29 Ibid., Article 81.
30 As for the mixed operation, further details can be found in Chapter 4.
31 Details see Chapter 6.
32 Securities Law, Article 180.
33 Ibid., Article 181.
34 Ibid., Article 184.
35 Ibid., Article 69.
36 Longman Dictionary of Contemporary English (2003 edition), Harlow: Longman, p. 834.

37 Brenda Hannigan, Insider Dealing (2nd edition), London: Longman (1994), p. 2.

38 Eugene Fama (1970). 'Efficient Capital Markets: A Review of Theory and Empirical Work'. *Journal of Finance* 25 (2), pp. 383–417. Details have been discussed in the later part of this chapter.

39 Details of the information disclosure issue will be discussed in future chapters.

40 Above definitions taken from: The new Palgrave Dictionary of Money & Finance, edited by Peter Newman, Murray Milgate, John Eatwell, London: Macmillan Press Ltd; New York: Stockton Press, 1992, pp. 213, 223, 302.

41 George A. Akerlof (1970), 'The Market for 'Lemons': Quality Uncertainty and the Market Mechanism', *The Quarterly Journal of Economics*, 84 (3), pp. 488–500.

42 The contents here were summarized from: Eugene Fama (1970). 'Efficient Capital Markets: A Review of Theory and Empirical Work'. *Journal of Finance* 25 (2), pp. 383–417.

43 Lishang. Zhang (2005), Information Disclosure and Analysis of the Listed Companies (Shangshi Gongsi Xinxi Pilu yu Fenxi), Chengdu: Southwestern University of Finance & Economic Press, p. 25. The author argued that based on the previous empirical research during 1995 to 1997, the Chinese capital market has reached weak form efficiency. Moreover, after 2001, due to the improvements of the market supervision structure, the Chinese capital market is moving towards the semi-strong efficiency.

44 Jianying Tian, Jianfeng Hu (2003), 'An Analysis of the Illegal Behaviors of the Chinese Listed Companies (Woguo Shangshi Gongsi Weigui Weifa Xianxiang Tanxi)', *China Zhejiang Academic Journal*, 4, p. 179.

45 Libin Tang (2004), 'Empirical Analysis of the Characteristics of Listed Companies Disobeying Information Dissemination Regulation (Xinxi Pilu Weigui Shangshi Gongsi Tezheng de Shizheng Fenxi)', *Statistical Research*, 5, p. 30.

46 Yanjun Huang (2005), 'An Empirical Study on the Influencing Factors of Listed Companies of China Disobeying Information Disseminating Regulation (Zhongguo Shangshi Gongsi Xinxi Pilu Weigui Yingxiang Yinsu de Shizheng Yanjiu)', *Journal Of Shanghai Finance College*, 2, p. 53. In a stratified sample the sampling frame is divided into non-overlapping groups or strata, e.g. geographical areas, age-groups, genders. A sample is taken from each stratum, and when this sample is a simple random sample it is referred to as stratified random sampling. See, Neville Hunt and Sidney Tyrrell (2004), 'Discuss Sampling Method', www.coventry.ac.uk/ec/~nhunt/meths/strati.html, last accessed: 1 November 2010.

47 Junwei Wang (2006), 'Analysis of Chinese Listed Companies' Violations based on Incomplete and Non-cooperate Game (Jiyu bu Wangquan Feihezuo Boyi de Shangshi Gongsi Weigui Xingwei Fenxi)' *Finance and Trade Research*, 6, p. 94.

48 Steven N. Durlauf and Lawrence E. Blume, ed. (2008). The New Palgrave Dictionary of Economics (2nd edition), Basingstoke, Hampshire; New York: Palgrave Macmillan. Game theory concerns the behaviour of decision makers whose decisions affect each other. Its analysis is from a rational rather than a psychological or sociological viewpoint. It is indeed a sort of umbrella theory for the rational side of social science, where 'social' is interpreted broadly, to include human as well as non-human players (computers, animals, plants). Its methodologies apply in principle to all interactive situations, especially in economics, political science, evolutionary biology and computer science. There are also important connections with accounting, statistics, the foundations of mathematics, social psychology, law, business and branches of philosophy such as epistemology and ethics.

49 Qiguang Li (2006), 'An Analysis of the Liability System of Illegal Disclosure by the Chinese Listed Companies (Woguo Shangshi Gongsi Xinxi Pilu Weigui zhi Falv Zeren Tixi Yanjiu)', *Market Modernization*, 12, p. 321.

50 Hongwei Tian, Jun Zhang (2001), 'The Analysis of the Quality of the Information Disclosed by the Listed Companies (Shangshi Gongsi Xinxi Pilu Zhiliang Diaocha Fenxi)',

www.cnstock.com/ssnews/2001–9–20/shiban/200109200181.htm, last accessed: 11 August 2010. The survey was conducted by the Shanghai Stock Exchange, Shanghai Securities News (Shanghai Zhengquan Bao), China Securities Journal (Zhongguo Zhengquan Bao) and Securities Times (Zhengquan Shibao) in 2001. The investigation period was from 21 June to 2 July 2001. The survey received around 2,100 answers from individual investors, and around 100 answers from institutional investors. (The percentages are accurate to the decimal point.)

51 Ibid.

52 The survey can only reflect the situation in 2001. No similar survey has been conducted recently.

53 Gongmeng Chen, Michael Firth, Daniel N. Gao and Oliver M. Rui, 'Is China's Securities Regulatory Agency a Toothless Tiger? Evidence from Enforcement Actions', *Journal of Accounting and Public Policy*, 24 (2005) pp. 451–488. Zheng Baiwen was regarded as a leading firm in the wholesale industry. In 1997, Zheng Baiwen reported a net profit of RMB812.9 million and a return on capital employed of 20.7 per cent. In 1998, the profits turned into large losses and the share price fell rapidly. The CSRC investigated the firm and found that sales revenues and profits had been falsified since 1995; the information published in the IPO prospectus was not true.

54 Ibid. Vitality (Huoli) 28 was listed in 1996 and had the image of a high quality 'blue chip' company. On 31 August 1999, the company reported a net loss of RMB200 million or RMB1.75 per share. Furthermore, having claimed that it would not engage in joint ventures, the company changed track in 1996. Ten days after listing, the company sold its core operations and established a joint venture with a German company Benckiser, in which it gave the other party a 50 years' right to its brand name ('Vitality 28'). It also failed to disclose this important information in the listing documents.

55 Ibid. The Qiong Minyuan case was explored on 29 April 1998, when the CSRC announced that the 1996 annual report of Qiong Minyuan was fraudulent; in particular, the RMB570 million profit was fictitious and RMB600 million capital reserves non-existent. Qiong Minyuan and its associated company Shenzhen Non-Ferrous were found to have manipulated their share price.

56 Xiaohu Tong (2005), Financial Services in China, the Past, Present and Future, Singapore: China Knowledge Press Private Limited, p. 223.

57 Shiguang Ma (2004), The Efficient of China's Stock Market, Aldershot Hants England; Burlington, VT: Ashgate p. 245.

58 Promulgation date: 29 June 2006, effective date: 29 June 2006.

59 Zhonglu Qin (2007), 'Amendments to Criminal Law of PRC(No. 6) and Reflection on Financial Crimes Legislation (Xingfa Xiuzhengan (Liu) yu Woguo Jinrong Fanzui Lifa de Sikao)', *Journal of Jinan University(Philosophy & Social Science Edition)*, 1, p. 79.

60 Amendment (VI) to the Criminal Law, Article XII. If the public fund management institutions such as social securities fund management institutions and housing accumulation fund management institutions, and insurance companies, insurance assets management companies and security investment fund management companies utilize the capital, which is contrary to the State provisions, the persons who are directly in charge and the other persons who are directly liable shall be punished according to the preceding provisions.

61 Amendment (VII) to the Criminal Law, promulgation date: 28 February 2009, effective date: 28 February 2009. Amendment (VIII) to the Criminal Law, promulgation date: 25 February 2011, effective date: 1 May 2011.

62 Xiaohu Tong (2005), Financial Services in China, the Past, Present and Future, Singapore: China Knowledge Press Private Limited, p. 225.

63 Securities Law, promulgation date: 27 October 2005, effective date: 1 January 2006.

64   Ibid., Article 66 (5).

65   Ibid., Article 67.

66   Ibid.

67   Ibid., Article 68.

68   Ibid., Article 69.

69   E. Bettelheim, H. Parry and W. Rees, Swaps and Off-Exchange Derivatives Trading: Law and Regulation, London: FT Law & Tax (1996), p.202. And, IOSCO (1995), Final Report From the Co-Chairman of the May 1995 Windsor Meeting to the Technical Committee of IOSCO. And, A.S. Bhalla (1 April 1995), 'Collapse of Barings Bank: Case of Market Failure', *Economic and Political Weekly*, 30 (13), pp. 658–662.

70   Qingjiang Kong (2006), 'International Regulation of Finance: is Regionalism a Preferred Option to Multilateralism for East Asia?' in The Regulation of International Financial Markets-Perspectives for Reform, edited by Rainer Grote & Thilo Marauhn, Cambridge: Cambridge University Press, p. 151.

71   Ibid.

72   The case will be discussed in detail in Chapter 6.

73   CSRC (2007), http://202.106.183.108/n575458/n575667/n818795/3978419.html, last accessed: 11 August 2010.

74   The www.163.com is a common Chinese Internet domain.

75   On the function of the administrative decision of the CSRC, further analysis can be found in Chapter 5.

76   CSRC (2007), http://202.106.183.108/n575458/n575667/n818795/3978419.html, last accessed: 11 August 2010.

77   Jim Drinkhall (1997), 'Internet Fraud', *Journal of Financial Crime*, 4 (3), pp. 242–244.

78   Robert. R. Pennington (1990), The Law of the Investment Markets, Blackwell Law, p. 305.

79   Ibid., p. 307.

80   Olu Omoyele (2005), 'Disclosure, Financial Misconduct and Listed Companies: A Critical Analysis of the UKLA's Continuing Obligation Regime', *Journal of Financial Crime*, 12 (4), pp. 310–326. The general requirements of continuing disclosure can be found in the UK Listing Rules, details see the Chapter 2.

81   Consolidated: 11 March 1985.

82   Date of Royal Assent: 7 November 1986, repeal date: 1 December 2001.

83   'Big Bang' refers to the structural reorganization of the London Stock Exchange in October 1986. Prior to the Big Bang, the brokers acted as agents on behalf of individual investors and borrowers; the jobbers fulfiled the market-making role of dealing in securities as principals. The essential change brought about by the Big Bang was the move from a single capacity system, under which there was a clear distinction between jobbers and brokers, to a dual capacity system whereby market makers not only quote prices in particular securities, but act as agents bringing borrowers and lenders to the market. Moreover, the stock exchange rules were also changed to allow foreign institutions to be members of the exchange. And, the trade shifted from the floor of the exchange to a screen based system using telephones to make transactions. See The new Palgrave Dictionary of Money & Finance, edited by Peter Newman, Murray Milgate, John Eatwell, London: Macmillan Press Ltd; New York: Stockton Press, 1992, p. 202.

84   Date of Royal Assent: 14 June 2000, implemented date: 1 December 2001.

85   Ibid., Section 2.

86   Made: 21 April 2004, came into force: 30 April 2004, implementation date in the UK: 1 November 2007.

87   Date of Royal Assent: 19 December 2012.

88   See PRA website, www.bankofengland.co.uk/pra/Pages/default.aspx, last accessed: 1 May 2013.

89 See FCA website, www.fca.org.uk/about/what, last accessed: 1 May 2013.

90 See FCA website, www.fca.org.uk/firms/markets/ukla, last accessed: 12 May 2013.

91 Berry Fong-Chung Hsu, Douglas W. Arner, Maurice Kwok-Sang Tse and Syren Johnstone (2006), Financial Markets in Hong Kong – Law and Practice, Oxford: Oxford University Press, p. 18. The contents of this part mainly took reference from the book. And, 'Hong Kong Stock Market Historical Events', www.hkex.com.hk/eng/stat/statrpt/factbook2002/documents/29.pdf, last accessed: 3 November 2010.

92 BAK Rider & HL French (1979), The Regulation of Insider Trading, London: Macmillan, p. 329.

93 Effective date: 1 July 1933, revised, please refers to the latest version.

94 Berry Fong-Chung Hsu, Douglas W. Arner, Maurice Kwok-Sang Tse, Syren Johnstone (2006), Financial Markets in Hong Kong – Law and Practice, Oxford: Oxford University Press, p. 19.

95 Ruhan Lü (1994), Securities Market (Gupiao Shichang), Hong Kong: Shangwu Yinshuguan, p. 29.

96 Berry Fong-Chung Hsu, Douglas W. Arner, Maurice Kwok-Sang Tse and Syren Johnstone (2006), Financial Markets in Hong Kong – Law and Practice, Oxford: Oxford University Press, p. 20.

97 See HKEx website, www.hkex.com.hk/eng/exchange/corpinfo/history/history.htm, last accessed: 15 September 2010.

98 SFC (2000), Introducing the SFC, p. 2.

99 See SFC website, www.sfc.hk/sfc/html/EN/speeches/public/others/main.html, last accessed: 15 September 2010.

100 See HKEx website, www.hkex.com.hk/eng/exchange/exchange.htm, last accessed: 15 September 2010.

101 Effective date: 1 April 2003 (since amended).

102 Updated: 3 June 2010, more discussion can be found in Chapter 2.

103 SFC HK, (March 2004), Retail Investor Survey 2003, www.sfc.hk/sfc/doc/TC/speeches/public/surveys/retail_investor_survey_040303_chi.pdf, last accessed: 11 August 2010.

104 See IOSCO website, www.iosco.org/about/, last accessed: 12 May 2013.

105 IOSCO (May 2003), Objectives and Principles of Securities Regulation.

106 IOSCO (10 June 2010), Global Securities Regulators Adopt New Principles and Increase Focus on Systemic Risk.

107 CSRC website, www.csrc.gov.cn/n575458/n575667/n818795/11090230.html, last accessed: 4 November 2010.

108 See www.iasb.org/NR/rdonlyres/E366C162–17E4–4FBE-80EB-7A506A615138/0/Framework.pdf, last accessed: 11 August 2010.

109 See the IASB website, www.iasb.org/NR/rdonlyres/8177F9A2-EB2F-45A3-BBF3–3DE7DCB13E1A/0/IFRS7.pdf, last accessed: 16 August 2010.

110 The OECD Principles of Corporate Governance, Chapter V.

111 TUAC Secretariat (October 2004), The OECD Principles of Corporate Governance, An Evolution of 2004 Review, www.tuac.org.

112 Ibid.

113 Promulgation date: 7 January 2001, effective date: 7 January 2001.

114 See UNCTAD website, www.unctad.org/Templates/Startpage.asp?intItemID=2531, last accessed: 16 August 2010.

115 See UNCTAD website, www.unctad.org/TEMPLATES/webflyer.asp?docid=7084&intItemID=2068&lang=1, last accessed: 16 August 2010.

116 Ibid.

2 Listed companies' disclosure and the role of stock exchanges

Introduction

Recently, extra attention has been given to the 'manipulators' or 'insiders' within the Chinese securities market. Apart from other traditional economic crimes, civil offences and securities crimes conducted by listed companies imposed strong negative impacts on the Chinese securities market. It not only demolished the image of the listed companies, but also brought massive losses to investors. Reasons for the phenomenon are various; numerous researchers have focused on this issue already. However, it is argued in this chapter that the information disclosure system and stock exchanges as a whole can serve the purposes of control and preventing illicit and illegal conduct by the listed companies.

As explained in Chapter 1, disclosure is one of the effective regulatory tools. Although, on the other hand, imperfect information disclosure may assist law breaking behaviour. The Chinese Criminal Law, Company Law, Securities Law and other laws and regulations have given a lot of attention to this issue. In this chapter the internal and external relationship between information disclosure rules, listed companies and stock exchanges will be analysed in order to suggest an effective regulatory regime.

First, this chapter will discuss the basic information required of listed companies. Second, detailed disclosure requirements will be examined. A comparative study between Mainland China, the UK and Hong Kong will be carried out. Following this, the function of the stock exchanges will be analysed. This chapter demonstrates that the information disclosure regime is an efficient approach to prevent and control the offences and crimes conducted by listed companies, and that the stock exchanges can perform a unique role in this respect.

The Chinese listed companies

Recent debates have argued that civil offences and crimes conducted by some listed companies are the 'original sins' within the Chinese securities market.[1] It has been argued that 'historical reasons (Lishi Yuanyin)' led to the phenomenon in which the controlling shareholders and their agents either on the board of directors or in the management corps of a company continued to operate in an historical mode: a large proportion of the listed companies in China are in fact transformed state-owned enterprises, recast as companies limited by shares that seek to finance themselves through the capital markets without really disturbing control by the original owner-operators.[2] Moreover, under the emerging and transitional nature of the Chinese securities market, securities and futures crimes are more complex than before, and the formats tend to be more concealed.[3] These arguments mainly focus on systemic or institutional dimensions. It must be admitted that the above opinions reflect the truth, that there are certain 'birth defects' in the Chinese securities market. And the incomplete regulatory environment and insufficient institutional input seems to have deepened the risk-orientations of some listed companies.

Chinese listed companies have experienced a fast development process. It can be seen from the Table 2.1 that the number of listed companies has increased significantly, starting from ten (in the year 1990) to 2,342 (in the year 2011). Moreover, the regional distribution of listed companies has changed. In 2010, the number of listed companies (A and B Shares) in Mainland China, Foreign Fund (B Shares) in the Mainland, H Shares overseas were 2,063, 108 and 165 respectively, while the figures in 2011 have been increased to 2,342, 108 and 171 respectively (Table 2.2).[4] Chinese listed companies have been participating actively in other markets.

Table 2.1 The number of listed companies (1990–2011)

Year	National	Shanghai Stock Exchange	Shenzhen Stock Exchange	A Shares	B Shares	A&B Shares
1990	10	8	2			
1991	14	8	6			
1992	53	29	24			
1993	183	106	77	177	41	35
1994	291	171	120	287	58	54
1995	323	188	135	311	70	58
1996	530	293	237	514	85	69
1997	745	383	362	720	101	76
1998	851	438	413	825	106	80
1999	949	484	465	922	108	81
2000	1,088	572	516	1,060	114	86
2001	1,160	646	514	1,140	112	92
2002	1,224	715	509	1,213	111	100
2003	1,287	780	507	1,277	111	101
2004	1,377	837	540	1,363	110	96
2005	1,381	834	547	1,358	109	86
2006	1,434	842	592	1,411	109	86
2007	1,550	860	690	1,527	109	86
2008	1,625	864	761	1,602	109	86
2009	1,718	870	848	1,696	108	86
2010	2,063	894	1,169	2,041	108	86
2011	2,342	931	1,411	2,320	108	86

Source: according to the National Statistics website.[5]

Table 2.2 The number of listed companies (geographic distribution)

Item	2010	2011
Number of Listed Companies (A and B Shares) in Mainland	2,063	2,342
Number of Listed Companies of Foreign Fund (B Shares) in Mainland	108	108
Number of Listed Companies (H Shares) Overseas	165	171

Source: according to the National Statistics website.[6]

Table 2.3 illustrates the financial figures for Chinese listed companies. It can be seen that these companies not only increased in number but also that they have maintained their wealth. In 1992, the total assets of listed companies were RMB48.1 billion while in 2011, the figure increased to RMB102,884.252 billion. In terms of the net assets, they increased from RMB16.827 billion (1992) to RMB13,576.778 billion (2011). Total profits improved from RMB3.164 billion in 1992 to RMB2,609.941 billion in 2011. Moreover, net profits increased from RMB2.403 billion (1992) to RMB1,911.074 billion (2011).

From the above figures, the importance of listed companies can be seen. Listed companies are the basic components of the securities market. The quality of their behaviour, together with their performance on the international or national capital markets, is fundamentally important to the financial system, and to the national economy. The fast growth of listed companies has contributed to

Table 2.3 Financial figures of listed companies (1992–2011)

Year	Total assets (100,000,000)	Net assets (100,000,000)	Revenue (100,000,000)	Total profit (100,000,000)	Net profit (100,000,000)
1992	481.00	168.27	225.55	31.64	24.03
1993	1,821.00	933.00	954.00	157.00	137.00
1994	3,309.00	1,628.00	1,680.00	256.00	214.12
1995	4,295.00	1,958.00	2,204.00	256.00	211.00
1996	6,352.00	2,940.00	3,235.00	344.00	282.00
1997	9,660.58	4,824.77	5,076.51	577.33	467.76
1998	12,407.52	6,266.76	6,269.71	614.40	466.97
1999	16,107.36	7,639.35	7,974.56	806.31	628.88
2000	21,673.88	10,079.77	10,783.87	1,007.43	769.22
2001	29,257.03	12,975.66	15,475.80	1,016.48	694.22
2002	41,526.17	14,636.98	19,001.97	1,298.89	826.95
2003	53,246.30	17,044.80	25,047.16	1,890.11	1,256.83
2004	63,472.40	19,261.59	34,064.44	2,671.98	1,757.06
2005	72,712.99	20,461.59	41,042.29	2,627.31	1,674.82
2006	218,489.62	33,418.35	50,774.97	5,109.75	3,400.76
2007	414,151.60	67,772.61	73,144.42	13,433.60	9,962.23
2008	486,892.35	72,228.88	88,241.06	10,738.72	8,199.28
2009	617,852.11	77,364.18	85,305.95	13,678.97	10,032.22
2010	862,227.27	114,143.88	144,619.94	22,208.87	16,457.13
2011	1,028,842.52	135,767.78	185,414.53	26,099.41	19,110.74

Source: according to the CSRC.[7]

the economic infrastructure and has further facilitated the establishment of a modern corporate culture. Based on these considerations, it is important to establish an effective regulatory regime for listed companies.

The development of regulatory structure

The regulation of listed companies has experienced several reforms. With the development of the Chinese capital market, legislation and other rules or regulations have been improved and enhanced. Starting from a relative weak point, the legal framework is moving towards a more comprehensive and modern structure.

As mentioned in the first chapter, before 1979, there were not many substantial clauses or sections concerning securities transactions. In 1993, the Interim Administrative Measures for the Issuing and Transaction of Securities[8] and the Interim Measures for the Prohibition of Issuing Securities by Fraudulent Means[9] produced the relevant offences; for instance, insider dealing and manipulating securities prices were regulated. Following this, the Criminal Law 1997 made significant improvements to these aspects of legislation. Together with the Securities Law 1998, a more comprehensive and effective regulatory framework had been established. Last but not least, in 2005, the revision and enforcement of the Company Law and the Securities Law brought extensive developments to the regulatory framework. The supervisory and regulatory regime reached a new level.[10]

The Securities Law primarily established the basic requirements for an information disclosure regime. Moreover, the enactment of a revised Securities Law and Company Law enhanced the system in order to accommodate the development of the Chinese capital market. Currently, the information disclosure regime is mainly under the supervision and regulation of these two laws. And, the regulation promulgated by the China Securities Regulatory Commission (hereafter CSRC) plays an important role.[11] The new laws and regulations showed the determination of the regulator to enhance the management of the information disclosure system. To a certain degree, the revised regime will promote a more efficient and transparent disclosure system.

Beside the above, there are various detailed rules that implement the basic Chinese laws. The Administrative Measures for the Disclosure of Information of Listed Companies (hereafter the Measures), that were adopted to meet the requirements and needs of the regulatory and supervisory purpose, have played an important role. Compared with the Securities Law, Company Law and Criminal Law, the Measures have more detailed requirements, focusing on the management of information disclosure. Under the Measures, a listed company is required to establish the relevant rules on the management of information disclosure, which contain the information that shall be disclosed and the criteria for disclosure; procedures for the transmission, check and disclosure of undisclosed information; the duties of the administrative department for information disclosure affairs and the person in charge of the work of information disclosure; the reporting and disclosure duties of the directors and the board of directors, supervisors and the board of supervisors, and senior managers; the rules on the records and preservation of records; the confidentiality measures for the undisclosed information, the range and confidentiality responsibilities of the insiders of the inside information; the internal control and supervision mechanism for the management of financial affairs and accounting calculations; the application for, check and announcement of information to be publicly released, and the information communication with the investors, investment service institutions, the media as well as the relevant rules; the archival management of documents and materials relating to information disclosure; the rules on the management and reporting of information disclosure affairs relating to the subsidiaries of the listed company; and the investigation and punishment mechanism regarding the liabilities for failure to disclose information as required, the measures for punishing violators.[12] Moreover, when the relevant personnel of a listed company violates the Measures, the CSRC may take the following supervisory actions: to order him to make a correction; to hold supervisory talks; to issue a letter of warning; to record the violation, non-performance of public commitment and other information in his credit archive, and make an announcement; to determine the individual as inappropriate to assume his position.[13]

It can be seen from the above laws and regulations that the basic regulatory framework for listed companies has experienced several reforms. The enforcement of the Measures abolished a batch of regulations: the Detailed Rules for the Disclosure of Information of Companies Offering Stocks Publicly (for Trial Implementation) (No. 43 [1993] of the CSRC), Notice on the Disclosure of Information about Public Offering of Stocks and Listed Companies (No. 19 [1993] of the CSRC), Notice on Strengthening the Examination of Temporary Reports of Listed Companies (No. 26 [1996] of the CSRC), Notice on Several Issues Concerning the Release of Clarification Announcements by Listed Companies (No. 28 [1996] of the CSRC), Notice on the Electronic Filing of Information Disclosed by Listed Companies (No. 50 [1998] of the CSRC), Notice on Strengthening the Supervision over Information Disclosed by Special Treatment and Particular Transfer Companies (No. 63 [2000] of the CSRC), Notice on the Issues Concerning the Interim Reports of Listed Companies to Issue New Stocks (No. 69 [2001] of the CSRC as well as the Notice on the Submission of Temporary Announcements of Listed Companies and Pertinent Annexes to the Institutions dispatched by China Securities Regulatory Commission for Archival Purposes (No. 7 [2003] of the CSRC).[14] These legal documents had set out different requirements for the corporate disclosure system.

Similarly with other sectors, the reform is continuing. One of the basic features of Chinese securities regulation regarding information disclosure is the revising, re-enacting and even restructuring of the law and regulations. On one hand, the result is derived from the economic reforms; on the other hand, it is devised to achieve better supervisory purposes. It should be borne in mind that the necessary improvements and developments are essential for a transitional market; however, one of the preconditions for maintaining effectiveness is that there shall be no significant gaps between rules and regulations. The information disclosure system is quite complex. With the development of financial globalization, the complexity may be further increased. Therefore, confusion or even conflict among the different legal requirements must be avoided.

The detailed disclosure requirements

The fundamental requirements for the information disclosure regime under the current regulatory structure can be headed into three categories: the information that is disclosed by issuers and listed companies shall be authentic, accurate and integrated;[15] the information disclosed by issuers and listed companies shall not have any false records, misleading statements or major omissions;[16] the information disclosed by issuers and listed companies shall reflect the latest situation, and this principle implies that listed companies shall provide the latest information in real time.[17]

Besides the above fundamental principles, the regime also sets down more detailed requirements. Principally, according to the Company Law, Securities Law and other regulations, the listed company shall publish the following information (Figure 2.1): listing announcement and prospectus; financial reports, including the midterm report, annual report and other financial statements, for instance, statement of profit appropriation; and temporary reports, in particular in terms of 'major events'.

Last but not least, besides the above basic requirements, the regime has also emphasized the methods of disclosure. According to Securities Law and other regulation, the reports and financial statements shall be published according to the formats which have been set down by the CSRC; and the listed companies shall publish the relevant information in the designated place within the prescribed period.[18] Moreover, the directors and senior managers of listed companies shall guarantee the authenticity, accuracy and integrity of the information.[19]

It can be seen from the above analysis that an information disclosure regime has been established in China. Moreover, the new laws and regulations show China's determination to enhance the application of the information disclosure system. Compared with the previous regime, this shows that more completed rules are now enforced. It should be possible to promote the disclosure regime to a certain degree as more efficient and transparent than before. Furthermore, the CSRC, financial institutions and investors have given a lot of attention to this issue. Surveillance from the whole of society may also lead the regime down a healthier path.

Application for listing

This part will only focus on the key issues relating to the information disclosure regime in particular, using the application for listing as a typical example to illustrate the regulatory regime.

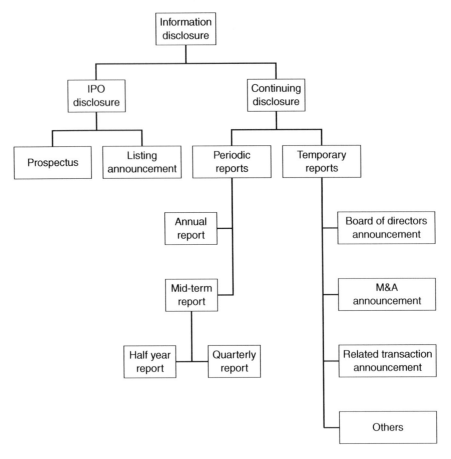

Figure 2.1 General requirement of information disclosure (source: Information Disclosure of the listed Companies and its Analysis[20]).

The mainland China perspective

Currently, the application for the initial public offering (IPO) shall be filed and submitted with the following documents to the CSRC: the business license of the company; the constitution of the company; the resolution of the general assembly of shareholders; the prospectus; the financial statements; the name and address of the bank that receives the funds as generated from the public offer of stocks on the behalf of the company; the name of the underwriting institution and the relevant agreements; when there is a sponsor, the Recommendation Letter of Issuance from him shall be submitted.[21] Moreover, the listing application shall be filed with a stock exchange in order to obtain the approval of the stock exchange, and a listing agreement shall be concluded by the company and stock exchange.[22] In the terms of documentation, when applying for the listing, the following documents shall be provided: the listing report; the resolution of the general assembly of shareholders regarding the application for the listing of stocks; the constitution; the business license; the financial statements of the company for the latest three years as audited by an accounting firm; the legal opinions and the Recommendation Letter of Listing; and the latest prospectus.[23] Apart from these, the listing rules of the Shanghai Stock Exchange (hereafter the SSE)[24] and Shenzhen Stock Exchange (hereafter the SZSE)[25] set out more comprehensive requirements.

In the SSE, an issuer applying for listing its IPO shares shall submit: listing application; the approval documents issued by the CSRC; the resolutions of the board of directors and the shareholders' general meeting with respect to its listing application; photocopy of the company's business license; the articles of association of the company; the financial reports of the company for the most recent three years audited in accordance with law by any Certified Public Accountant (hereafter CPA) firm with the qualification for practice in securities and futures related business; sponsorship agreement and the letter of listing sponsorship produced by a sponsor; legal opinion issued by a law firm; document evidencing the registration of all its shares with China Securities Depository and Clearing Corporation Limited (hereafter the CSDCC);[26] capital verification report produced by a CPA firm with the relevant qualification; particulars on the shareholdings of directors, supervisors and senior officers and the declaration and undertaking with regard to directors (supervisors, senior officers); relevant information about the person who is intended to be appointed or has been appointed as the board secretary by the issuer; the financial information newly added during the period since the public offering up to the listing pursuant to relevant regulations, and a statement on relevant material events, if applicable; the controlling shareholder and de facto controller's undertaking that within 36 months of listing of the issuer's shares, they shall not transfer the issuer's shares issued before the IPO and held by them either directly or indirectly, or appoint others for the management of such shares, and such shares shall not be repurchased by the issuer; the latest prospectus and full set of IPO application documents; document evidencing the lock-up of the shares issued and held before the public offering; listing announcement.[27]

In the SZSE, an issuer applying to the Exchange for listing its IPO shares shall submit the following documents: listing report (listing application); the resolutions of the board of directors and the general meeting with respect to its listing application; photocopy of the company's business license; the articles of association of the company; the audited financial reports of the company for the most recent three years; sponsorship agreement and the letter of listing sponsorship produced by a sponsor; legal opinion issued by a law firm; capital verification report produced by a competent CPA firm; document evidencing the registration of all its shares with the SD & C; report on the shareholdings of directors, supervisors and senior management and the declaration and undertaking with regard to directors (supervisors, senior management or the controlling shareholder and de facto controller); relevant information about the person who is intended to be appointed or has been appointed as the board secretary by the issuer; the undertaking letter of the controlling shareholder and de facto controller; document evidencing the lock-up of the shares issued and held before the public offering; the financial information newly added during the period since the public offering up to the listing, and a statement on relevant material events, if applicable; the latest prospectus; listing announcement.[28]

After the stock exchange approves the issuer's application for listing its IPO shares, in the SSE, the issuer shall disclose the relevant documents in the designated website within five trading days prior to the listing: listing announcement; the articles of association of the company; legal opinion; letter of listing sponsorship and other documents.[29] While in the SZSE the issuer shall disclose: the listing announcement; the articles of association of the company; the resolution of the shareholders' general meeting with respect to its listing application; legal opinion; letter of listing sponsorship.[30] It can be seen that the SSE did not specify the requirement of disclosing the resolution of shareholders concerning listing, instead used 'other documents'.

From these provisions, it can be seen that there are no material differences between the listing rules regarding an IPO application in the SSE and SZSE. As stated earlier, to maintain a consistent corporate disclosure system is crucially important for the Chinese securities market. Although the main focus of the stock exchanges are slightly different (for instance, the SSE puts more emphasis on state-owned enterprises,[31] while the SZSE is concentrating more on developing a multi-layer capital market system[32]) the basic regulatory structure will remain similar. In this context, it will be less time consuming for Chinese companies. Furthermore, it will be more cost effective. More details of the function of the SSE and SZSE will be discussed in the later part of this chapter.

The UK perspective

After the recent regulatory structure reform, the UK Listing Authority (hereafter the UKLA), which is a part of the Financial Conduct Authority (hereafter FCA) is currently responsible for regulating all bonds listed in the financial services market.[33]

The FCA oversees the admission process to a Regulated Market, to assess issuers' eligibility and to ensure the relevant rules are met. More specifically, it monitors market disclosure by issuers and others under the FCA Disclosure and Transparency Rules; reviews and approves of prospectuses published by issuers and offerors of securities under the FCA Prospectus Rules; and operates the UK listing regime under FCA Listing Rules.[34]

According to the Listing Rules (hereafter the LR),[35] when a company is applying to list equity shares, relevant documents need to be submitted. All documents to be submitted to the FCA by midday, two business days before for the application: a completed Application; the prospectus or listing particulars that has been approved by the FCA, or a copy of the prospectus, a certificate of approval and a translation of the summary of the prospectus, if another European Economic Area (EEA) State[36] is the home Member State for the shares; the circular that has been published in connection with the application; the approved supplementary prospectus or approved supplementary listing particulars, if applicable; written confirmation of the number of shares to be allotted (pursuant to a board resolution allotting the shares); if a prospectus or listing particulars have not been produced, a copy of the Regulated Information Service (RIS) announcement detailing the number and type of shares that are the subject of the application and the circumstances of their issue.[37]

Documents signed by a sponsor (if applicable) or by a duly authorized officer of the applicant (if a sponsor is not required) must be submitted to the FCA before 9 a.m. on the day the FCA is to consider the application: a completed Shareholder Statement, if an applicant is applying for a listing of a class of shares for the first time; or a completed Pricing Statement, in the case of a placing, open offer, vendor consideration placing, offer for subscription of equity shares or an issue out of treasury of equity shares of a class already listed.[38]

If a written confirmation of the number of shares to be allotted pursuant to a board resolution cannot be submitted to the FCA by the deadline or the number of shares to be admitted is lower than the number notified according to the LR, written confirmation of the number of shares to be allotted or admitted must be provided to the FCA by the applicant or its sponsor at least one hour before the admission to listing is to become effective.[39] Furthermore, if the FCA has considered an application for listing and the shares that are the subject of the application are not all allotted and admitted following the initial allotment of the shares (for example, under an offer for subscription), further allotments of shares may be admitted if before 4 p.m. on the day before admission is sought the FCA has been provided with: written confirmation of the number of shares allotted pursuant to a board resolution; and a copy of the RIS announcement detailing the number and type of shares and the circumstances of their issue.[40]

Last but not least, written confirmation of the number of shares that were allotted (pursuant to a board resolution allotting the shares) must be submitted to the FCA as soon as practicable after admission, if the number is lower than the number that was announced under LR 3.2.7 G as being admitted to listing.[41]

Additionally, an applicant must keep copies of the following for six years after the admission to listing: any agreement to acquire any assets, business or shares in consideration for or in relation to that which the company's shares are being issued; any letter, report, valuation, contract or other documents referred to in the prospectus, listing particulars, circular or other document issued in connection with those shares; the applicant's constitution as at the date of admission; the annual report and accounts of the applicant and of any guarantor, for each of the periods which form part of the applicant's financial record contained in the prospectus or listing particulars; any interim accounts made up since the date to which the last annual report and accounts were made up and prior to the date of admission; any temporary and definitive documents of title; in the case of an application in respect of shares issued pursuant to an employees' share scheme, the scheme document; where listing particulars or another document are published in connection with any scheme requiring court approval, any court order and the certificate of registration issued by the Registrar of Companies; and copies of board resolutions of the applicant allotting or issuing the shares.[42]

The Hong Kong perspective

Currently, in addition to the Company Ordinance[43] and Securities and Futures Ordinance,[44] the Rules Governing the Listing of Securities on the Stock Exchange of Hong Kong Limited (hereafter Listing Rules) includes detailed requirements for issuers to provide timely information to the shareholders and public.[45] Similar to other jurisdictions, the information required to be disclosed by issuers under the Listing Rules can be grouped into the following categories: announcements and notices; corporate communications; and the prospectus and application forms. For the purpose of comparative study, the information provided for the listing sought for the equity securities of a Main Board issuer that does not already have share capital listed will be examined here.

In order to allow the Exchange to have sufficient time to consider an application for listing, the applicant must normally make an application for listing to the Exchange not less than 25 clear business days prior to the date on which it is expected that the Listing Committee will meet to consider the application.

As for the required information, the following shall be provided with the application: general information about the issuer, its advisers and the listing document; information about the securities for which listing is sought and the terms and conditions of their issue and distribution; information about the issuer's capital; general information about the group's activities; financial information about the group and the prospects of the group; information about the issuer's management; use of proceeds; material contracts and documentation for inspection.[46]

The Listing Rules set out the details for the documents to be inspected (not less than 14 days): the memorandum and articles of association or equivalent documents of the issuer; each contract disclosed pursuant to the Listing Rules, in the case of a contract not reduced into writing, a memorandum giving full particulars; all reports, letters or other documents, balance sheets, valuations and statements by any expert any part of which is extracted or referred to in the listing document; a written statement signed by the reporting accountants setting out the adjustments made by them in arriving at the figures shown in their report and giving the reasons; and the audited accounts of the issuer or, in the case of a group, the consolidated audited accounts of the issuer and its subsidiaries for each of the two financial years immediately preceding the issue of the listing document together with (in the case of a Hong Kong issuer) all notes, certificates or information required by the Companies Ordinance.[47]

The discloseable transaction

The mainland China perspective

Chapter 1 of this book introduced the reform of the regime of major events under the revised Securities Law as one of the important improvements. Moreover, the

Administrative Measures for the Disclosure of Information of Listed Companies went further to define the term major event. When a major event occurs that may considerably affect the trading price of a listed company's shares, but is not yet known to the investors, the listed company shall disclose it, stating the cause, the present situation, and the possible legal consequence of such an event. The major event includes (in addition to the items defined under Article 67 of Securities Law[48]): any newly promulgated law, regulation, rules or industrial policy that may considerably affect the company; a resolution of the board of directors on the new stock offering plan or any other financing plan or equity incentive plan; a court ruling which prohibits the controlling shareholder from transferring its shares; 5 per cent or more of the shares held by any shareholder is pledged, frozen, judicially auctioned, kept in custody or in trust, or the voting rights of such shareholder are limited; the main assets have been sealed up, detained, frozen, mortgaged or pledged; the main or all businesses have stopped; providing any important external guarantee; obtaining a large sum of government subsidy or any other extra proceeds which are likely to produce important effects on the assets, liabilities, rights and interests or business achievements of the company; changes in the accounting policies or accounting estimates; if there is any error in the information disclosed previously or because the company fails to disclose information as required or because the information disclosed contains any false record so that the company is ordered to make a correction by the relevant organ or the board of directors of the company decides to make a correction.[49] Moreover, after a listed company discloses the major event, if the progress or change of this major event may considerably affect the transaction prices of its securities and the derivatives, it shall disclose the progress or change and its possible consequences in a timely manner.[50]

More specifically, the SSE Listing Rules state that listed companies shall promptly disclose a transaction when it reaches the following standard: the total amount of assets involved in the transaction (if such assets have both book value and valuation, the higher shall be applied) accounts for more than 10 per cent of the listed company's latest audited total assets; the transaction amount (including the debt and expenses incurred) accounts for more than 10 per cent of the listed company's latest audited net assets, with the absolute amount of the transaction exceeding RMB10 million; profit derived from the transaction accounts for more than 10 per cent of the listed company's audited net profit for the most recent financial year, with the absolute amount of the profit exceeding RMB1 million; operating income related to the subject matter of the transaction for the most recent financial year accounts for more than 10 per cent of the listed company's audited operating income for the same period, with the absolute amount of the income exceeding RMB10 million; or the net profit related to the subject matter of the transaction for the most recent financial year accounts for more than 10 per cent of the listed company's audited net profit for the same period, with the absolute amount of the net profit exceeding RMB1 million.[51]

Moreover, when a transaction reaches the following level, the listed companies shall promptly disclose the relevant information, and shall submit the transaction to the shareholders' general meeting for consideration: total amount of assets involved in the transaction (if such assets have both book value and valuation, the higher shall be applied) accounts for more than 50 per cent of the listed company's latest audited total assets; transaction amount (including the debt and expenses incurred) accounts for more than 50 per cent of the listed company's latest audited net assets, with the absolute amount of the transaction exceeding RMB50 million; profit derived from a transaction that accounts for more than 50 per cent of the listed company's audited net profit for the most recent financial year, with the absolute amount of the profit exceeding RMB5 million; operating income related to the subject matter of a transaction for the most recent financial year accounts for more than 50 per cent of the listed company's audited operation income for the same period, with the absolute amount of the income exceeding RMB50 million; or net profit related to the subject matter of a transaction for the most recent financial year accounts for more than 50 per cent of the listed company's audited net profit for the same period, with the absolute amount of the net profit exceeding RMB5 million.[52]

The Listing Rules also set up the standard for the disclosure concerning guarantee by listed companies.[53] The above figures are quoted from the SSE Listing Rules, as stated earlier, the Main Board Listing Rules of the SZSE have similar provisions and standards.

The UK perspective

Under the current regime of the UK, in order to ensure the shareholders of companies with equity shares listed are aware of certain transactions entered into by a listed company, the Listing Rules empowered the FCA with the authority to determine whether a transaction is in the ordinary course of business or not.[54] Moreover, the transaction is classified by assessing its size relative to that of the listed company proposing to make it, and the comparison of size is made by using percentage ratios.[55] These tests are: the gross assets test, the profit test, the consideration test and the gross capital test.[56] The gross assets test is calculated by dividing the gross assets the subject of the transaction by the gross assets of the listed company.[57] The profits test is calculated by dividing the profits attributable to the assets the subject of the transaction by the profits of the listed company.[58] The consideration test is calculated by taking the consideration for the transaction as a percentage of the aggregate market value of all the ordinary shares (excluding treasury shares) of the listed company.[59] The gross capital test is calculated by dividing the gross capital of the company or business being acquired by the gross capital of the listed company.[60]

In general, these transactions are divided into two classes. The Class 2 transaction refers to a transaction where any percentage ratio is 5 per cent or more but each is less than 25 per cent; Class 1 transaction: a transaction where any percentage ratio is 25 per cent or more.[61] Furthermore, according to the different classes, the notifications are various. In the case of Class 2, the notification shall include details of the transaction, including the name of the other party to the transaction; a description of the business carried on by, or using, the net assets the subject of the transaction; the consideration, and how it is being satisfied (including the terms of any arrangements for deferred consideration); the value of the gross assets the subject of the transaction; the profits attributable to the assets the subject of the transaction; the effect of the transaction on the listed company including any benefits which are expected to accrue to the company as a result of the transaction; details of any service contracts of proposed directors of the listed company; for a disposal, the application of the sale proceeds and, if securities are to form part of the consideration received, a statement whether the securities are to be sold or retained; finally, details of key individuals important to the business or company the subject of the transaction.[62]

For the Class 1 notification, in addition to the compliance of the Class 2 requirements, the company must send an explanatory circular to its shareholders and obtain their prior approval in a general meeting for the transaction; and ensure that any agreement effecting the transaction is conditional on that approval being obtained.[63]

The Hong Kong perspective

In Hong Kong, the continuing obligations are designed to ensure the maintenance of a fair and orderly market in securities and that all users of the market have simultaneous access to the same information.[64]

More specifically, the Listing Rules introduced that all noticeable transactions shall be disclosed. Table 2.4 sets out the basic method for the classification of the transactions. An issuer shall disclose details of acquisitions and realizations of assets and other transactions as required by the listing rules. According to the standards, there are different types of transaction: share transaction, means an acquisition of assets (excluding cash) by a listed issuer where the consideration includes securities for which listing will be sought and where all percentage ratios are less than 5 per cent; the disclosable transaction, means a transaction or a series of transactions by a listed issuer where any percentage ratio is 5 per cent or more, but less than 25 per cent; the major transaction, means a transaction or a series of transactions by a listed issuer where any percentage ratio is 25 per cent or more, but less than 100 per cent for an acquisition or 75 per cent for a disposal; the very substantial disposal means a disposal or a series of disposals of assets by a listed issuer where any percentage ratio is 75 per cent or more; the very substantial acquisition means an acquisition or a series of acquisitions of assets by a listed issuer where any percentage ratio is 100 per cent or more.[65] Moreover, the percentage ratios used here are the figures, expressed as percentages resulting from the following calculations: assets ratio, means the total assets which are the subject of the transaction divided by the total assets of the listed issuer; profit ratio, means the profit attributable to the assets which are the subject of the transaction divided by the profit of the listed issuer; revenue ratio, means the revenue attributable to the assets which are the subject of the transaction divided by the revenue of the listed issuer;

Table 2.4 Classification and percentage ratios for the transaction (HK)

Transaction type	Assets ratio	Consideration ratio	Profits ratio	Revenue ratio	Equity capital ratio
Share transaction	Less than 5 per cent	Less than 5 per cent	Less than 5 per cent	Less than 5 per cent	Less than 5 per cent
Discloseable transaction	5 per cent or more but less than 25 per cent	5 per cent or more but less than 25 per cent	5 per cent or more but less than 25 per cent	5 per cent or more but less than 25 per cent	5 per cent or more but less than 25 per cent
Major transaction – disposal	25 per cent or more but less than 75 per cent	25 per cent or more but less than 75 per cent	25 per cent or more but less than 75 per cent	25 per cent or more but less than 75 per cent	Not applicable
Major transaction – acquisition	25 per cent or more but less than 100 per cent	25 per cent or more but less than 100 per cent	25 per cent or more but less than 100 per cent	25 per cent or more but less than 100 per cent	25 per cent or more but less than 100 per cent
Very substantial disposal	75 per cent or more	75 per cent or more	75 per cent or more	75 per cent or more	Not applicable
Very substantial acquisition	100 per cent or more	100 per cent or more	100 per cent or more	100 per cent or more	100 per cent or more

Source: HKEx. [66]

consideration ratio, means the consideration divided by the total market capitalization of the listed issuer; and, the equity capital ratio, means the nominal value of the listed issuer's equity capital issued as consideration divided by the nominal value of the listed issuer's issued equity capital immediately before the transaction.[67]

The format of the disclosure

The mainland China perspective

Currently, in Mainland China, according to the requirements of law and regulation, a listed company, or others obliged to publish, shall publish the draft announcements and other reference documents in the medium designated by the CSRC.[68] For instance, the Securities Daily (Zhengquan RiBao), Securities Times (Zhengquan Shibao), Shanghai Securities News (Shanghai Zhengquan Bao), and China Securities Journal (Zhongguo Zhengquan Bao) are the major designated newspapers. The main designated websites are the SSE and SZSE websites and the relevant newspapers' websites (www.cninfo.com.cn, www.cs.com.cn, www.cnstock.com, www. secutimes.com, www.ccstock.cn, etc.). Moreover, the investors may contact the relevant departments of the listed companies or stock exchanges.

Since 2009, the launch of the ChiNext has brought some new changes to the disclosure mode.[69] ChiNext can be seen as the Growth Enterprise Board (hereafter GEB). The CSRC designated five websites as the legal platforms for information disclosure: http://chinext.cninfo.com.cn/, http://chinext.cs.com.cn/index.htm, http://chinext.cnstock.com/, http://chinext.secutimes.com/, http://chinext.ccstock.cn/index.html. Compared with the GEB, these specialized websites will be free of charge for the listed companies. It will reduce the costs for disclosing the required information, and further provide a convenient platform for investors to obtain information.

The UK perspective

In the UK, one significant issue to be noted is that the function of the Regulatory News Service (hereafter RNS).[70] The RNS, as a provider of regulatory disclosure distribution services to the UK listed and AIM companies,[71] offering them the channel to communicate with investors and fulfil the regulatory obligations through just one partner immediately and accurately in full text and in industry leading formats.[72] These announcements are visible to market professionals, databases and financial websites across the world, including Thomson Reuters, Bloomberg, Dow Jones and the LSE's own corporate website.

For the purpose of this book, aspects concerning regulatory services will be examined here. The RNS provides a comprehensive service, which allows companies to meet the regulatory obligations in the UK, Europe and the US in an accurate and secure manner. Considering the complexities of the financial market, international filings need to fulfil different requirements and formats, the RNS is user friendly. For instance, for regulatory purposes, the regulatory headlines include: company appointments, directors and meetings; deals, transactions and operational updates; offers; financial statements, dividends and corporate actions; other statements and announcements; shareholder and panel on takeovers and mergers (takeover panel) disclosures; equity, debt and investment trusts; market, RNS and related announcements; documents and circulars; and prospectus directive filings.[73] Moreover, the LSE also provide a submit demonstration in order to illustrate the announcement submission process.[74] By this method, the features of the RNS service can be demonstrated.

The Hong Kong perspective

In Hong Kong, the Electronic Disclosure Project was introduced on 25 June 2007.[75] After the implementation of the Electronic Disclosure Project, listed issuers had to submit announcements to HKEx for publication via the E-Submission System (hereafter ESS).[76] The ESS is the internet-based information submission and dissemination system launched by HKEx in October 2001, to facilitate issuers and their agents to submit information to HKEx for vetting or publication on the Exchange's websites.

Figure 2.2 shows the operation of ESS. It can be seen from the figures that the working procedures of ESS are easy to follow. Submission simply follows five steps: entry of submission details, submission preview, uploading files, approving submission and acknowledgement. Moreover, retrieval of a previously saved submission for approval can be achieved by taking the following steps: logging onto the system, searching submission history, submission history retrieval, approval submission and acknowledgement. Finally, once the approval and submission have been successful, the original submission number will be displayed again.

In fact, in Hong Kong, there was a reform in the information dissemination regime as well. Initially, the main board issuers needed to distribute all announcements; for instance, announcements and circulars, corporate communication and prospectus and application forms through a variety of channels, including: newspapers (by way of paid announcements as required under the main board Listing Rules), the Exchange Website, the third generation of the Automatic Order Matching and Execution System of the Exchange, the Exchange's information services such as the Market Data Feed, the Issuer Information Feed System and the Electronic Mailing Stock Information Service. This issuer information disclosure regime was designed at a time when disclosures were still largely paper based and most investors obtained market information from newspapers. The increasing popularity of the Internet has provided opportunities for more timely disclosure and better market transparency. The paper process is inefficient, time consuming and presents unnecessary risks. To satisfy the market's demand for timely information disclosure by issuers, electronic submission through the ESS has been made mandatory and publication of announcements in the newspapers optional.[77]

Submission and approval of files in single session

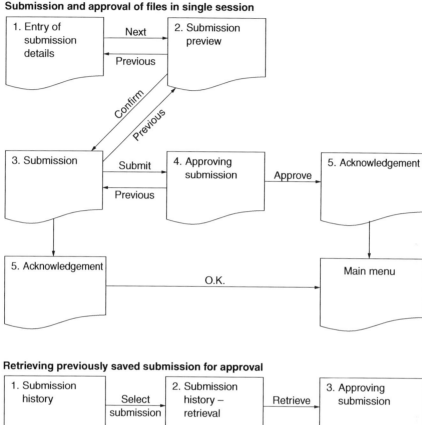

Retrieving previously saved submission for approval

Figure 2.2 ESS system working procedures (source: HKEx[78]).

The similarities and differences

The previous part of this chapter focuses on the legal requirements on information disclosure in the three jurisdictions. The selected three perspectives cannot constitute a complete regulatory framework. However, they can represent the regulatory regime from a certain degree.

First of all, it can be seen from the requirements of the three jurisdictions that there is no material difference in the required information for the general listing application. In fact, throughout the development procedures of the information disclosure regime, either nationally or internationally, the information to be disclosed is continuously being reformed, enhanced and redesigned. Different time periods, diverse regulatory structures, various industrial perspectives, even under the same time and supervisory structures the classification of investment may lead to different disclosure requirements. However, this situation can be changed, and although different problems arose in the unfair disclosure, the format and contents of the disclosure itself, compared with the enforcement, is not a deadlock issue, as these are easily corrected and amended, even if there are some deficits in the formats and contents themselves.

There is a difference between the three jurisdictions: in the UK and Hong Kong, the listing procedures take international characteristics into account, while in China, the main focus is still on domestic issues. The operations of the UK and Hong Kong markets have involved more international or transnational corporations, therefore, the listing procedures are tailored to their needs. As the world's most international and diverse market for the listing and trading of equity, debt and other securities, the London Stock Exchange's Main Market hosts over 2,600 companies from 60 countries, including many of the world's largest companies.[79] As for Hong Kong, as an international financial centre, it is always in a leading position; for instance, according to the Global Financial Centres Index (GFCI), it ranked in 3rd place in 2012.[80] Therefore, to establish and maintain a regulatory regime with a global focus is crucially important for the UK and Hong Kong. The rules and regulations provide the stable environment required by the international institutions and further promote financial innovation. Compared with the UK and Hong Kong, less international elements are to be found in Mainland China. However, with the development of the market structure, the information required in Mainland China may tend to move in line with international standards. China is becoming more of a global economic power house, and in particular Shanghai is aiming to perform as an international financial centre; therefore, the corporate regulations will need to take more account of international issues. Incorporating the consideration of the international element is one of the necessary initial steps.

Second, it can be noted from the three jurisdictions that there are some similarities in the regimes for the 'must disclose' events. The most significant common feature is that the three jurisdictions pay close attention to the influences on the trading prices of these events. In fact, throughout different jurisdictions, the main focuses on the temporary report can be reflected in two dimensions: the significance and the timescale, namely, what to disclose and when to disclose. Nevertheless, these two standards are not easy to establish. Taking the significant standard as an example, the securities market changes frequently and is full of unexpected events. Even the same event will have various impacts on different receivers. Due to the diversification of the business nature, operating style, assets and profits scale of the receivers, the 'significance' may be classified differently by them. However, eventually for the financial market, the impacts will be reflected by the changing of trading prices. Therefore, together with the consideration of the basic function of the securities market, most of the jurisdictions have equal significance in the influence on trading prices.

When the UK and Hong Kong regimes are examined carefully, it is not difficult to observe that they have set out more detailed and comprehensive classification standards. For the developed markets, such a method may be seen as suitable. First of all, the markets themselves are comparatively mature and functioning well; the prices in the market can make certain adjustments according to the information disclosed.[81] Therefore, to adopt different requirements for corporate disclosure will be necessary. Since the information disclosure itself will create costs, this method can be less time consuming and cost effective for the listed companies. Second, the investors are more rational than those in the developing markets. They are able to make reasonable responses to the disclosed information. Third, the detailed classification method will benefit the supervisory bodies. It will facilitate them to fulfil the regulatory function economically and efficiently.

These methods of calculation can be seen as examples from which Mainland China can learn. Besides the above reasons, eventually it is important to reach a balanced level for the standard of 'significance'. On one hand, listed companies shall disclose information that will influence the trading prices; on the other hand, over-disclosure of information can create noise, further reducing market efficiency.[82] To reduce market noise could be a crucial issue for the Chinese market. The quality of information concerning the listed companies must be improved in China. In the past two decades, it was not difficult to find false, misleading information in the Chinese securities market. Therefore, it is necessary to establish a comprehensive classification method for disclosable events. However, being a new emerging market, the Chinese market may benefit from the model but cannot simply copy it. The figures and classification standards that are suitable for the Chinese market need to take into account many elements. There needs to be some more experimental initiatives.

Third, it can be seen from the above comparison study that there are some differences in aspects of the disclosure method. Currently, in Mainland China, listed companies still need to pay to publish their information in the designated places. It is not difficult to understand the necessities for this method; in particular, at the start of the development of a market. When a market was newly formed, a fair and efficient operational system was not easy to achieve. In this context, the information disclosure regime needs to be closely monitored by a strong legal framework and certain necessary administrative measures. Designated media had their unique influences and high ratios of market possession; accordingly, through this method, the authority of the publicized information could be maintained.[83] However, it is not suitable for today's situation. Notably, with the development of the information disclosure regime, the disclosure requirements are more complex and subsequently become more costly. As for the designated media of the disclosure system, different problems needed to be noted, namely the issues of the independence of these media and potential conflicts of interests.[84] Information disclosure in the Chinese securities market has experienced certain dark ages, unfair, misleading and false disclosure in various dimensions has penetrated the market in the past. In order to prevent the reoccurrence of such risks, the reformed information disclosure method should be taken into account in China. The newly effective platform, for instance, of the internet, has been involved more actively. The website disclosure system for ChiNext can be seen as a significant improvement. Similarly with other sectors, the reforms shall be conducted in a steady manner. This conclusion was based on the current developing status of the Chinese securities market. Compared with the developed markets, one of the main consumers of the disclosure information, the retail investors are not yet mature enough. There are some who cannot master the operation of a computer. Given that, a radical step such as the abolishing of the paper-based disclosure system may not be acceptable to them. In fact, in Hong Kong, some voices were raised against the abolition of the paid announcement requirement.[85] Moreover, it shall be noted that this method must be backed up by fast and safe internet services. Taking Hong Kong as an example, the stability and safety issues have been resolved as is demonstrated by support for the ESS.[86]

Overall, from the experiences of the LSE and HKEx, electronic dissemination through the stock exchanges' website, a single, official, centralized location that can be easily accessed by both local and overseas investors, will ensure that information disclosure and securities investment efficiency are more secure than previously. A similar system could be one of the solutions for China. As a consequence, it could bring Mainland China's information dissemination system into line with other leading international equity markets. China could implement this approach, in a steady and reasonable manner.

The role and function of stock exchanges

Disclosure requirements are increasingly complicated. From the above analysis it can be seen that the Chinese information disclosure system is moving towards higher standards. Even if, the current regime cannot be fully in line with the level of the mature markets, it is predictable that there will be continuing improvements. However, as mentioned before, although the Chinese information disclosure regime has been improved, some problems remain. The problems of information disclosure are not isolated. As a social scientific phenomenon, to find the cause that led to this problem, it is necessary to consider the other relevant elements.

Reasons for the problems may be various. One central point that cannot be ignored is the compliance issue. Without full compliance awareness by the listed companies, an efficient level of information disclosure cannot be easily achieved. In addition, the issue of business ethics has not been fully addressed in China. It is not easy in China, to expedite the ethics of a 'fair culture' in the securities market. As can be seen from the theory study in Chapter 1, there is an imbalance inside the securities market. In fact, besides the general economic theories, some market players have a significant status advantage over retail investors. Therefore, an effective and strict supervisory and regulatory framework must be established. The CSRC, as the government body, should pay more attention to this issue.[87] In addition, real time monitoring is required to facilitate the regulatory regime. Being the 'front line regulator', the stock exchange's function cannot be ignored. The roles of the SSE and SZSE will be examined; in particular, their responsibility concerning information disclosure.

From a legal perspective, the stock exchanges are the providers of trading venues. Therefore, they have been endowed with certain powers. As for the Chinese securities market, what is the source of its powers? How efficient are the stock exchanges in discharging their power? Unlike other mature markets, the Chinese stock exchanges appeared only ten years after the opening up of reforms aimed at restructuring the national economy; this restructuring occurred due to the failure of ill-conceived economic policy and political disruption over previous decades.[88] Hence, the birth of the Chinese stock exchanges had certain political features. Therefore, it can be argued that this system has an inherent Chinese nature. So, will these Chinese characteristics influence the function of the stock exchanges, particularly with regard to information disclosure?

Currently, the term 'stock exchange' in China refers to a legal entity that provides the relevant place and facilities for concentrated securities trading, organizes and supervises the securities trading and applies a self-regulated administration.[89] Moreover, the establishment and dissolution of a stock exchange shall be subject to the decision of the State Council.[90] Based on the above provisions, the Chinese securities exchanges can be seen as self-regulatory bodies under the government's supervision. Together with the governmental regulators, the self-regulatory bodies can perform their unique roles to enhance regulation of the listed companies.

Generally, the authority of the stock exchanges is derived from the following aspects, by law and by contractual relationship. First, the Securities Law sets out the basic functions and powers: formulating business rules;[91] receiving and handling listing issues;[92] organizing and monitoring the trading;[93] managing public market information.[94] Second, the listing agreements signed between the companies and stock exchanges endow the latter with certain regulatory and monitoring authority. In fact, these two aspects are not isolated. In Mainland China, the law and regulation directly designate certain regulatory roles to the exchanges, while the approved rules and business codes formulated by the stock exchanges support the governmental regulatory structure. Moreover, agreements between the listed companies and stock exchanges set out detailed self-regulatory matters.

In detail, the role and function of the SSE and SZSE illustrates the above analysis. The SSE is a membership institution directly governed by the CSRC, which endeavours to perform a variety of functions: providing a marketplace and facilities for securities trading; formulating business rules; accepting and arranging listings; organizing and monitoring securities trading; regulating members and listed companies; managing and disseminating market information.[95] In particular, its Market Surveillance Department is in charge of real time monitoring on the trading market, responsible for the timely discovery of extraordinary trading behaviour, and conducting investigations and dealing with violations.[96]

Similarly, the SZSE is a national stock exchange that provides a venue for securities trading. Proposing to create a market which meets diversified financing needs, the SZSE works to ensure the listed issuers meet continuous listing standards and comply with the exchange rules.[97] Taking the market surveillance team as a typical example, this team monitors everyday trading activity in a real time and post trade manner by using the trading and settlement data; helps to detect unreasonable trading volume, price volatility and other irregularities; and prevents insider trading and market manipulation.[98] The organization and functions of the team are displayed in Figure 2.3. It is clear that this team is well established and covers the most important aspects of supervision. Based on the discovery of malpractices, the team makes due diligence inquiries and submits their findings to the CSRC for the necessary investigation or disciplinary action.[99]

It can be seen from the above analysis how the basic roles of the stock exchanges have been defined in China. A closer examination at the implementation and enforcement is particularly necessary. In 2009, there were numerous

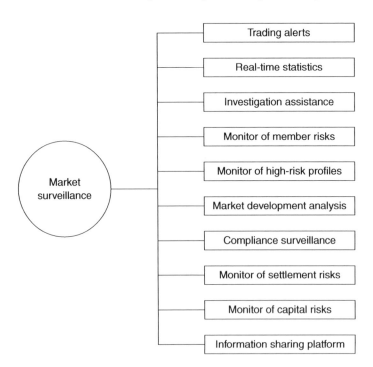

Figure 2.3 Market surveillance in the SZSE (source: SZSE[100]).

incidents of misconduct by listed companies concerning information disclosure identified by the stock exchanges. Table 2.5 analyses the 28 disciplinary punishments handed down by the SZSE caused by untimely disclosure, three punishments caused by false recording, two punishments caused by misleading statements, and two punishments caused by major omission in statement, which together accounted for 53 per cent of the disciplinary punishments, which were: criticism; public censure; disqualification. In fact, the stock exchanges have played an important role in preventing and controlling illicit disclosure and trading by the listed companies. As mentioned earlier, a compliance culture has not been fully established in China, therefore, the front line monitoring of the listed companies is quite important. The SSE and SZSE have respectively established their Honest Record of the listed companies.[101] The Honest Record re-enforces the self-regulatory regime. Last but not least, similar action is being taken in other industrial sectors of Mainland China, and the establishment of the credit culture and compliance culture is being proposed. For instance, in order to strengthen the supervision on insider dealing, the SSE held a meeting on supervisory work required in order to combat insider dealing.[102] In this meeting, the SSE proposed seven regulatory measures: internal supervision resources to be integrated; the capability to discover clues to insider dealing to be strengthened; the supervision of information disclosure to be intensified; the supervision role of the media to be given full play; the training for listed companies and the education of investors to be enhanced; supervision cooperation to be enhanced to promote the construction of comprehensive prevention and control systems for insider dealing; finally, the client management responsibility of brokers to be strengthened. The proposed supervisory enhancement can further improve

Table 2.5 Disciplinary punishments in 2009 (SZSE)

Reason	Times
Untimely Disclosure	28
Illicit Transaction by Senior Executives	6
Short Selling	4
Holding Securities Exceeding the Ratio	4
Illicit Related Transaction	4
False Record	3
Illicit Application of Funds	3
Appropriating Funds	2
Misleading Statement	2
Illicit Guarantee	2
Major Omission in Statement	2
Breach of Duty by Sponsors	2
Breach of Takeover Offer	1
Refusing to Cooperate with Supervisory Body	1
Illicit Allotment of Funds	1
Others	1

Source: SZSE.[103]

regulatory abilities. In fact, the registration system of insiders in significant assets reorganization of listed companies has been introduced in the SSE.[104] This system is an important initiative to control and prevent inside dealing.

However, currently in the Chinese securities market, the occurrences of misleading disclosure and insider dealing are not rare. There are some aspects in the regulatory regime that need to be improved. First of all, the stock exchanges lack effective tools to monitor the listed companies. The disciplinary punishments, i.e. criticism, public censure and disqualification, do not appear to have had a great effect.[105] Therefore, the impact of these sanctions is relatively weak, even on those who have been fined. In fact, the low cost of breaching law and regulation is not a rare phenomenon in the Chinese legal system. Public censure has limited influences. A comparison may be made with the UK. In January 2008, the FSA brought its first criminal prosecution for insider dealing.[106] Apparently, the FSA took steps to strengthen the deterrent effect against insider dealing.

The ambiguity on the power division between the CSRC and stock exchanges is a crucial issue in China. The power and authority endowed by the law and regulations are too general and lack the necessary implementing methods and operational measures; empowerment is ambiguous in certain aspects, for example, the power to exert the authority of investigation is not clear.[107] It has been argued that the control of the CSRC is 'excessive'.[108] The Chinese stock exchange functioning under the mandate of the CSRC has been criticized. Moreover, the exchanges must also meet the CSRC's three general reporting requirements: the stock exchanges need to request the CSRC's approval for matters regarding personnel, financial accounts, fees, new listings and other logistical areas; the exchanges must report record keeping matters to the CSRC, for instance, performance assessments of department managers or expenditures over budget; the reporting requirement involves operational decisions.[109] Furthermore, it has been observed that although the CSRC has taken steps to grant more autonomy to the exchanges since 2002, the exchanges are still considered part of the CSRC bureaucracy.[110]

Obviously, as trading houses, the stock exchanges are also business operators. Therefore, the lack of independence creates certain restrictions on daily business operations. These conflicts may create certain negative impacts on the supervisory regimes. For instance, the ambiguity may lead to the wasting of supervisory resources, and the excessive control may decrease the enthusiasm of the self-regulatory bodies. Eventually, the waste of resources may result in over burdening the regulated, while lack of enthusiasm may induce the regulated into illicit behaviour.

The CSRC has significant influence on the operation of the stock exchanges in China. For example, the CSRC nominates the chairman and deputy chairman of the decision making body (Lishihui), and appoints the General Manager and Deputy General Manager of the stock exchanges.[111] This may be necessary; in particular during the initial development stage of the Chinese financial market. Being trading houses, the stock exchanges themselves are in a delicate position. Deriving from the surveillance function, they are self-regulatory bodies; on the other hand, from the commercial side, they are business dealers; moreover, the stock exchanges are under the regulation of government bodies. Compared with the governmental regulators, the self-regulatory bodies can perform unique roles, the low regulatory cost and high efficiency of them cannot be ignored. However, it should be admitted that only relying on the self regulatory bodies to supervise and monitor the market is not enough. The failure of self-regulation by the financial institutions has led to the government's involvement. The shortcomings of the self-regulatory framework, in particular conflicts of interests, require a government overview. Given the background of conflict of interest, the stock exchanges should endeavor to create a more favourable trading environment for the listed companies. During the transitional stage of the Chinese securities market, it is important to have supervision from a macro level.

On the other hand, with the development of a market structure, Chinese stock exchanges need to be endowed with sufficient and clear authority in order to fulfil their front line regulatory functions. However, the power must be well structured in order to avoid confusion with other regulatory bodies. Furthermore, from the earlier analysis, it can be seen that legislating techniques on the regime for information disclosure is just one of the issues. Improvement in real time regulation and supervision is also crucial. In order to enhance their function, the stock exchanges should consolidate the coordinating mechanism between real time monitoring and information disclosure supervising. Once malpractice is discovered, the exchanges should explore relevant behaviour and report to the competent authority. The cooperation between the governmental and self-regulatory bodies should be improved in an efficient manner.

Summary

In the last few years, improving the efficiency of the regulating regime of the Chinese securities market has becomes more important than ever. Among the different issues, how to ensure the real time and accurate dissemination of the latest information on listed companies is a major concern. Ideally, accurate, rapid and efficient information disclosure can ultimately benefit the financial system. However, disclosure requirements are increasingly complicated. In order to fulfil domestic and international regulatory obligations, effectively communicate with regulators, shareholders, and institutional or individual investors it is more important today than in the past, in particular, trans-border acquisitions and mergers are more common for Chinese companies. Thus, the legal procedures must fulfil different requirements for the different jurisdictions. How to avoid this kind of problem will be an issue requiring study by China.

In fact, it can be seen from the early part of this chapter. There are no material differences between the disclosure requirements of the three jurisdictions. Mainland China is continuingly improving its regime. However, legislative technique is only the first step. As mentioned before, although the information disclosure regime has been improved, there are some problems still remaining. The problems of information disclosure are not isolated. As a social scientific phenomenon, to find the causes that led to the problems, consideration must be given to multiform elements. There are some typical cases that have happened in the Chinese securities market, and such cases have some common features, particularly, from the aspect of information disclosure. They can be summarized into the following categories: the disclosure is inaccurate; the disclosure is insufficient and incomplete; the disclosure is not timely.[112]

Besides the government regulatory bodies, the stock exchanges, through their daily function, have the abilities to continually monitor the listed companies' information disclosure. As the front line market regulators, they are crucially important to the comprehensive and effective supervisory system. Integrated monitoring measures should be enhanced. In order to use the resources in the most efficient and economic way, proper and clear structured regulating power needs to be given to the stock exchanges. Thus, together with an advanced disclosure regime, the stock exchanges can better regulate the listed companies in Mainland China.

Notes

1 Lei Li (2009), 'Examining the Original Sins of Chinese Capital Market from 'Huang Guangyu' Case (You 'Huang Guangyu Shijian' Kan Zhongguo Ziben Shichang Yuanzui)', *Social Outlook*, 1 (2009), p. 59.
2 Nicholas C. Howson (2005), 'Regulation of Companies with Publicly Listed Share Capital in the People's Republic of China', *Cornell International Law Journal*, 38 (2005), p. 242.
3 CSRC (19 May 2010), 'International Conference of 'The Reforming of Securities Administrative Punishment System and Investor Protection' has been held in Beijing (Zhengquan Xingzheng Chufa Tizhi Gaige he Touzizhe Baohu' Guoji Yantanhui zai Jing Zhaokai)', www.csrc.gov.cn/pub/newsite/bgt/xwdd/201005/t20100519_180696.htm, last accessed: 10 June 2010.
4 In China, securities can be divided into A and B shares. A share is denominated in Chinese currency, the RMB. B share refers to foreign invested shares, issued domestically by Chinese companies. B shares are denominated in RMB but traded in foreign currencies. H shares refer to shares issued in Hong Kong.
5 National Statistics website, www.stats.gov.cn/, last accessed: 21 May 2013.
6 National Statistics website, www.stats.gov.cn/, last accessed: 21 May 2013.
7 CSRC (2012), China Securities and Future Statics 2012, www.csrc.gov.cn/pub/newsite/xxfw/cbwxz/tjnj/zqqhtjnj/2012/main/nj2011/5–13.htm, last accessed: 8 June 2010.
8 SCSC, promulgation date: 22 April 1993, effective date: 22 April 1993, Article 72, Article 78, Article 81, repealed.
9 SCSC, promulgation date: 2 September 1993, effective date: 2 September 1993, repealed.
10 For details, see Chapter 1.
11 The CSRC has published a series of requirements for the format of information disclosure. A list can be seen at: www.csrc.gov.cn/n575458/n4239016/n6634558/n9768098/n9768480/index.html, last accessed: 24 August 2009. The CSRC is a ministry-level unit directly under the State Council, regulates China's securities and futures markets with an aim to ensure their orderly and legitimate operation. See the CSRC official website, www.csrc.gov.cn/pub/csrc_en/about/, last accessed: 7 January 2010.

12 Administrative Measures for the Disclosure of Information of Listed Companies, promulgation date: 30 January 2007, effective date: 30 January 2007, Article 37.
13 Ibid., Article 59.
14 Ibid., Article 72.
15 Securities Law, promulgation date: 27 October 2005, effective date: 1 January 2006, Article 63.
16 Ibid.
17 Wanyi Zhao (2006), Securities Law (Zhengquan Fa), Beijing: Legal Publishing House, p. 116.
18 Securities Law, Article 70.
19 Ibid., Article 68.
20 Lishang. Zhang (2005), Information Disclosure and Analysis of the Listed Companies (Shangshi Gongsi Xinxi Pilu yu Fenxi), Chengdu: Southwestern University of Finance & Economic Press, at p. 66.
21 Securities Law Article 14.
22 Ibid., Article 48.
23 Ibid., Article 52.
24 The SSE was founded on 26 November 1990. The SSE aims for development on the principle of 'legislation, supervision, self-regulation and standardization' to create a transparent, open, safe and efficient marketplace. See the SSE website, http://static.sse.com.cn/sseportal/en_us/ps/about/bi.shtml, last accessed: 21 June 2012.
25 Created in 1990 as China's second stock exchange, as part of the continued development of the Shenzhen Special Economic Zone, the SZSE has a market capitalization around RMB 1 trillion. Based on the principle of 'Regulation, Innovation, Cultivation and Service', the SZSE will continue to maintain its focus on developing the Small and Medium Enterprises Board, while seeking for a tier market. See the SZSE website, www.szse.cn/main/en/aboutsse/sseoverview/, last accessed: 21 June 2012.
26 Established in 2001, the CSDCC was created pursuant to the Securities Law and Company Law. The SSE and SZSE each holds 50 per cent of the CSDCC' shares. Headquartered in Beijing, the CSDCC has two branches in Shanghai and Shenzhen. Its main functions are: establishing and managing the securities accounts and settlement accounts; deposit and transfer of securities; registration of securities holders' names and rights; managing the securities and financial clearing and settlement; distributing the warrants on behalf of the issuers; and providing securities registration and settlement business related queries, information, advisory and training services. The CSRC is the competent authority of the CSDCC. See www.chinaclear.cn/main/02/0203/0203.html, last accessed: 21 August 2012.
27 Rules Governing the Listing of Stocks on Shanghai Stock Exchange, Article 5.1.2, 5.1.5, effective date: January 1998, the 7th revision in July 2012. For breach of undertakings, the punishment can be: criticism, public censure or disqualification.
28 Rules Governing the Listing of Stocks on Shenzhen Stock Exchange, effective date: January 1998, the 7th revision July 2012, Article 5.1.3. The Listing Rules shall be applied to listing on the main board and the Small and Medium Enterprises board of SZSE. As for listing on the ChiNext, the listing requirements are different. The disclosure for ChiNext can be found in the later part of this chapter and in Chapter 5.
29 Rules Governing the Listing of Stocks on Shanghai Stock Exchange, Article 5.1.8.
30 Rules Governing the Listing of Stocks on Shenzhen Stock Exchange, Article 5.1.9.
31 See SSE website, www.sse.com.cn/sseportal/en/c01/p996/c1501_p996.shtml, last accessed: 27 August 2010. It stated that the SSE is fully committed to the goal of state-owned industrial enterprises reform and developing Shanghai into an international financial centre with great confidence.
32 See SZSE website, www.szse.cn/main/en/aboutsse/sseoverview/, last accessed: 27 August 2012. It stated that the SZSE gives full support to development in small and

medium businesses and implementation of the national strategy of independent innovation. The SME Board was launched in May 2004. The ChiNext market was inaugurated in October 2009.

33 It should be noted that, until April 2013, the Financial Services Authority had acted as the securities regulator, and was referred to as the UKLA. It took over the function of admitting to the Official List from the London Stock Exchange in May 2000.

34 See FCA website, www.fca.org.uk/firms/markets/ukla, last accessed: 12 May 2013.

35 The Listing Rules are part of the FCA Handbook. The Handbook sets out the FCA's rules, guidance and other documents. The new Handbooks came into force on 1 April 2013.

36 The European Economic Area consists of the 27 Member States of the European Union plus Iceland, Liechtenstein and Norway.

37 FCA Handbook, Listing Rules, Section 3.3.2R.

38 Ibid., Section 3.3.3R.

39 Ibid., Section 3.3.4R.

40 Ibid., Section 3.3.4 AR. Companies are required to make announcements to investors. These announcements must be made via a Regulated Information Service. Companies making announcements can choose from a range of providers who have been approved to act as a Regulated Information Service; for instance, One, Business Wire Regulatory Disclosure, etc. See, www.fsa.gov.uk/Pages/doing/ukla/ris/contact/index.shtml, last accessed: 16 November 2010.

41 Ibid., Section 3.3.5 R.

42 Ibid., Section 3.3.6 R.

43 Effective date: 1 July 1933, revised.

44 Effective date: 1 April 2003, revised.

45 Rules Governing the Listing of Securities on the Stock Exchange of Hong Kong Limited, latest revision: 31 December 2012.

46 Ibid., Appendix 1.

47 Ibid., Articles 52, 53.

48 Please refer to Chapter 1.

49 Administrative Measures for the Disclosure of Information of Listed Companies, promulgation date: 30 January 2007, effective date: 30 January 2007, Article 30.

50 Ibid., Article 32.

51 Rules Governing the Listing of Stocks on Shanghai Stock Exchange, Article 9.2.

52 Ibid., Article 9.3. This article does not apply to the providing of a guarantee, receipt of cash donations, or any other transaction that simply relieves the listed company from its obligatory debt.

53 Ibid., Articles 9.10, 9.11.

54 Listing Rules, Section 10.1.5G.

55 Ibid., 10.2.1G.

56 Ibid., 10 Annex 1, 1G.

57 Ibid., 10 Annex 1, 2R.

58 Ibid., 10 Annex 1, 4R.

59 Ibid., 10 Annex 1, 5R.

60 Ibid., 10 Annex 1, 7R.

61 Ibid., 10.2. 2. R.

62 Ibid., 10.4.1R.

63 Ibid., 10.5.1R.

64 Rules Governing the Listing of Securities on the Stock Exchange of Hong Kong Limited, Chapter 13, Article 13.03.

65 Ibid., Chapter 14, Article 14.06.

66 Ibid., Chapter 14.

67 See ibid. Article 14.07.

68 Securities Law, Article 70.

69 ChiNext provides a new capital platform for the needs of enterprises engaged in independent innovation and other growing venture enterprises. The difference between ChiNext and the main board are their financing mechanisms, investment and risk management for issuers at various stages of development. ChiNext facilitates: perfecting the financing chain for Small and Medium Enterprises (hereafter the SMEs) engaged in independent innovation and facilitating industrial upgrade; promoting demonstrative and multiplier effects of the capital market in driving economic growth, and enhancing development in venture capital investment; stimulating public enthusiasm for entrepreneurship, innovation, and employment; enriching capital market products and providing investors with a wider range of financial instruments for wealth management and risk hedges. See, SZSE, 'About ChiNext', www.szse.cn/main/en/ChiNext/aboutchinext/, last accessed: 5 January 2013.

70 After 'Big Bang', the securities trading moved from face to face dealings on the market floor to computer and telephone dealings. A new approach of distributing information fairly and widely was required. The LSE enabled market users to view full text announcements on the Company News Service (CNS) and summaries on the Edited Text News Service (ETNS). In 1988 the edited service, Commercial Company News Service (CCNS) was sold. The full text service was re-named the Regulatory News Service (RNS) and remains the London market's official news platform. The new computer to computer submission method, Direct Input Provider (DIP) was also introduced in 1988. Companies could deliver announcements to RNS electronically and to key vendor and market audiences via RNS. The information here about RNS can be found at: www.londonstockexchange.com/products-and-services/rns/history/history.htm, last accessed: 20 July 2012.

71 The AIM is the LSE's international market for smaller growing companies. A broad range of businesses including early stage, venture capital backed and more established companies join the AIM seeking access to growth capital. Since its launch in 1995, over 3,000 companies from world have chosen to join the AIM. See www.londonstockexchange.com/companies-and-advisors/aim/aim/aim.htm, last accessed: 15 September 2012.

72 See RNS website, www.londonstockexchange.com/products-and-services/rns/about/rns-remove.htm, last accessed: 15 September 2010.

73 See RNS website, www.londonstockexchange.com/products-and-services/rns/regulatory/headline/explained.htm, last accessed: 20 May 2013.

74 See RNS website, www.londonstockexchange.com/products-and-services/rns/rns-submit/demo/demo.htm, last accessed: 20 May 2013.

75 On 18 November 2005, HKEx published an 'Exposure Paper on the Abolition of Requirement for Main Board Issuers to Publish Paid Announcements in Newspapers and Related Matters'. The comment period for the Exposure Paper closed on 13 January 2006. HKEx received 35 sets of comments from a total of 40 respondents. Supports for the proposal to abolish the paid announcement requirement were 36, while there were four responses against the proposal. Based on these responses, the abolition of the requirement for paid announcements in newspapers moved towards the international practice. See 'Exposure Conclusion – Abolition of Requirement for Main Board Issuers to Publish Paid Announcements in Newspapers and Related Matters (July 2006)'.

76 See HKEx website, www.hkex.com.hk/eng/listing/edp/ess/ess_online.htm, last accessed: 5 July 2010.

77 Contents in this paragraph were summarized from: HKEx (November 2005), 'Exposure Paper on the Abolition of Requirement for Main Board Issuers to Publish Paid Announcements in Newspapers and Related Matters'.

78 HKEx, 'Submitting a Document for Publication through e-Submission – Quick Reference Guide', Version 1.1.

79   See LSE website, www.londonstockexchange.com/companies-and-advisors/main-market/main/market.htm, last accessed: 15 September 2012.

80   Z/Yen (September 2012), The Global Financial Centres Index 12.

81   This can be seen as the reflection of the Efficient Capital Market Hypothesis. See Chapter 1.

82   Fischer Black (1986), 'Noise', *Journal of Finance*, 41, pp. 529–543. According to Black, noise is contrasted with information; noise is what makes observations imperfect; noise is the arbitrary element in expectations that leads to an arbitrary rate of inflation consistent with expectations; noise makes financial markets possible, but also makes them imperfect.

83   Wenwei Hu, Deguang Mai, Wenying Lu, Guangwen Kong, Zhe Shao (October 2007), 'The Comparison and Analysis between the Information Disclosure System for the Listed Companies in the SSE and HKEx (Hu Gang Shangshi Gongsi Xinxi Pilu Zhidu de Bijiao Yanjiu yu Fenxi)', p. 23. The paper was the No. 17 of the SSE's cooperative research project, form the Hong Kong Dafu Securities Group Research Team.

84   Ibid., the authors argued that to designate media for the information disclosure system reflected excessive administrative intervention, it might influence the independence of these media and further influence the supervision and objective judgement for the listed companies by these media. Moreover, the authors argued that the major incomes for the media came from the listed companies' disclosure and advertisement fee, which led to the close relationship between the two parties; hence, there was a risk that would affect the independence. And, pursuant to the economic profits, some of the media might take unduly approaches to obtain the designated status.

85   HKEx (July 2006), 'Exposure Conclusion – Abolition of Requirement for Main Board Issuers to Publish Paid Announcements in Newspapers and Related Matters', p. 11. Some respondents in the survey expressed views in favour of maintaining the status quo whereby main board issuers are required to publish announcements in the newspapers under the Listing Rules. They also suggested alternative proposals short of the total abolition of the paid announcement requirement; for example, the requirement to publish in the newspapers should be abolished only for certain announcements with the requirement being maintained for the others.

86   Ibid. In September 2005, the HKEx Website Disaster Recovery Site project was completed. The project helped strengthen the backup arrangements for the HKEx's website so service can be restored more quickly in the event of an incident disabling the primary website.

87   The analysis of the CSRC is found in Chapter 5.

88   Carl E. Walter, Fraser J.T. Howie (2003), Privatizing China: The Stock Markets and Their Role in Corporate Reform, Singapore: John Wiley and Sons, IX, p. 20–30.

89   Securities Law, Article 102.

90   Ibid.

91   Ibid., Article 118. It states that a stock exchange shall, pursuant to the laws and administrative regulations on securities, formulate rules on listing, trading and membership administration as well as any other relevant rules, and shall report them to the securities regulatory authority under the State Council for approval.

92   Ibid., Article 48. It states that an application for the listing of any securities shall be filed with a stock exchange and shall be subject to the examination and approval of the stock exchange according to law, and a listing agreement shall be concluded by both parties. Stock exchanges shall, according to the decision of the department as authorized by the State Council, arrange for the listing of government bonds.

93   For instance, the Securities Law, Article 114 states that when any normal trading of securities is disturbed by an emergency, a stock exchange may take the measures of a technical suspension of trading. In the case of an emergency of force majeure or

for the purpose of preserving the normal order of securities trading, a stock exchange may decide a temporary closure. And Article 115 stated that the stock exchanges shall exercise a real time monitoring of securities trading and shall report abnormal trading to the CSRC; shall carry out supervision over the information disclosed by the listed companies or the relevant obligors, supervise and urge them to disclose information in a timely and accurate manner according to law.

94 Ibid., Article 113 states that the stock exchanges shall guarantee a fair centralized trading, announce up-to-the-minute quotations of securities trading, formulate the quotation tables of the securities market on the basis of trading days, and make announcements for it.

95 SSE website, http://static.sse.com.cn/sseportal/en_us/ps/about/bi.shtml, last accessed: 21 June 2012.

96 SSE website, http://static.sse.com.cn/sseportal/en_us/ps/about/os.shtml, last accessed: 21 June 2012.

97 See SZSE website, www.szse.cn/main/en/aboutsse/sseoverview/, last accessed: 21 June 2012.

98 SZSE website, www.szse.cn/main/en/aboutsse/regulatoryfunctions/, last accessed: 23 June 2012. In order to perform the self-regulatory purpose, a market surveillance team with auto-alert and trade analysis functions is established in SZSE to deter market abuse.

99 Ibid.

100 SZSE website, www.szse.cn/main/en/aboutsse/regulatoryfunctions/, last accessed: 23 June 2012.

101 See SSE website, www.sse.com.cn/disclosure/listedinfo/credibility/home/, and the SZSE website, www.szse.cn/main/sme/ssgs/cxdd/jgjcjjl/,last accessed: 21 June 2012. The Honest Record of the listed companies is being published on the stock exchanges' websites. The disciplinary punishments, information concerning the senior management and other relevant records about a listed company can be found online. In SZSE, the quality rating of the disclosed information can also be accessed.

102 Lu Wang (24 August 2010), 'SSE Takes Seven Measures to Crack down on Insider Dealing (Shangjiaosuo Caiqu Qixiang Cuoshi Yanda Neimu Jiaoyi)', *Shanghai Securities News* (Shanghai Zhengquan Bao), English version is available at: www.sse.com.cn/sseportal/en/home/home.shtml, last accessed: 27 August 2010.

103 According to the: SZSE Self-regulation Working Report 2009 (Shenzhen Zhengquan Jiaoyisuo 2009 Zilü Jianguan Gongzuo Baogao), p. 12.

104 Ibid.

105 Wenli You, Yinglin Luo (2009), 'A Research on the Supervisory Law System over Information Disclosure of Listed Companies in Chinese Stock Exchanges (Woguo Zhengquan Jiaoyisuo dui Shangshi Gongsi Xinxi Pilu Jianguan de Falü Zhidu Yanjiu)', *Humanities & Social Sciences Journal of Hainan University*, 27 (5), p. 509.

106 *R. v McQuoid* [2009] 4 All E.R. 388; [2009] EWCA Crim 1301.

107 Zhihua Liu (2008), 'The Problems and Possible Improvements for the Self-regulation of the Chinese Stock Exchanges (Zhongguo Zhengquan Jiaoyisuo Zilü Jianguan Tizhi de Wenti ji qi Gaijin)', *Theory Front*, 11, p. 41.

108 Chenxia Shi (2007), 'Protecting Investors in China through Multiple Regulatory Mechanisms and Effective Enforcement', *Arizona Journal of International & Comparative Law*, 24 (2), p. 477.

109 Ibid.

110 Ibid.

111 Measures on the Administration of Stock Exchanges, promulgation date: 10 December 1997, revised: 12 December 2001, Article 21 and 24.

112 For details, see Chapter 1.

3 Securities companies and information disclosure

Introduction

Under the current emerging and transitional nature of the Chinese securities market, the securities companies are still in the process of developing. Though significant improvements have been achieved, typical problems remain; for instance lack of transparency, misappropriation of clients' funds, misleading and false disclosure or non-disclosure. Considering the importance of the securities companies, questions have been raised: are these companies well regulated in the securities market? How can we enhance the regulatory regime of securities companies?

Information disclosure regulation is of essential importance to the regulatory regime of securities companies. There are various reasons for applying disclosure requirements to securities companies. Considering their business nature, securities companies are in a more advantageous position compared to the general public. They are also responsible for considerable amounts of funds. Furthermore, some securities companies are also listed companies. Last but not least, the mixed operation system has emerged in Mainland China.[1] Under these circumstances, when securities companies conduct business, prevention and control of the conflict of interests becomes an important consideration. A Chinese Wall or Firewall mechanism, that aims to separate the different branches, and prevent leaks of information inside an institution is required to be established, and when necessary, enhanced. All these factors call on companies to improve information disclosure in an effective, but practical manner.

In this chapter, the disclosure regime for securities companies will be examined. Initially, the development of securities companies will be studied. The second part will focus on the detailed disclosure requirements. Finally, conflict of interest in the mixed operation systems will be analysed.

The development of securities companies

The term 'securities companies', in a general sense, refers to a limited liability company or joint stock limited company that has been established and engages in the business operation of securities according to the law.[2] The establishment of a securities company needs to meet the requirements set by law and regulation.[3] Furthermore, the establishment of a securities company shall be subject to the examination and approval of the CSRC, no entity or individual may engage in any securities operations without such approval.[4]

Securities companies have a broad business scope. According to the Securities Law, a securities company can undertake the following business operations: securities brokerage, securities investment consulting, financial advice relating to activities of securities trading or securities investment, underwriting and sponsoring of securities, self operation of securities, securities asset management, and other business operations concerning securities.[5] From the business perspective, it can be seen that securities companies are very similar to investment banks (within the range of securities business) in other jurisdictions. However, unlike investment banks in other jurisdictions, investment banking business is just one branch or stream for securities companies in China. Also, according to the Securities Law, a securities company shall undertake its operations of securities brokerage, underwriting, self operation and asset management in a separate manner.[6] Currently, mixed operation is in the trial stage in Shanghai, or only allowed for some specially authorized financial institutions (a detailed analysis is contained in the later part of this chapter); therefore, most of the securities companies will only deal with business relating to securities.

The current model in China requires investors to register with securities companies or their business branches in order to carry out securities transactions. According to the Securities Law, an investor shall conclude an entrustment agreement with a securities company, open an account for trading in a securities company and entrust the company to purchase or sell securities by an instruction in writing, by telephone or other means.[7] The transaction and settlement funds are deposited with securities companies.[8] In a background of lack of systemic control, this situation used to result in the misappropriation of the clients funds in the early development stages of the Chinese securities market. Law and regulation now require that the transaction and settlement funds of clients shall be deposited in a commercial bank and be managed separately under the name of each client; a securities company shall not incorporate any of these funds into its own assets; when a securities company goes bankrupt or goes into liquidation, these funds shall not be defined as its insolvent assets or liquidation assets.[9] The aim of the Article 139 is to protect investors' assets. However, some people argued that the deposit bank is like a warehouse, that merely 'stores assets' for its customers.[10] In other words, the securities companies are still in a more favourable position as they retain control.

By the end of 31 December 2012, the total assets of the 114 securities companies reached RMB1.72 trillion, with net assets of RMB694.346 billion, net capital of RMB497.099 billion, the balance of securities transaction and settlement funds of RMB600.271 billion, the market value of custody securities of RMB13.76 trillion and the total capital of trusteeship management of RMB1.89 trillion.[11] Table 3.1 is the balance list for clients' transaction and settlement funds held by the securities companies in 2012. From this table, it can be seen that the securities companies are in control of a huge amount of wealth.

Table 3.1 Balance of the Clients' Transaction and Settlement Funds Ranking (2012) (Unit: RMB10,000)

No.	Securities companies	Balance
1	Galaxy Securities Co., Ltd	3,323,878
2	Guotai Junan Securities Co., Ltd	2,941,281
3	Huatai Securities Co., Ltd	2,820,237
4	Guangfa Securities Co., Ltd	2,807,875
5	Shenyin & Wanguo Securities Co., Ltd	2,713,246
6	Guosen Securities Co., Ltd	2,474,169
7	Haitong Securities Co., Ltd	2,452,142
8	China Merchants Securities Co., Ltd	2,423,331
9	(CITIC) China Securities Co., Ltd	2,137,057
10	Everbright Securities Co., Ltd	1,587,210

Source: The Securities Association China.[12]

From the above analysis, it can be seen that business scope and operational characteristics decide that securities companies manage a large amount of wealth. Moreover, the function and impact of self disciplinary measures is limited. So, during the last two decades, there have been several scandals in this respect.

One important factor needing to be noted is that the securities companies themselves are quite wealthy. Table 3.2 lists the top ten securities companies in China, according to total assets in 2012. As a result, their behaviour has a significant impact on the Chinese economy.

Securities companies are part of the most important financial institutions in the Chinese securities market. They are the bridges between fund raisers and investors. Their conduct and business are important to the steady and prosperous growth of the capital market as a whole. Given the lack of an effective regulatory and supervisory regime, there will be risks posed for financial system stability. These risks may have long-term, complicated and systemic negative

Table 3.2 Securities companies' total assets list (2012) (Unit: RMB10,000)

No	Securities companies	Total assets
1	CITIC Securities Co., Ltd.	13,020,150
2	Haitong Securities Co., Ltd	10,860,803
3	Guotai Junan Securities Co., Ltd	8,986,033
4	Guangfa Securities Co., Ltd	8,253,162
5	Huatai Securities Co., Ltd	6,941,791
6	China Merchants Securities Co., Ltd	6,900,763
7	Galaxy Securities Co., Ltd	5,810,530
8	Guosen Securities Co., Ltd	5,782,655
9	Everbright Securities Co., Ltd	5,344,209
10	Shenyin & Wanguo Securities Co., Ltd	4,917,556

Source: The Securities Association of China.[13]

impacts on the social economy. Drawn from the experiences of the recent financial cirsis, the recognition of the importance of financial regulation has been taken to a new level.[14] Newly reformed regulatory approaches have been adopted at a domestic and international level. For the Chinese securities market, although it has not been fully influenced by the crisis, the lessons learned from other jurisdictions should be taken as reference points for future development. International experiences have illustrated the importance of transparency in the financial system. The Chinese regulatory regime may also gain advantages by learning from the experiences of others.

In order to promote a healthy securities market and in particular a healthy disclosure regime, it is necessary to prevent and control the risks derived from securities companies. Investors desire to obtain relevant corporate information to facilitate their decision making. For the company itself, disclosure will be very helpful to establishing a good corporate governance system. Some securities companies are also listed companies; for instance, Haitong Securities Co., Ltd,[15] Sinolink Securities Co., Ltd (Guojin),[16] Changjiang Securities Co., Ltd,[17] Southwest Securities Co., Ltd.[18] Being a securities company, it will be subject to the relevant regulations on the supervision and administration of securities companies. As a listed company, it will also be subject to the relevant regulations on the listing and offering of stocks. Under these conditions, it is beyond any doubt that there must be an open, fair and immediate disclosure structure.

Compared with the general listed companies, historically, due to various reasons, limited attention has been placed on the securities companies. Based on the failure of some securities companies, Chinese law and regulation has enhanced the disclosure and risk control regime for securities companies in the last few years. In general, information disclosure for securities companies has two layers: On one hand, the securities companies must disclose their own information according to the law and regulation. On the other hand, as a trading services provider, they must deal with the relevant information supplied by their business counterparts.

Information concerning the securities companies

General requirements for the securities companies

As stated earlier the securities companies are playing an important role in the Chinese capital market. Therefore, the legal and regulatory regime pays a great deal of attention to them. Disclosure is a necessary and vital requirement for an effective regulatory and supervisory regime. In practice, a securities company must disclose the information relating to its business on the company's website, the 'investors' field' of its business sites. According to the Notice of the Relevant Issues about Information Disclosure of Securities Companies, securities companies shall disclose the following information: general information of the company; for instance, the branches, licensed business, senior managers; if a company is under the risk disposal procedures, relevant information shall be disclosed; sufficient risk indication and necessary information; securities companies shall be responsible for the authenticity, accuracy and integrity of the disclosed information.[19] Finally, according to the Notice of Enhancing the Information Disclosure of Securities Companies, the Securities Association of China shall establish the information column for Securities Companies on its official website (www.sac.net.cn). Moreover, the Shanghai Stock Exchange (SSE), Shenzhen Stock Exchange (SZSE) and China Securities Depository and Clearing Corporation Limited (CSDCC) shall establish the relevant web links to the information column.[20]

It can be seen from these legal requirements, that the regulatory bodies are attempting to establish a comprehensive system of information disclosure. These measures have encouraged securities companies to transform themselves into modern and reliable financial institutions. According to these legal requirements, the general information disclosed by the securities companies needs to be displayed at the relevant places. More often (apart from the company name, business address, relevant qualification required, legal representative) other information, for instance: the statement on product information of the securities company, information on the senior executives and information on corporate social responsibilities can also be found.

In the last few years, there have been some scandals and cases occurring due to untimely and false disclosure in securities market.[21] Therefore, the law and regulation has attempted to enhance the regime. The Securities Law placed strict liabilities on false records, misleading information and major omissions in the disclosure procedures. When a securities company, its shareholders or actual controller provides false records, misleading statements information or materials regarding its business and management or there is a major omission in the information or materials, it shall be ordered to correct the information, given a warning and a fine from RMB30,000 up to RMB300,000 will be imposed; moreover, the relevant business license of the securities company may be suspended or cancelled; the person in charge and other person directly responsible shall be given a warning and fined no more than RMB30,000 and the relevant post holding qualification or securities practice qualification shall be canceled.[22] If such a person breaches the criminal law, a term of up to ten years' fixed-term imprisonment will be applied.[23]

Based on these standards and requirements, the information disclosure regime for general securities companies has been established. In fact, this regime does facilitate the regulation and supervision of the securities companies, although there are some aspects that need to be further enhanced. Financial restructuring and law reform are the basic requirements of market development. The relatively short history, incomplete market structure, and weak regulatory framework has resulted in the inherent problems of the Chinese financial market. Therefore, to settle these issues needs a gradual progress. Chinese legal reform has come an 'extraordinary distance, further than anyone could have foreseen',[24] and has demonstrated China's achievements.

Requirements for listed securities companies

Information disclosure for listed securities companies has two different dimensions, as a listed company and as a securities company. Therefore, disclosure shall be established according to the multiple requirements: the Company Law,[25] Securities Law and Rules of Corporate Governance of Securities Companies,[26] Administrative Measures for the Risk Control Indexes of Securities Companies[27] and other laws and regulations setting up the basic standards. Moreover, the Contents and Formats of Information Disclosure by Companies Offering Securities to the Public No. 2 – Contents and Format of an Annual Report,[28] Standards on the Contents and Format of an Annual Report of a Securities Company[29] outline more detailed obligations.

The contents and format of information disclosure have been attracting the attention of the financial regulators. In general, the contents required by the law and regulation may vary, however the following facts must be disclosed in the annual report: basic information about the company; summaries of accounting data and business data; changes in stock capital and information about shareholders; information about directors, supervisors, senior executives and employees; corporate governance structure; brief introduction of the general assembly of shareholders; reports of the directors, report of the supervisors; important events; financial report; catalogue of reference documents.[30]

In 2009, following the financial crisis, in order to strengthen the supervision and administration of listed securities companies, the Provisions on Strengthening the Supervision and Administration of Listed Securities Companies were enacted.[31] This document has numerous articles concerning information disclosure. According to these provisions, a securities company shall notify all the shareholders in writing of the company's or a company officer's suspected involvement in any major violation of law or regulation; the deterioration of the company's financial status; the intent to change the chairman of the board of directors, general manager or chairman of the board of supervisors; the particular changes in the risk control indexes and other situations. Moreover, the listed securities company shall promptly announce the above situations on the designated information disclosure media, so as to perform its obligation of notifying all shareholders in writing.[32]

Furthermore, a securities company must obtain the approval from the CSRC in order to initiate a new business or operate an innovative business. When a listed securities company announces a resolution of the board of directors or the general meeting of shareholders regarding the operation of a new business, it shall disclose to the investors the risks by stating that it remains subject to the examination and approval of the regulatory body, and the approval may not be obtained if the company fails to meet the requirements of the laws and regulations.[33]

In addition, a listed securities company shall also disclose the major events which cause changes in its risk control indexes and any regulatory measures that have been taken against it. In particular, the securities company shall disclose the information about all risk control indexes in its annual report and semi-annual report. If during the operation of the business, the risk control indexes do not conform to the standards required by law and regulation, the company shall in a timely manner disclose the information in an interim report to explain the reasons, status quo and possible consequences. Another consideration is, if any major regulatory measure or risk disposal measure has been taken against the listed securities company, that may affect its business operation or have a significant impact on the share price, the company shall confirm the occurrence of a major event, disclosing it in an interim report, semi-annual report and annual report.[34]

As with general listed companies, the information provided by the listed securities companies must be accurate, authentic and integrated. When the prospectus, measures for financing through issuance of corporate bonds, financial statement, listing report, annual report, midterm report, temporary report or other information disclosed has any false record, misleading statement or major omission, and this results in losses to investors, the issuer or the listed company shall be subject to the liabilities of compensation. The director, supervisor, senior manager or other person directly responsible shall be subject to joint and several liabilities for compensation. Furthermore, when the shareholder or actual controller of the company is at fault, he shall be subject to joint and several liabilities for compensation together with the relevant issuer or listed company.[35]

It should be noted that listed securities companies have a relatively short history in China. Regarding the special nature of listed securities companies, imposing strict corporate disclosure requirements is a necessary step for the purpose of better regulation, in particular, with respect to major events; significant business changes; risk control indexes; and administrative disposal procedures. These disclosure measures will provide the investors with a clear scenario, and will facilitate the establishment of a better governance structure for the securities companies.

Protecting the clients' funds

From the above analysis, it can be seen that the law and regulation has paid more attention to the disclosure of information from securities companies. This was either decided by the business nature of securities companies or for historical reasons. Earlier in the twenty-first century, it was argued, that some securities companies in China tended to perform on the edge of risk.[36] The insufficient regulatory system can be seen as one of the major reasons. Newly emerging and transitional situations deepened this phenomenon. The Chinese securities market was formed with 'birth defects', in particular, for the management and settlement system of clients' transaction funds.[37]

Historically the financing sources for the securities companies were limited. One reason was the separated operational system in the Chinese financial market. Therefore, at the earlier stage, it had been argued that the major financing sources for the securities companies were the funds deposited by the clients.[38]

This phenomenon, started after the 5.19 Bull Market.[39] One of the reasons for the event was the approval of the policy proposal submitted by the CSRC to the State Council. These six policies included: reforming the IPO system; allowing insurance capital to enter the financial market; gradually setting the legal financing channels for securities companies; allowing some of the eligible securities companies to issue financial bonds; extending the experimental scope for securities investment funds; invigorating the B share Market, allowing eligible B shares and H shares to carry on re-purchase. Moreover, according to the Financial Statistics Book of Shanghai, in 2001, the amount of entrusted funds from clients reached RMB24 billion, plus the entrusted funds from state owned companies and private companies, the actual amount was around RMB250 billion.[40] It can be seen from the figures that the behaviour of the securities companies was vitally important for the whole social economy.

Traditionally for the securities companies, their incomes mainly came from the underwriting business, self operation and securities brokerage. With the development of the Chinese securities market, this situation could not satisfy the growing demands of the securities companies, in particular, for midterm and long-term financing demands. The problem faced by the securities companies was the limited channels for them to borrow funds.[41] At that time, the Chinese securities market was in the initial stage, the institutional establishment was relatively weak, therefore, the financing channels were limited. Moreover, research showed that, in 2002, the self operational funds of securities companies needed to reach 20 times capital turnover ratio in order to occupy around 10 per cent of the trading amounts in the second market, which was in fact 'performing the main stream institutional function'; however, the 20 times capital turnover ratio was very difficult to achieve (nearly three times the actual turnover ratio in the securities market); even if the target could be achieved, it would be dangerous for market stability.[42] If such a turnover rate had become a reality, the stabilization function of the securities companies as institutional investors could not be fulfilled, and the operational risks of the securities companies would be increased.[43] Therefore, some securities companies would turn to unlawful channels. In this context, broadening the financing channels could improve the efficiency of securities companies, prevent illegal fund raising and maintain financial stability.

In this aspect, there was a very important step that cannot be ignored. In the Opinion of the State Council on Promoting the Reform, Opening and Steady Growth of Capital Markets has declared the channel for the securities companies should be broadened to raise funds. It stated that:

> Financing channels of securities companies must be expanded. Continuing support will be given to the qualified companies' efforts in raising long-term funds through public offering of shares and bonds. We should improve the administrative measures for pledged borrowing of securities companies as well as their entry into the inter-bank market, and formulate the review and approval standards for acquisition and merger of securities companies as

well as loans for securities underwriting. We should, on the basis of improving the mechanism for risk control, create favourable conditions for securities companies to use loans and raise funds. Experiments will be steadily conducted on the financing of fund management companies.[44]

This document stated the further development of strategies for the Chinese capital market.[45] Since then, the financing channels for securities companies have quickly expanded. Subsequently, the number of securities companies also reached a new level. Nevertheless, problems also emerged, in particular, with regard to managing and controlling the clients' transaction and settlement funds. As can be seen from the earlier analysis, the securities companies are in charge of a considerable amount of these funds. Therefore, without an efficient regulatory system, the funds may be misused.

Virtually, from 2001, the financial regulators in China have already paid attention to the issue of regulating and managing securities companies. In order to protect clients' funds, the Measures on the Management of Clients' Transaction and Settlement Funds were issued in 2001.[46] According to these Measures, clients' transaction and settlement funds must be totally deposited in commercial banks with qualifications for engaging in deposition and management of securities trading settlement funds, and be managed with separated accounts.[47] The commercial banks and the settlement companies for securities registration shall supervise the directional transfer of clients' funds.[48] Moreover, the CSRC will supervise the business activities on deposition and management of securities trading settlement funds.[49]

In order to oversee and manage the use of the funds, the Measures went further and required a reporting system.[50] First of all, the account opened by a securities company or its securities trading department for clients' transaction and settlement funds and for its own funds shall be reported to the CSRC for recording within three working days after being opened, and may not be used until the return receipt of the account records has been obtained. Second, the account for a securities company's self-operated securities shall be reported to the CSRC and the settlement company. If a settlement company finds that a securities company has misappropriated a large amount of clients' transaction settlement funds, it must report to the CSRC immediately. Third, a securities company shall report to the CSRC monthly, on the balance of clients' transaction settlement funds in its book account and copy to the settlement company. Finally, a securities company, a settlement company, a deposition-management bank, or a settlement bank shall report to the CSRC in good time regarding its requirements, or immediately, in the case of important unconventional circumstances affecting to these accounts.

It can be seen that the reporting and disclosure system for the clients' funds has been established. Moreover, this system is gradually improving. However, there were still some securities companies misappropriating client funds. One of the early cases was the bankruptcy of the NewChina Securities Co., Ltd (hereafter NewChina Securities). NewChina Securities licence was cancelled in

December 2003.[51] It was a shocking event at that time. A combination of highly risky investment, excessively high leveraged operations and loose internal control were believed to be the main reasons; in particular, most of this behaviour was based on the misappropriation of clients' funds.[52] The Board Chairman, however, disappeared and therefore could not be pursued personally.

Furthermore, by December 2005, 23 securities companies had their business licences cancelled or were required to close.[53] The main problems were concentrated on the misappropriation of the funds in a client's account, market manipulation and exceeding the licenced business scope. Nanfang Securities Co., Ltd (hereafter Nanfang Securities) was another typical case. In April 2005, the CSRC decided to cancel the business license of Nanfang Securities and ordered it to close.[54] After investigation, the CSRC found that Nanfang Securities had misappropriated huge amounts of clients' transaction and settlement funds, could not repay the funds, and this led to serious results. Therefore, it was not allowed to continue operations. In March 2006, two CEOs (appointed respectively in June 2002, June 1998) and one Deputy CEO (appointed in March 1997) of Nanfang Securities were arrested for market manipulation, which created an 'earthquake' in the Chinese securities market.[55] From then on, the law enforcement agencies of China started a new period of supervising and management of the senior management of securities companies.

The result of the case has been described as 'the tiger's head but a snake's tail', a Chinese expression meaning to start as a huge event but finish as a small matter. The statement that quashed the indictments to two of the former CEOs caused arguments regarding, who will pay the price, for the RMB21 billion economic losses and RMB8 billion central bank's injection?[56] It can be seen from this case that although the reporting and disclosing system for clients' funds has been significantly improved, there is still a long way to go.

Risk disclosure

Besides the risks resulting from the financing channel, there are some other contributions leading to the high risks of securities companies; for instance, weak corporate governance, loose internal control, historically unresolved problems, and external or macroeconomic environments. From a broader sense, the market risk, liquidation risk, credit risk, operational risk and other systemic risks are all faced by securities companies. More importantly, the character of the Chinese capital markets, newly emerging and transitional nature itself may create some uncertainty. Experiences illustrate that when the law and regulation are not sufficient and effective enough in a market, unlawful behaviour may increase.

These circumstances require that the risk management for the Chinese securities companies must be improved. The experiences drawn from China and other jurisdictions have emphasized the importance of enhancing the risk control of securities companies. Under this background, the Measures for the Risk Control Indexes of Securities Companies were revised in 2008.[57] In the last two decades, the development and reform in the Chinese financial market, has promoted and facilitated the innovation of financial products. Subsequently, the securities companies started to provide new types of services. Therefore, the risk control index needed to be redesigned to meet the latest market situation.

According to the Measures, the securities company shall establish a dynamic supervision and complementary mechanism of risk control indexes according to its assets, liability structure and business development. Based on this approach, the company shall ensure that each and every aspect of the risk control index is in compliance with the law and regulations. Moreover, the company shall conduct a sensitivity analysis on the index before carrying out each business transaction or distributing any profit, in order to rationally determine the maximum scale of relevant business and the profits to be distributed. Finally, the company shall also set up a 'stress test' mechanism and constantly improve it, so as to make stress tests on the company's risk control indicators in the light of the fluctuations of the market in a timely manner.[58]

As for the risk control index, the Measures state that a securities company shall comply with the required standards.[59] A detailed examination of the risk control index is beyond the scope of this chapter, the disclosure of the risk control index is the main focus.

A securities company which has subsidiaries shall prepare the net capital calculation sheets and risk control index supervisory statements, based on the data of the parent company.[60]

The directors and senior managers of a securities company shall sign the semi-annual and annual net capital calculation sheets, risk capital reserve calculation sheets and risk control index supervision statements for confirmation. The principal chief and the financial chief that are in charge of the operation and management shall sign the monthly net capital calculation sheets, risk capital reserve calculation sheet and risk control index supervisory statements for confirmation. The person who signs the documents must guarantee the authenticity, accuracy and integrity of the content, and ensure that there is no false record, misleading statement or significant omission therein.[61]

For the time allowed for submitting the required report, the company shall within seven working days after the end of each month, file the monthly net capital calculation sheet, risk capital reserve calculation sheet and risk control indicator supervision statement to the regulatory bodies. Moreover, when the net capital index changes more than 30 per cent compared to the previous month, or does not meet the regulatory standards, the securities company shall send a report in writing to all the directors within five working days and, to all the shareholders within ten working days.[62]

Finally, in the case of when the net capital index or other risk control index changes by more than 20 per cent compared to the previous month, the securities company shall send a written report stating the basic information and possible reasons to the CSRC and its detached offices within three working days.[63] Furthermore, when the risk control index reaches the alert level or fails to comply with the stipulated standard, the securities company shall send a written report to the CSRC within three working days and to the detached offices within one working day respectively, the report shall provide the basic information, the reasons, specific solutions and the time requirement for such solution.[64]

Risk control is an essential element of the regulatory regime for the securities companies. The risk control index system which is based on the net capital is an important standard to evaluate the securities company's risk bearing abilities. The Chinese financial market is different from other mature markets. Thus, to discover a quantitative measurement model which is suitable to the market is crucially important. Moreover, the western model cannot be transplanted directly into China. It has been argued that the reasons for this are: first, the financial products are less varied than in the mature markets; second, the price formation system of the Chinese capital market is not perfect.[65] In fact, this argument reflected the situation in the earlier stages of the Chinese securities market; however, it should be noted that these methods can provide useful examples and models for the Chinese market. Therefore, quantitative analysis is an important tool to enhance risk control. The Chinese securities market emerged with unique Chinese features. Most significantly, the continuing reform according to the market situation, facilitates the modernization of the Chinese financial market. As a consequence, at this stage, the financial products are not as diversified as those in mature markets; moreover, the price of securities, under the current circumstance, may not be determined by the market itself. Under these conditions, the timely adjustment and disclosure of the risk control index may help to prevent individual and systemic risks. It can be seen from the above laws and regulations, that the risk disclosure framework has been enhanced. The next task is to build a regime which could promote the securities companies' growth in a modern, steady and safe manner.

Innovation disclosure

Concerning the special nature of the Chinese listed securities companies, attention has been given to innovative businesses disclosure. The term is not clearly prescribed in the Securities Law and other regulations, simply being referred to as 'innovative businesses'.[66] Some of the innovative businesses may not be new in other mature markets. Recalling the earlier stage of the securities market, some ideas were directly borrowed or transferred from other countries. The results were that such financial operations did not correspond with the Chinese market situation. Therefore, the State Council stopped certain types of business; for instance mixed operations, which is analysed in greater detail in the later part of this chapter. In fact, the core issue of financial innovation, in the current stage, under the emerging and transitional nature, is how to conduct innovation in a healthy, stable and safe mode.

Similar to the other financial institutions, the securities companies are participants of financial reforms in China. In fact, securities companies themselves are also the products of financial reforms. With the growth of the Chinese securities market, the government worked out a more suitable timetable to introduce innovative businesses. In 2004, in the document, Some Opinions of the State Council on Promoting the Reform, Opening and Steady Growth of Capital Markets, the State Council stated its intention to promote the healthy development of the Chinese securities market.[67] Also, in the Notice of Several Issues Concerning the Promotion of Innovation Activities in Securities Industry, the CSRC stated the importance of financial innovation:

> Securities companies shall be encouraged to give full play to the enthusiasm, initiative of innovation, carry out innovation in business, operation mode as well as organizations according to market requirements and their own practical needs, improve the quality of service, and better the profit mode with a view to growing excellent to become powerful in market competition and pushing forward the integral development of securities industry.[68]

Moreover, considering financial stability and existing cases, the CSRC decided to start the innovative reform on a trial base. Based on these experiences, the CSRC would draw conclusions in order to establish an efficient but safe approach for innovation. The CSRC also set up the terms and conditions for the pilot securities companies; for instance good corporate governance, advanced internal risk control systems, higher level of capital adequacy and operation conforming to law, furthermore, the innovative activities should start based on the precondition that the risks of these activities are measurable, controllable and sustainable.[69]

According to law and regulation, the innovative business must receive approval, for example, the 'Innovative Pilot Broker' qualification. The Securities Association of China was responsible for reviewing the proposals, and established the detailed measures for the appraisal; legal representatives and principal persons who are responsible for operation and management of the securities company shall maintain the authenticity, accuracy and integrity of the information in the application.[70] Moreover, currently, upon the approval of the CSRC, a securities company may engage in innovative businesses; the operation of innovative businesses by a securities company according to the existing laws, administrative regulations and provisions of the CSRC, the risks of which can be calculated, controlled and endured, shall relate closely to the current securities businesses, and contribute to the full use of the present business outlets, customer resources, business expertise, or management experiences of the company, and optimizing customer services and improving the profit model of the company; to operate innovative businesses, a securities company shall establish an internal assessment and examination mechanism, conduct full assessment and study of the compliance, feasibility and possible risks of the innovative businesses, formulate rules for business management, and clarify the operating procedures, risk control measures and measures for protecting the legitimate rights and interests of customers.[71] It can be seen that the regulatory bodies take a very cautious attitude towards innovation business. Therefore, in order to secure market stability, enhanced disclosure requirements are needed.

For innovative disclosure, according to the Provisions on Strengthening the Supervision and Administration of Listed Securities Companies, a securities company shall obtain approval from the CSRC to initiate a new or innovative business immediately. When a listed securities company announces a resolution of the board of directors or the general meeting of shareholders regarding this, it shall warn the investors of the risks by stating that it remains subject to the examination and approval of the regulatory body, and the approval might not be obtained if the company fails to meet the requirements of the law and regulations.[72]

Moreover, as for the risk index, when a new product or business for which the risk adjustment ratio or risk capital reserve calculation ratio fails to meet the requirements of law and regulations, the securities company shall report to the CSRC or its authorized officer before investing in the product or operating the business. The CSRC shall determine the corresponding risk adjustment ratio and the risk capital reserve calculation ratio according to the characteristics and risk status of the new product or business of the securities company.[73]

It can be seen from the above analysis that, due to the importance of securities companies, the law and regulations are taking a very cautious attitude to the innovative securities business. From this point of view, innovation disclosure is a helpful tool for both the financial regulators and securities companies. It can provide a steady and safe approach for the regulatory bodies through a transparent regime. Innovation itself is an attractive feature to investors. Therefore, such disclosures will create potential business opportunities and bring benefits to the securities companies. The promotion of innovative businesses is a long-term undertaking; therefore, it should be carried out in a manner fully transparent to the whole of society. Based on these disclosures, relevant information can encourage the securities companies to develop an innovative business in a realistic manner.

Information concerning the business counterparts

As stated earlier, securities underwriting is one of the major businesses for the securities companies. Table 3.3 lists the ranking of net incomes of underwriting, sponsoring, M&A and other consultant business of the securities companies in 2012.

When dealing with securities businesses, the securities companies shall also verify the information available to them, in order to obtain and supply accurate information to other parties. When a securities company underwrites any securities, it shall conclude an agreement with the relevant issuer on sale by proxy or exclusive sale. The general agreement shall include the following information: the name, domicile and the name of the legal representative of the parties concerned; the classes, quantity, amount and issuing prices of the securities; the term of sale, the starting and termination date; the method and date of payment; the expenses for and settlement method; and the liabilities.[74]

Moreover, according to the law and regulations, the securities company that is engaged in the underwriting of securities shall verify the authenticity, accuracy

Table 3.3 Securities companies ranking (2012) (net incomes of the underwriting, sponsoring, M&A and other consultant business) (Unit: RMB10,000)

No.	Securities companies	Net incomes of the underwriting, sponsoring, M&A and other consultant business
1	Citic Securities Co., Ltd	248,521
2	Guosen Securities Co., Ltd	166,608
3	Guangfa Securities Co., Ltd	106,506
4	(CITIC) China Securities Co., Ltd	102,787
5	China International Capital Corporation, Ltd	94,171
6	Ping An Securities Co., Ltd	93,914
7	Hongyuan Securities Co., Ltd	87,427
8	Guotai Junan Securities Co., Ltd	77,283
9	Galaxy Securities Co., Ltd	67,495
10	Huatai Securities Co., Ltd	66,585

Source: The Securities Association of China.[75]

and integrity of the financial documents. When any false record, misleading statement or major omission is found, no sales activity can be processed, when any securities have been sold under such circumstances, the sales activity shall be immediately terminated and correcting measures shall be taken.[76] Furthermore, if the information disclosed by listed companies has any false record, misleading statement or major omission and further resulted in losses to investors, the underwriting securities companies shall be subject to joint and several liability for compensation unless the underwriting company is able to prove exemption of any fault.[77]

Law and regulation went further to state that the relevant personnel of securities companies engaging in underwriting are categorized as 'insiders'.[78] Therefore, they may not purchase or sell the securities of the relevant company, or unlawfully disclose such information, or advise any other person to purchase or sell the securities; by engaging in this prohibited behaviour, the perpetrator shall make compensation for any loss incurred by the relevant client; the illegal proceeds shall be confiscated and a fine from one, up to five times of the illegal proceeds shall be imposed; where there are no illegal proceeds or the illegal proceeds are less than RMB30,000, a fine of RMB30,000 up to RMB600,000 shall be imposed.[79] Moreover, the Criminal Law has provided relevant penalties regarding insider trading: if the circumstances are serious, the person shall be sentenced to a fixed term of imprisonment of not more than five years or criminal detention and shall also, or shall only, be fined not less than one times, but not more than five times the illegal gains; if the circumstances are especially serious, he shall be sentenced to fixed-term imprisonment of not less than five years, but not more than ten years and shall also be fined not less than one times, but not more than five times the illegal gains.[80]

It is strictly prohibited for the securities companies and their practitioners to commit fraudulent acts in the process of securities trading, which may damage the interests of clients, by making use of mass media or any other approach to provide or disseminate false or misleading information to investors; by acting in a prohibited manner, the perpetrator shall make compensation of any loss incurred by the relevant clients.[81] Also, if serious consequences have resulted, the person shall be sentenced to a fixed-term imprisonment of not more than five years or criminal detention and shall also, or shall only, be fined not less than RMB10,000 but not more than RMB100,000; if the circumstances are especially serious, he shall be sentenced to a fixed-term of imprisonment of not less than five years but not more than ten years and shall also be fined not less than RMB20,000 but not more than RMB200,000.[82]

However, considering the special nature of the Chinese securities market, the information disclosure system is not advanced enough, and a large number of investors are retail investors. Therefore, in order to maintain the fairness and health of the market, strict criminal and civil liabilities should be imposed. The primary issue is to establish detailed and operational supplementary rules and regulations for securities crimes, for instance, insider trading and market manipulation. Inside these rules and regulations, the method for calculating losses, proving of evidence and compensation schemes shall be covered.

The business nature of securities companies means that comprehensive regulatory requirements must be imposed on them from different dimensions. In particular, with the improvement of the Chinese securities market, more and more innovative businesses have been introduced into the market. Processing information by securities companies will reach a new level. Underwriting, M&A and other types of securities services will more often be required by business partners. Therefore, the system demands that this type of disclosure must be sufficient and accurate. Examining the current system, it will not be difficult to find that the law and regulations have paid more attention to the disclosure of self-owned information by the securities companies, but not their business counterparts. Practically, the investment banking branches of securities companies can perform at the front line. Based on this consideration, the financial regulators may need to enhance the relevant supervisory regime.

Conflict of interest and information disclosure

It can be seen from the above analysis, that the law and regulation has put intensive attention on the issues of internal control, corporate governance and the managing of clients' assets by the securities companies. Some of the regulatory measures are relatively new and modern. However, there is still one issue needing to be addressed: the conflict of interest.

The management of conflict of interest is a difficult topic, even in mature markets. The situation in China is slightly different from other countries. Currently, according to the Securities Law, the divided operation and management shall be adopted by the industries of securities, banking, trust and insurance; the securities companies and the business organizations of banks, trust and insurance shall be established separately, unless otherwise provided for by the state.[83]

However, it does not mean that there are no mixed operations existing in Mainland China.

To examine this issue, it is interesting to focus on the existing mixed operation system of financial institutions. Currently, China has maintained a firewall mechanism within the financial system: commercial banks shall not undertake the businesses of trust and investment and securities dealing business, nor shall they invest in the non-self-use real property or non-bank financial institutions and enterprises within the territory of China, unless it is otherwise prescribed by the state.[84] According to Mingkang Liu, China still insists that the main funding source of banks should always come from deposits.[85] Second, from the regulatory aspects, banking, insurance, securities business are monitored by separate regulatory commissions, each of which reports directly to the State Council.

At present, there are two types of Financial Holding Company in Mainland China. The first type is non-banking institutions based on a financial holding company. The second is an industrial capital based financial holding company. Among the first type, CITIC Group is a typical example.[86] Its core business ranges from financial industry, industrial investment to service industries; and its financial service consists of the China CITIC Bank Corporation Ltd, CITIC International Financial Holdings Ltd, CITIC Prudential Life Insurance Co., Ltd, CITIC Trust & Investment CO., Ltd, and CITIC Securities Co., Ltd etc.[87]

Another example is, Ping An Insurance (Group) Company of China, Ltd (hereafter Ping An).[88] In June 2009, ShenZhen Development Bank filed its Non-Public Offering (NPO) plan to Ping An with Shenzhen Stock Exchange.[89] It was one of the most significant events in the first half year of 2009 in the Chinese financial system. Today Ping An's business scope already covered the banking, insurance and securities business.

The second type of mixed operation is the industrial capital based financial holding company: for instance, the Haier Group. Haier has tapped into the finance and real estate business in the last few years: in 2001, Haier launched its insurance business. 'Sincere Forever' entered the financial field.[90] Moreover, Hongta Tobacco Group Corporation (hereafter Hongta Group) is a very typical case in this category.[91] One of the examples of Hongta Group's steady strategy on financial industry is the Hongta Securities Co., Ltd (hereafter Hongta Securities). Based on the securities business of three investment trust companies in Yunnan, the Hongta Securities was launched by Hongta Group and another twelve corporations together in 2002.[92]

Furthermore, the other important example is the BOC International (China) Limited (hereafter BOCI).[93] It is jointly controlled by BOC International Holdings Limited and five other Chinese enterprises; namely, China National Petroleum Corporation, State Development & Investment Corporation, Hongta Tobacco Group Corporation, China General Technology (Group) Holding Limited, and Shanghai State-owned Assets Operation Corporation. It obtained the 'Innovative Pilot Broker' qualification on 12 May 2006. Figure 3.1 shows the shareholders' structure of BOCI:

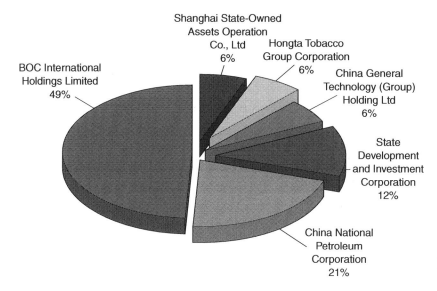

Figure 3.1 The shareholder structure of BOCI (source: BOC International (China) Ltd[94]).

Taking a close look at the shareholders' structure, it is not difficult to discover that all these shareholders are leading corporations in their own industrial field. For example, established on 5 May 1995, State Development & Investment Corporation (hereafter SDIC) is the largest state owned investment holding company in China. Currently, SDIC Trust Co., Ltd (hereafter SDIC Trust), a subsidiary company of SDIC, is mainly in charge of its financial service business. The SDIC Trust is one of the largest trust and investment companies in China. The UBS SDIC Fund Management Co., Ltd, in which SDIC Trust has a share holding, launched the UBS SDIC Core Companies Equity Fund and UBS SDIC Dynamic Innovation Fund in 2006. In the meantime, SDIC also has participation in other financial enterprises of securities, funds and banks; for instance, the China Bohai Bank.[95]

Furthermore, according to the BOCI's own description, it has the solid background of a commercial bank, effectively the Bank of China. With the diversified financial platform, BOCI is able to coordinate with Bank of China's resources and offer its clients comprehensive and one stop financial services. Meanwhile, Bank of China's broad and multilayered customer base and sales network also provide BOCI China with greater potential to expand its business.[96]

It can be seen that all the companies listed above as examples are playing an increasingly important role in the development of the national economy. And it is not difficult to imagine that with the expansion of the business, they may participate in the world economy with a more important function.

Moreover, it seems that the tide towards a mixed operation in financial market is inevitable. In particular, China is aiming to make Shanghai an international financial centre, developing cross-institution and cross-market financial products.[97] Therefore, a comprehensive operation, or mixed operation, in financial industry shall be carried out in Shanghai on a formal trial basis. As a result, conflict of interest will be a crucial problem needing to be settled in the near future. The main concern in this field is lack of regulation. Apparently, just relying on the general provisions of the Company Law, Commercial Bank Law, Securities Law and Insurance Law is not enough; comprehensive legal framework and strict criminal liabilities should be enforced. China, should learn from the control of other types of securities crime, to solve this issue at an earlier stage. Without regulating this area, it will not be difficult to imagine that when the mixed operation becomes more popular in the future, there will be some difficulties ahead.

Disclosure of the senior management

Some experiences may be learned from existing models in other jurisdictions. Also previously, the overseas listing and cross listing of Chinese companies have promoted the establishment of a corporate governance culture. In fact, managing conflict of interest has been given an important place in individual financial industries; securities companies can be examined as an example. Since there is not a complete legal framework to regulate mixed operations, internal control and corporate disclosure could be effective mechanisms.

The securities companies have a comprehensive business scope. Therefore, conflict management becomes very important. In other jurisdictions, law and regulation have managed the issue of conflict of interest from the following perspectives: corporate governance; internal control; risk management; protection of client assets; employer training and external supervision.

Based on the experiences of earlier scandals, the law and regulation have put the probity of the management and the personnel of a securities company in an important position; in particular, for directors, supervisors and senior managers. In general, the requirements for them can be summarized as follows: honest; with good level of morals; be suitably qualified; be approved by the CSRC; accepting compulsory auditing on leaving post; must be under continuing supervision. Moreover, the person who is subject to the following circumstances cannot be a director, supervisor or senior manager of a securities company; a person in charge of a stock exchange or securities registration and clearing institution or a director, supervisor or senior manager of a securities company who has been removed from his post for his irregular or disciplinary breaches of behaviour within five years of the offence; a professional of a law firm, accounting firm or investment consulting organization, financial advising organization, credit rating institution, asset appraisal institution or asset verification institution who has been disqualified for his irregular or disciplinary breaching behaviour within five years.[98]

With people who are unable to comply with the above stipulations, the CSRC may revoke their post-holding qualification and order the company to remove them from their post and replace them.[99]

The Regulation on the Supervision and Administration of Securities Companies went further to regulate directors, supervisors and senior managers.[100] According to Article 25, when the legal representatives or senior managers of securities companies leave their posts, the securities companies shall submit audit reports about them to the CSRC within two months; moreover, when the legal representatives or major principals in operation and management of the securities companies leave their posts, accounting firms qualified for handling relevant securities or futures businesses shall be engaged to audit their track record.

Importantly, according the Administrative Measures on the Qualification of Directors, Supervisors and Senior Managers of Securities Companies, the CSRC will establish and complete the database for directors, supervisors and senior managers, other securities companies can search the database when considering someone for employment.[101] Apparently, the database is an effective tool to control senior management. Moreover, the stock exchanges have also disclosed relevant information about them. For instance, Table 3.4 is a sample of the list of candidates for independent directors from the SZSE. The details are for listed companies. The same details are required for listed securities companies.

The database is designed to enhance the regulatory system for independent directors. After the company discloses the candidate's name, the SZSE will publish the relevant information on the website. Any corporation or person can submit his opinions concerning the qualification and independence of the candidate. The SZSE will examine and verify the candidates with reference to such opinions.[102] In practice, online searching, as a unique tool with 'Chinese characters', facilitates the establishment of a supervisory environment for the whole of society.

Internal control and Chinese walls

Having a complete risk management system as well as an internal control system is an important approach to prevent conflict of interest. According to the Securities Law, a securities company shall establish and improve an internal control

Table 3.4 Database for the candidate of independent directors

No.	Code	Company	Disclosure period	Candidate name	CV	Your opinion
1	XXXXXX	XX Company	2009–09–12 ~ 2009–09–18	XXX	Browse	Submit
2	XXXXXX	Same as above	2009–09–12 ~ 2009–09–18	XXX	Browse	Submit
3	XXXXXX	XXX Co., Ltd	2009–07–22 ~ 2009–07–29	XXX	Browse	Submit
2	XXXXXX	Same as above	2009–09–12 ~ 2009–09–18	XXX	Browse	Submit
2	XXXXXX	XX Company	2009–09–12 ~ 2009–09–18	XXX	Browse	Submit

Source: Shenzhen Stock Exchange.[103]

system, adopt an effective measure of separation so as to prevent any interest conflict between the company and its clients or between different clients; moreover, a securities company shall undertake its operations of securities brokerage, underwriting, self operation and asset management in a separate manner but not in a mixed manner.[104]

A separate account can also prevent conflict of interest. The securities company shall undertake its self-operation in its own name.[105] The trading settlement funds of the clients of a securities company must be deposited in a commercial bank and be managed through separate accounts.[106]

The importance of a Chinese Wall has been addressed in the different sections under the Chinese regulatory regime. It aims to separate the different branches and further prevent leaks of information inside an institution. In the Guidance on Internal Control for Securities Companies, it states that a complete information separation wall shall be established among major business departments inside securities companies to ensure the independence of businesses such as brokerage, self operation, entrusted investment management, investment banking, research and consultancy service.[107] Also, the Regulation on the Supervision and Administration of Securities Companies requires that securities companies engaged in the management business of securities assets must not conduct transactions between the self operation accounts and management accounts of securities assets, or between different management accounts without adequate separation.[108]

As for the liabilities, when a securities company fails to carry out its securities operation for brokerage, underwriting, self operation or asset management in a separate manner, it shall be ordered to make a correction; the proceeds shall be confiscated and a fine of between RMB300,000 and RMB600,000 may be imposed; in serious circumstances, the relevant business licence can be cancelled, the person in charge and any other person directly responsible shall be given a warning and imposed a fine of between RMB30,000 and RMB100,000, and the relevant post holding qualification or securities practice qualification shall be revoked.[109]

It can be seen that the control of conflict of interest has been emphasized in different legal documents for the securities companies. Information disclosure plays a sensitive role here. Interestingly, on one hand, there shall be a Chinese Wall or Fire Wall mechanism to prevent information transfer between different business branches; for example, from the investment banking sectors to other securities dealing sectors. On the other hand, there must be an effective and accurate disclosure system in every sector, according to law and regulation, as set out in the earlier part of this chapter.

With the development of the Chinese securities market, mixed operation may be necessary. However, under the new emerging and transitional nature, the market itself may not be able to regulate and adjust moral hazards and other systemic risks. In particular, the financial holding companies are in an obviously advantagous position because they have more access to relevant financial information. Therefore, to establish a powerful internal control is crucially important. Furthermore, the risks index and relevant corporate information such as senior management must be available for the whole of society.

For mixed operations, as can be seen from earlier analysis, an insufficient system is the chief hidden danger. Externally, the initial target is to establish a complete and effective regulatory regime. The three financial regulators shall cooperate actively, based on their own specialties. Internally, the risk culture shall be restructured: emphasis being placed on different industrial aspects. The China Banking Regulatory Commission (CBRC) is currently developing a regulation that will require firewalls to be established between commercial banks and their controlling shareholders and between commercial banks and their non-banking subsidiaries, in order to prevent risk contagion.[110] Another major step is the issuing of Guidelines on Chinese Wall Systems of Securities Companies by the SAC.[111] This document gives recognition of the importance of the establishment of a Chinese Wall, and further gives guidelines on how to operate; for instance, the management of the work place, information system, communication between employees. Nevertheless, it shall be borne in mind that the SAC is a self-regulatory body. While the self-regulatory bodies have less influence in the Chinese securities market. Therefore, more detailed rules and guidance from the governmental bodies are required. It will be a particularly tricky issue, under the background of mixed operation, to prevent and control related transactions.

Furthermore, the remuneration policy must be taken into account. In the Circular on Issues Concerning Executive Remuneration in State-owned Financial Institutions released on 10 April 2009, China's Ministry of Finance has indicated that total executive pay for state-owned financial institutions in 2008 must not exceed 90 per cent of 2007 levels; if there was a decline in the business in 2008, then the senior manager's remuneration shall be reduced by 10 per cent or more.[112] It may be helpful to limit other financial institutions in a similar way. The incomes of senior executives shall be disclosed according to law. However, under the current situation in China, it may be not be easy to achieve this aim. The fundamental issue, 'transparent awareness', has thus been placed in an important position. There is a long way to go.

A comparative perspective on company director disqualification

As stated earlier in this chapter, the securities company is operating significantly differently from the investment banks in the UK and Hong Kong markets. However, there is one concern on which the three jurisdictions have put the same emphasis. It can be seen from earlier analysis that the law and regulations have paid attention to the qualification issue of directors, supervisors and senior managers. Beside the specific regulation concerning the securities companies, in China, the Company Law also set down the general requirements.[113] The disqualification method has also been applied on different occasions.[114]

In the UK, the Company Directors Disqualification Act 1986 (hereafter Act) has established the regulatory regime upon the qualification system.[115] According to the Act, the court has authority to make a disqualification order; and, under such order, the person shall not be a director of a company, or directly or indirectly concerned or taking part in the promotion, formation or management of a company, for a specific period prescribed in the order.[116]

The grounds of disqualification may vary: the court may disqualify a person for general misconduct in connection with companies; for instance, disqualification on conviction of indictable offence,[117] for persistent breaches of company's legislation,[118] for fraud in winding up,[119] and on summary conviction.[120] Another important ground is 'unfitness'.[121] It covers not just dishonesty or deliberate wrongdoing but also mere incompetence, in context, a finding of unfitness may lead to a disqualification order.[122] Moreover, participation in wrongful trading, undischarged bankrupts and failure to pay under county court administration order may lead to disqualification.[123]

Furthermore, the period of disqualification that has been set up, which can be a maximum of 15 years.[124] The consequences of acting in contravention of a disqualification penalties order are imprisonment for not more than two years or a fine, or both.[125]

The regulatory structure in Hong Kong is very similar to the UK approach.[126] The section 168E, F, G, J and L of Companies Ordinance set the provisions under which a person may be disqualified from acting as a director. Furthermore, Section 168 H, states the circumstances where the court shall make a disqualification order. The disqualification period can be up to 15 years. Furthermore, Section 168 M states that where a person acts in contravention of a disqualification order, he is guilty of an offence and is liable to imprisonment and a fine.

On 7 March 2012, the Hong Kong's Court of First Instance in a case ordered two of the defendants to pay HK$85 million in total, and disqualified from being a company director for 12 years.[127] In this landmark ruling, the court gave the longest disqualification orders ever made in such proceedings.[128] Clearly, this case showed that the listed company directors must conduct the business in a responsible way in managing their companies. Just as the SFC has noted:

> The directors flouted their responsibilities, abused shareholders' funds and sought to prevent steps being taken to make them accountable. The compensation order means they must now account for shareholders' funds that were misappropriated and the lengthy disqualification periods send a deterrent message. Companies and shareholders may lose money for all sorts of reasons but misconduct by directors is not one of those reasons.[129]

As can be seen from the above, the three jurisdictions set up the regulatory regime for qualification of directors respectively. Clearly, China has put effort into this aspect. However, the law and regulations are not detailed enough. Compared with the Chinese law, UK and Hong Kong law provide more information on the procedural issues; for instance, the courts' involvement. Though the Chinese law and regulation, at this stage, place more focus on the passive qualification, i.e. in what circumstances the person in question cannot take up a position. Article 7 of Measures for the Supervision and Administration of the Professional Qualifications of Directors, Supervisors and Senior Managers of Securities Companies illustrated this situation.[130] A further issue to be considered is that whether these laws and regulations can be enforced effectively in China.

Summary

From the above analysis, it can be seen that the securities companies are crucially important for the Chinese securities market. Their fast growth will have great positive impacts on the economy. However, due to the business nature of the securities companies, they control more information and sources than the general public. Therefore, they may take relevant advantages and further abuse the information they have obtained. With this background, it has been argued that the relevant information for securities companies should be disclosed at the point of client business, and relevant information about main branches should also be available.[131] Nevertheless, it will increase the costs for financial institutions, which may not be realistic. A high level of regulatory standards that may not be practical and may not be suitable for the current market situation.

Information disclosure of the securities companies is an important and necessary mechanism for the open and fair disclosure regime. This system will bring benefits to the Chinese securities market. It can enhance market transparency, improve the efficiency of supervision and regulation, and promote the healthy and steady growth of the securities companies.

Disclosure for the securities companies has two layers. However, it is not 'A Tale of Two Cities'. On the contrary, the two different aspects are internally linked. Management of clients' transaction and settlement funds, was, is and will be a sensitive and important issue. Risk disclosure is now in a central position. Innovative disclosure, in the current market climate, is an issue that needs to have more attention. Financial innovation can bring new profits to the securities companies. In fact, innovative abilities may decide the survival of a financial institution. However, it should be carried out in a steady and safe manner. The securities companies should establish a scientific and mature attitude to development: enlargement or expansion is not the aim; healthy growth is more important.

As for mixed operations, as can be seen from the earlier analysis, insufficient systems are the chief hidden danger. The initial target is to establish a complete and effective regulatory regime. A system of a single regulator may not be suitable for the Chinese market, or at least will take time to achieve. Currently, the divided financial regulators concentrate on their specific roles, which is more cost effective and less time consuming. However, supervisory cooperation is vitally important with this background. Further consideration must be given to enhance communication between financial regulators. At the same time, corporate governance and internal control can perform unique roles. Moreover, corporate disclosure is another approach that allows financial institutions to be monitored by the whole of society.

Last but not least, the current financial crisis has provided China with very useful experiences. China has really showed its ability to learn quickly. However, on the way towards a modern, mature financial system, balancing financial stability and innovation is crucially important. In the control and management of the information disclosure system of securities companies, the code of ethics itself is not enough; the complete legal environment is central. Previous analysis in this chapter has illustrated that besides the information disclosure regime, the supervisory system for senior management will be an important approach to enhance the regulation of securities companies.

Notes

1 Details of the mixed operation system will be discussed in the later part of this chapter.
2 Securities Law, promulgation date: 27 October 2005, effective date: 1 January 2006, Article 123. A limited liability company is a company where the shareholders are responsible for the company to the extent of the capital contributions they have paid, and the company bears the liabilities for its debts with all its property. A joint stock limited company, is a company that the shareholders are responsible for the company to the extent of the shares they have subscribed to, and the company bears the liabilities for its debts with all its property. See Company Law, Article 3.
3 Securities Law, Article 124. The establishment of a securities company shall meet the following requirements: have a corporation constitution that meets the relevant laws and administrative regulations; the major shareholders have the ability to make profits continuously, enjoying good credit standing, and have no irregular or rule-breaking record over the last three years, and its net asset being no less than RMB0.2 billion; have a registered capital that meets the provisions of law; the directors, supervisors and senior managers have the qualification for assuming such posts and its practitioners having the qualification to engage in the securities business; have a complete risk management system as well as an internal control system; have a qualified business place and facilities for operations.
4 Ibid., Article 122.
5 Ibid., Article 125.
6 Ibid., Article 136.
7 Ibid., Article 111.
8 According to the Measures on the Management of Clients' Transaction Settlement Funds, promulgation date: 16 May 2001, effective date: 1 January 2002, Article 37 (2): Clients' transaction settlement funds include the funds deposited by clients for the purpose of ensuring full amount of delivery and receipt, all money obtained from selling negotiable securities (the brokerage commission and other proper expenses shall be deducted), the bonus shares, cash, dividends on shares or bonds obtained from the holding of securities, interest obtained from the above said funds, and other funds confirmed by the CSRC.
9 Securities Law, Article 139.
10 Xian Tang (2006), 'Some Thoughts on Establishing the Information Disclosure System of Securities Companies in China' (Goujian Woguo Zhengquan Gongsi Xinxi Pilu Zhidu de Sikao), *Reform of Economic System*, 4, p. 39.
11 SAC (2013), 'SAC Released Operating Statistics of Securities Companies of the Year 2012', www.sac.net.cn/en/update/201302/t20130206_61584.html, last accessed: 30 May 2013. The Securities Association of China (SAC) is a self-regulatory organization for securities industry established on 28 August 1991. The main objectives of the SAC are: conducting self-regulation over the securities

industry under the government's centralized and comprehensive supervision and management; bridging between the government and the industry; providing services to members, protecting the lawful rights and interests of members; maintaining the fair competition order in the securities industry, promoting transparency, justice and fairness of the securities market and pushing forward the healthy and steady development of the securities market.

12 See the SAC website, www.sac.net.cn/ljxh/xhgzdt/201305/P020130530532560243 261.pdf, last accessed: 17 May 2013.

13 Ibid.

14 G20 (15 November 2008), Declaration on Summit on Financial Markets and the World Economy, inter alia: 'Enhancing Sound Regulation: We pledge to strengthen our regulatory regimes, prudential oversight, and risk management, and ensure that all financial markets, products and participants are regulated or subject to oversight, as appropriate to their circumstances. We will exercise strong oversight over credit rating agencies, consistent with the agreed and strengthened international code of conduct. We will also make regulatory regimes more effective over the economic cycle, while ensuring that regulation is efficient, does not stifle innovation, and encourages expanded trade in financial products and services. We commit to transparent assessments of our national regulatory systems.'

15 Haitong Securities Co., Ltd was founded in 1988 as one of the earliest securities companies in mainland China. Haitong was transformed to a limited liability company in 1994 and gradually developed itself into a national securities firm. It was wholly transformed to a joint stock company at the end of 2001. On 31 July 2007, Haitong officially went public in Shanghai Stock Exchange. See www.htsec. com/htsec/Channel/1505835, last accessed: 12 November 2009.

16 Sinolink Securities Co., Ltd (also known as Guojin Securities) was founded in 1990 as one of the earliest securities companies in mainland China. In February 2008, Sinolink Securities was listed in Shanghai Stock Exchange. See www.gjzq.com.cn/ gjzq/about/about-us.jsp?menuType=6_2, last accessed: 12 November 2012.

17 Changjiang Securities Co., Ltd (formerly Hubei Securities Co., Ltd) was founded in 18 March 1991 and listed in Shenzhen Stock Exchange on 27 December 2007. See www.cjsc.com.cn/, last accessed: 12 November 2012.

18 Southwest Securities Co., Ltd was founded in 28 December 1999 and listed in Shanghai Stock Exchange on 26 February 2009. Southwest Securities is the first listed financial type company in Chongqing. See www.swsc.com.cn/portal/ homepage.jsp#, last accessed: 12 November 2012.

19 CSRC (20 April 2006), www.csrc.gov.cn/pub/newsite/xxfw/fgwj/bmgz/200803/ t20080303_78163.htm, last accessed, 17 September 2009.

20 CSRC (20 April 2006), http://old.csrc.gov.cn/n575458/n776436/n804950/n827698/ 2052952.html, last accessed, 17 September 2012.

21 See Chapters 1, 5 and 6.

22 Securities Law, Article 222.

23 Criminal Law, promulgation date: 14 March 1997, effective date: 1 October 1997, Article 181.

24 Donald C. Clarke (2007), 'Legislating for a Market Economy in China', *China Quarterly*, No. 191: pp. 567–585.

25 Revised date: 27 October 2005, effective date: 1 January 2006.

26 Issued date: 11 December 2012, effective date: 1 January 2013. Rules of Corporate Governance of Securities Companies (Trail), issued date: 15 December 2003, effective date: 15 January 2004, was repealed.

27 Issued date: 5 July 2006, revised: 24 June 2008.

28 Latest revision date: 19 September 2012, effective date: 1 January 2013.

29 CSRC, promulgation date: 19 November 1999, revised: 4 February 2002, revised: 14 January 2008.

30 Contents and Formats of Information Disclosure by Companies Offering Securities to the Public No. 2 – Contents and Format of an Annual Report, latest revision date: 19 September 2012, effective date: 1 January 2013.
31 Promulgation date: 3 April 2009, effective date: 3 April 2009, revised: 30 June 2010.
32 Ibid., Article 7.
33 Ibid., Article 9.
34 Ibid., Article 10. The regulatory and risk disposal measures, in general, are: restricting the business operation of the company, ordering the company to suspend some business, stopping the approval of a new business, stopping the approval of new establishment or acquisition of a business branch, restricting the distribution of bonus, restricting the payment of remunerations and offering of benefits to the officers, directors and supervisors, revoking the business licenses, ordering the controlling shareholder to transfer equities or restricting the shareholders' rights, temporarily taking over the company.
35 Securities Law, Article 69.
36 Jiemin Pang, Qingren Wang (2003), 'The Risk Management of Chinese Securities Firms during the New Emerging and Transitional Period (Xinxing jia Zhuanggui Tiaojian xia Zhongguo Zhengquan Gongsi de Fengxian Chengyin ji Jiankong)', *Economic Research Journal*, 12, p. 60. They claimed that one of the reasons that resulted in the securities companies' illicit behaviour was the system defection and insiders' control.
37 Ibid., they claimed that the 'brokerage model' which means 'the brokerages managing securities; the brokerages managing transaction and settlement funds' led to the misappropriation of clients' funds.
38 Xian Tang, see note 10, p. 39. The author further argued that, because of this reason, the securities companies were similar with the commercial banks to a certain extent: to absorb the public funds.
39 Information about 5.19 Bull Market was from: Wenlin Xie (22 September 2008), 'Zhou Zhengqin: the Whole Story of 5·19 (Zhou Zhengqin: 5.19 Hangqing Shimo)', *Chinese Securities Journal* (Zhongguo Zhengquanbao). The 5.19 Bull Market refers to the Bull Market started from 19 May 1999. During the Bull Market period, the prices of more than 95 per cent of the securities in the Chinese market rose. In the Shanghai Stock Exchange, daily transactions reached RMB44.5 billion, and the index reached 1756.18.
40 Junguang He (2005), 'Establishing the Information Disclosure System for the Securities Companies (Jianli Zhengquan Gongsi Xinxi Pilu Zhidu)', *Productivity Research*, 12, p. 76.
41 Wenlin Xie (22 September 2008), see note 39. According to Mr Zhou Zhengqing, the former Director of the State Council Securities Commission (SCSC) and Chairman of the CSRC: there was limited channel for the securities companies to borrow funds around 1999; nobody wanted to lend, nobody was in charge of the matter; even the general industrial companies can borrow funds, so why not securities companies? Therefore, the 'front door' should be open to the securities companies and the 'back door' should be shut.
42 Shusong Ba (25 May 2004), 'Ba Shusong: To Broaden the Financing Channels for Securities Companies-Understanding of 'Yijian' (Ba Shusong: Tuozhan Zhengquan Gongsi Rongzi Qúdao de Zhongda Tupo- Jiedu 'Yijian' Zhiyi)', www.macrochina.com.cn/zhtg/20040525064608.shtml, last accessed: 17 September 2009.
43 Ibid.
44 31 January 2004, Point 3.
45 Ibid. It focused on: fully understanding the importance of developing capital markets; the guidelines and tasks of promoting reform, opening and steady growth of capital markets; further improving the relevant policies and promoting the

steady growth of capital markets; improving the systems of capital markets and diversifying securities products; further upgrading the quality of listed companies and promoting the standardized operation of listed companies; promoting the regulated development of intermediary institutions on capital markets and upgrading their practicing level; enhancing the construction of sound legal and credit systems and improving the supervision and administration of capital markets; enhancing coordination and cooperation and preventing and defusing market risks; earnestly summing up experiences and promoting openness in a positive and reliable manner.

46 Promulgation date: 16 May 2001, effective date: 1 January 2002.
47 Ibid., Article 2.
48 Ibid., Article 3.
49 Ibid., Article 4.
50 Ibid., Article 9, 19, 20, 21.
51 NewChina Securities Co., Ltd was one of the biggest securities companies in Jilin Province. Based on Changchun Securities Co., Ltd, it was established on 14 December 2000, and its license cancelled on 5 December 2003.
52 Weibin Yu, 'The Bankruptcy of The NewChina Securities Co., Ltd (Jiekai Xinhua Zhengquan Cusi de Neimu)', *The Banker*, 2 (2004), p. 126.
53 Zhengqing Zhou, Securities Knowledge Handbook (Zhengquan Zhishi Duben), www.csrc.gov.cn/n575458/n870586/n1335340/n8200134/10644047.html, last accessed: 17 Sep 2009.
54 CSRC [2005] No. 9, 28 Apr 2005.
55 Ning Yu, 'The Arrest of Kan Zhidong, Liu Dong and Guo Yuanxian (Kan Zhidong, Liu Dong, Guo Yuanxian Beibu)', *Caijing*, 5 (2006).
56 Ning Yu (2007), 'Nanfang Securities Case: the Tiger's Head but a Snake's Tail (Nanfang Zhengquan Hutou Shewei)', *Caijing*, 10. According to the author, the Procuratorate of Luohu District, Shenzhen City quashed the litigation of two of the CEOs on the grounds of 'changes in the facts and evidences'.
57 Promulgation date: 5 July 2006, revised: 24 June 2008.
58 Ibid., Article 6.
59 Ibid., Article 20. A securities company shall comply with the following standards: the proportion between the net capital and the sum of all risk capital reserves shall not be lower than 100 per cent; the proportion between net capital and net assets shall not be lower than 40 per cent; the proportion between the net capital and the liabilities shall not be lower than 8 per cent; the proportion between the net assets and the liabilities shall not be lower than 20 per cent.
60 Ibid., Article 26.
61 Ibid., Article 27. Risk capital reserve shall be calculated on a certain basis and establish a corresponding relationship between such reserves and net capital so as to ensure that each risk capital reserve is backed by corresponding net capital. See Article 40.
62 Ibid., Article 28, 29.
63 Ibid., Article 30.
64 Ibid., Article 31.
65 Jiemin Pang, Qingren Wang (2003), see note 36.
66 For instantce, the Interim Provisions on the Examination and Approval of the Business Scope of Securities Companies, promulgation date: 30 October 2008, effective date: 1 December 2008, Article 5.
67 31 January 2004.
68 CSRC, 12 August 2004, repealed on 10 April 2009, Point 1.
69 Ibid., Point 2.
70 Ibid., Point 3.
71 The Interim Provisions on the Examination and Approval of the Business Scope of

Securities Companies, promulgation date: 30 October 2008, effective date: 1 December 2008, Article 5.

72 Article 9.
73 Administrative Measures for the Risk Control Indexes of Securities Companies, promulgation date: 5 July 2006, effective date: 5 July 2006, revised: 24 June 2008, Article 3.
74 Securities Law, Article 28, 30.
75 SAC, www.sac.net.cn/newcn/home/info_detail.jsp?info_id=1244193338100&info_type=CMS.STD&cate_id=81183692051100, last accessed: 17 May 2013.
76 Ibid., Article 31.
77 Ibid., Article 69.
78 Ibid., Article 74(6).
79 Ibid., Article, 202.
80 Criminal Law, Article 180. The period of criminal detention shall be not less than one month but not more than six months, and will be served through the public security organization in the vicinity. During this period, a criminal under criminal detention, in contrast to imprisonment, may go home for one to two days each month; an appropriate remuneration may be given to those who participate in labour. The fixed-term imprisonment shall be not less than six months but not more than 15 years, which shall be served in prison or another designated place. See Criminal Law, Article 42, 43, 45, 46.
81 Securities Law, Article 79.
82 Criminal Law, Article 181.
83 Securities Law, Article 6.
84 Commercial Bank Law, promulgation date: 10 May 1995, revised: 27 December 2003, Article 43. In 2003, when the Commercial Bank Law under revising, the phrase 'unless it is otherwise prescribed by the state' had been added. The purpose of such amendment was to pre-arrange room for the future development, in particular, in the aspect of mixed operation. See 'Interpretation of Commercial Bank Law', available at: www.lawinfochina.com/, last accessed: 15 November 2009.
85 MingKang Liu (28 Jun 2009), 'Basic Rules Helped China sidestep Bank Crisis', Financial Times.
86 The information about CITIC group was obtained from its website: www.citic.com/wps/portal/encitic, last accessed: 20 September 2009. The CITIC Group, formerly China International Trust and Investment Corporation, using its own words, is a window on China's opening to the outside world. CITIC group now is a large transnational conglomerate which owns 44 subsidiaries (banks) including those in Hong Kong, the United States, Canada, Australia, and New Zealand.
87 CITIC, www.citic.com/wps/portal/encitic/gyzx/jtjj?lctn=1&flag=11, last accessed: 17 September 2012.
88 The information about Ping An was obtained from the website: www.pingan.com/homepage/index.jsp, last accessed: 20 April 2013. Ping An is the first integrated financial services conglomerate in China that blends its core insurance operations into securities brokerage, trust and investment, commercial banking, asset management and corporate pension business. The Group was established in 1988 and headquartered in Shenzhen, Guangdong Province, China.
89 SDB, www.sdb.com.cn/website/page/66696c6573/77636d73/534442/7072696d6172 79/7a685f434e/534442496e666f/e6b7b1e58f91e5b195e5bfabe8aeaf/323030393036 3239e882a1e4b89ce5a4a7e4bc9a2e68746d, last accessed: 17 September 2009.
90 Haier Group, www.haier.cn/, last accessed: 20 September 2009. Haier is the world's 4th largest white goods manufacturer and one of China's Top 100 IT Companies. 'Sincere forever' is Haier Group's business slogan.
91 The information was obtained from the website www.hongta.com/model_ht/index.jsp, last accessed: 17 September 2009. The Hongta Group was established in 1956

as a Tobacco Re-curing Factory. Currently, it is the largest modern multinational tobacco enterprise group in China. Besides the traditional tobacco industry, Hongta Group has established foot in energy and transportation, banking, insurance, real estate, medicine and the light chemical industry.

92 www.hongtazq.com/htmlpage.aspx?serial=141000&html=gsjs&height=900, last accessed: 17 September 2009.

93 The information was obtained from the website of BOCI, www.bocichina.com/boci/bocienglish/aboutBOCI/gk_in1.html, last accessed: 20 September 2012. With the approval of the CSRC, BOCI was established on 28 February 2002 with a registered capital of RMB1.5 billion.

94 BOC International (China) Ltd, www.bocichina.com/boci/aboutBOCI/stockholder-Intro.jsp?thirdMenu=qtcd_aboutBOCI_BOCIsurvey_gdjs, last accessed: 20 September 2012.

95 The information was obtained from the State Development & Investment Corporation, www.sdic.com.cn/en/about/A0201index_1.htm, last accessed: 20 September 2012. By the end of 2012, the SDIC had total assets of RMB311.3 billion.

96 The information was obtained from the website of BOCI, www.bocichina.com/boci/bocienglish/aboutBOCI/gk_in4.html, last accessed: 20 September 2009.

97 State Council (29 April 2009), Issues on Opinions of the State Council on Promoting the Development of Shanghai's Modern Service Industry and Advanced Manufacturing Industry, and Promoting the Construction of Shanghai International Financial Centre and International Shipping Centre.

98 Securities Law, Article 131.

99 Ibid., Article 152.

100 Promulgation date: 23 April 2008, effective date: 1 June 2008.

101 Promulgation date: 30 November 2006, effective date: 1 December 2006, revised date: 19 October 2012, Article 49.

102 SZSE, www.szse.cn/main/disclosure/bulliten/npdldsgs/2008123139739059.shtml, last accessed: 20 September 2009.

103 SZSE, www.szse.cn/main/disclosure/bulliten/npdldsgs/, last accessed: 20 May 2013. CVs of the candidates can be viewed on website by clicking 'Browse'. Opinions about the candidates can be submitted on the website by clicking 'Submit'.

104 Securities Law, Article 136.

105 Ibid., Article 137.

106 Ibid., Article 139.

107 Promulgation date: 15 December 2003, effective date: 15 December 2003, Article 16.

108 Promulgation date: 23 April 2008, effective date: 1 June 2008, Article 46 (4).

109 Securities Law, Article 220.

110 MingKang Liu (28 June 2009), 'Basic Rules Helped China sidestep Bank Crisis', *Financial Times*.

111 Issued date: 29 December 2010, effective date: 1 January 2011.

112 MOF (April 2009), www.mof.gov.cn/jinrongsi/zhengwuxinxi/gongzuodong-tai/200904/t20090410_131395.html, last accessed: 15 November 2009.

113 Company Law, Article 147. It states that anyone who is in any of the following circumstances shall not assume the post of a director, supervisor or senior manager of a company: being without civil capacity or with only limited civil capacity; having been sentenced to any criminal penalty due to an offence of corruption, bribery, encroachment of property, misappropriation of property or disrupting the economic order of the socialist market and five years have not elapsed since the completion date of the execution of the penalty; or he has ever been deprived of his political rights due to any crime and three years have not elapsed since the completion date of the execution of the penalty; he was a former director, factory director or manager of a company or enterprise which was bankrupt and liquidated, whereby he was

personally liable for the bankruptcy of such company or enterprise, and three years have not elapsed since the date of completion of the bankruptcy and liquidation of the company or enterprise; he was the legal representative of a company or enterprise, but the business license of this company or enterprise was revoked and this company or enterprise was ordered to close due to a violation of the law, whereby he is personally liable for the revocation, and three years have not elapsed since the date of the revocation of the business license thereof; he has a relatively large amount of debt which is due, but has not been paid.

114 Securities Law, Article 131 stated that: a person shall not hold the qualification of director, supervisor or senior manager: where a person in charge of a stock exchange or securities registration and clearing institution or a director, supervisor or senior manager of a securities company has been removed from his post for his irregularity or disciplinary breach and five years have not elapsed as of the day when he is removed from his post; and (2) where a professional of a law firm, accounting firm or investment consulting organization, financial advising organization, credit rating institution, asset appraisal institution or asset verification institution has been disqualified for his irregularity or disciplinary breach and five years have not elapsed as of the day when he is removed from his post.

115 Company Directors Disqualification Act 1986, made: 25 July 1986, came into force: 29 December 1986.

116 Ibid., Section 1.

117 Ibid., Section 2. The section states that the court may disqualify a person if he is convicted of an indictable offence (whether on indictment or summarily) in connection with the promotion, formation, management or liquidation of a company, or with the receivership or management of a company's property.

118 Ibid., Section 3. The section states that the court may disqualify a person if he has been persistently in default in relation to provisions of the companies legislation requiring any return, account or other document to be filed with, delivered or sent, or notice of any matter to be given, to the registrar of companies.

119 Ibid., Section 4. The section states that the court may disqualify a person if, in the course of the winding up of a company, he is liable for fraudulent trading or has been guilty while an officer or liquidator of the company or receiver or manager of its property, of any fraud in relation to the company or of any breach of his duty as such officer, liquidator, receiver or manager.

120 Ibid., Section 5. The section states that the court may disqualify a person if he is convicted of a summary offence prescribed under the Act.

121 Ibid., Section 6. The section states that the court may disqualify a person if he is or has been a director of a company which has at any time become insolvent and that his conduct as a director of that company makes him unfit to be concerned in the management of a company.

122 Re. Richborough Furniture Ltd. [1996] 1 BCLC 507.

123 Company Directors Disqualification Act 1986, Section 10, 11, 12. Wrongful trading occurs when the directors of a company have continued to trade a company past the point when they knew, or ought to have concluded that there was no reasonable prospect of avoiding insolvent liquidation; and they did not take every step with a view to minimizing the potential loss to the company's creditors. See Insolvency Act 1986, Section 214, date of Royal Assent: 25 July 1986. It is different to fraudulent trading, since it does not require any 'intent to defraud'. If any business of a company is carried on with intent to defraud creditors of the company or creditors of any other person, or for any fraudulent purpose, every person who is knowingly a party to the carrying on of the business in that manner commits an offence of fraudulent trading. See Insolvency Act 1986, Section 213 and also Companies Act 2006, date of Royal Assent: 8 November 2006, came into force: 1 October 2009, Section 993.

124 Ibid., Section 2.
125 Ibid., Section 13.
126 Companies Ordinance, promulgation date: 1 July 1933, Part IVA, Disqualification of Directors.
127 Securities & Futures Commission v Cheung, Yeung, Li, Chan and Styland Holdings (HCMP 1702 of 2008).
128 Cliffed Chance (20 March 2012), 'Record-breaking Compensation and Disqualification orders made against Listed Company Directors in Hong Kong by the Court of First Instance under section 214 of the Securities and Futures Ordinance'.
129 Ibid.
130 Efective date: 1 December 2006, revised date: 19 October 2012, Article 7. It states that anyone who is under any of the following circumstances shall not take the position of director, supervisor, senior manager or person in charge of a branch of a securities company: the circumstances as prescribed in paragraph 2 of Article 131, Article 132 and Article 133 of the Securities Law; it is less than three years after the expiration of the administrative punishment imposed on such person by the financial regulatory authority for severe violation of any law or regulation; it is less than three years from the day when the person's professional qualification is revoked by the CSRC; it is less than two years from the day when such person is identified as unfit for a position by the CSRC; or other circumstances as determined by the CSRC.
131 Guojun Zhang (2006), 'Establishing and Improving the Information Disclosure of Securities Companies (Zhengquan Gongsi Xinxi Pilu Zhidu de Jianli yu Wanshan)', *Financial Accounting*, 4, p. 52.

4   Regulating financial intermediaries

Introduction

Since its establishment, the Chinese securities market has made many improvements; in particular, after the new Securities Law came into force, the regulatory
regime reached a more effective level. But it should be admitted that the securities regulation in China is still in need of improvement.

In respect of securities professionals, on one hand, they constitute an essential
part of the market, and facilitate the establishment of a healthy and active securities market. On the other hand, they may assist illegal securities transitions.
Some of the existing scandals have illustrated these issues. It should be noted
that in these scandals, it was common that the professionals took advantage of
information, which was obtained directly from their employment. The main aim
of this chapter is to analyse the internal and external relationship between
information disclosure and securities professionals in order to establish an
effective regulatory regime.

In this chapter, historical and current regulatory approaches will be examined.
The Securities Law, Chapter VIII (Securities Trading Service Institutions) established the fundamental legal requirements for securities professionals. It focuses
on the investment consulting institutions, financial advising institutions, credit
rating institutions, asset appraisal institutions, accounting firms and their staff.[1]
Furthermore, other legislation and regulatory rules will be examined, for
example, the Lawyer's Law. Moreover, the function of the Credit Rating Agencies (hereafter the CRAs) and securities lawyers will be analysed in detail. As
typical examples of the above professionals, the regulatory approaches of the
CRAs and securities lawyers are important issues to be examined.

Regulating the credit rating agencies

The financial crisis has put the CRAs in the front line. It has been questioned
whether these agencies have performed their function in an open and fair
manner. According to the survey conducted by Allen & Overy Global Survey,
over three-quarters (76 per cent) of respondents to the global survey agreed that
greater regulation of rating agencies is necessary, in particular, this was felt most

strongly by respondents in Asia (86 per cent), followed by the USA (84 per cent), Continental Europe (79 per cent) and the UK (78 per cent).[2] In the Declaration of the G20 Summit on Financial Markets and the World Economy, it also stated that the regulators will exercise strong oversight over credit rating agencies, consistent with the agreed and strengthened international code of conduct.[3] IOSCO and the European Commission have made amendments on the regulation of CRAs respectively.

However, compared with other mature markets, the history of CRAs in China is relatively short. Consequently, the laws and regulations are new. It may be questioned whether this regime is effective enough to supervise and regulate the activities of CRAs in China. A further question could be raised over whether the CRAs in Mainland China could be part of the regulatory system or quasi-regulatory mechanism. This chapter will concentrate on the study of law and regulation. Starting with a brief introduction to the function of CRAs, it will further examine the history of CRAs in China. Moreover, other models will be analysed in order to illustrate the latest situation in more detail.

To supervise the information disclosure regime, the quasi-regulatory mechanism cannot be ignored as a special force. In the mature capital markets, these financial institutions together with the public authorities perform the regulatory and supervisory functions. Basically, the rating agencies should enable all parties in the financial markets to have access to accurate, comprehensible and concise information on the credit risk of the financial instruments in which they are dealing. 'Information is goods, and rating agencies are the providers of the goods.'[4] However, this role has now been greatly expanded from that of mere information providers.

According to Moody, one of the biggest CRAs in the world, in their opinion, the main and proper role of credit rating is to help to enhance transparency and efficiency in debt capital markets by reducing information asymmetry between borrowers and lenders. They believe that this benefits the market by increasing investor confidence and allowing borrowers to have broader access to funds.[5] From this point of view, the CRAs can be seen as part of the financial regulators. In fact, this argument was generally accepted in the developed capital market before the recent financial crisis. The major US debt rating agencies were called the 'quasi-regulatory mechanisms'.[6] If performing duly, the CRAs can promote the integrity and stability of the financial market, by 'piecing the fog of asymmetric information that surrounds lending relationships' and 'helping borrowers emerge from that same fog'.[7] On the other hand, however, it is globally accepted that the CRAs bear a certain responsibility for the recent financial crisis. An enhanced regulatory regime has been enforced in major jurisdictions.

Processing information is the core content of the work of the credit rating agencies. Most of the rating procedures have involved information on: (a) quantitative data provided by the issuer about its financial position; (b) quantitative data gathered by the agency about the industry, competitors and economy; (c) legal advice relating to specific issues; (d) qualitative data provided by the issuer on policy, management, business outlook, accounting practices; and

(e) qualitative data collected by the agency on competitive positions, quality of management, long-term industry prospects and economic environment.[8] After comparing the methodologies of different credit rating agencies, it is not difficult to find that there are some common features.[9] Generally, the analytical framework is divided into both qualitative and quantitative aspects. The rating agencies will examine the companies from a macroeconomic aspect, industry development prospects, legal environment, public policies, financial risks and corporation operating risks. Based on the analysis, rating agencies will issue the rating report. Moreover, the rating company will monitor the rated entities on a continuous basis and make timely reviews. Finally, it will inform the market and the rated entities about the rating results.

Taking the Xinhua Finance and Shanghai Far East Credit Ratings Co., Ltd (hereafter Xinhua Far East China Ratings) as an example, their rating analysis focuses on assessing whether the company can generate adequate future cash flow, particularly on a recurrent basis and during stress scenarios, to meet the financial commitments of its essential funding needs, and the certainty and stability of a company to generate a positive cash flow. The analytical framework takes into account all the qualitative and quantitative information including the following areas: economy, industry trends and developments, regulations and government policies, management, operating risk, financial risk, availability of contingency liquidity sources, organization structure, and support from parent company, major shareholders and government. Moreover, as for the sources of information, the Xinhua Far East China Ratings will consider: the adequacy of public information disclosures by the rated companies (relative to the general disclosure requirements in the capital market which the companies operate); the audited financial statement of the rated entity and its notes; the disclosures of major transactions and events of the rated entity (the disclosure fund raising activities, and change of operating business; the detailed description of corporate guarantees and litigations; the disclosures of default on debt particularly the reasons for inability to make due payments); and disclosures of other significant events.[10]

In general, the agency will collect the information to assess the credit risks of the corporations. Second, it will analyse all the relevant factors and risks. Third, the rating agency will monitor the rated entities on a continuous basis and give rating reviews with respect to the fundamental changes in company or business environments. Finally, it will inform the market and the rated entities on the rating rationale and results. It can be seen from this procedure, that information is one of the core issues.

In fact, CRAs are consumers of information, and at the same time, providers of information. To provide a convenient approach for investors to judge credit quality, the CRAs gather and analyse the financial, industry, market and economic information, synthesize the information, and publish assessments of the creditworthiness of securities and issuers. Thus, credit rating is a market product and rating methods shall be created according to the needs of market practices. Moreover, the rating methodologies of individual rating companies shall cover, consider and analyse the essential elements listed earlier in the chapter. Ideally, the rating method shall be consistent with the primary aim of credit rating. It is true that the financial market is continuing to evolve, so the rating principles and methods should be adjusted and further improved, according to the latest changes in the market.

The ratings are based on the information obtained directly from issuers, underwriters, and other relevant sources that the CRAs believe to be accurate and reliable. Then the CRAs process such information. Before recent financial crisis, the CRAs generally declared that they do not audit or verify the truth or accuracy of such information, and have no obligation to do so, or to perform investigative diligence into the completeness or accuracy of the information. Therefore, all the ratings rely on information supplied by the clients. However, the current financial crisis and previous scandals led people to question the function of CRAs. Beside the rating method itself, other issues need to be considered, for instance, the rating bias, conflict of interests and liabilities of CRAs. More details will be examined in the later part of this chapter. A clear set of regulations, including a code of conduct and best practices need to be developed and enhanced for the CRAs.

The regulatory framework

While the CRAs in the mature market are called 'embedded knowledge networks (EKNs)',[11] the Chinese CRAs seem more likely to develop a different approach. EKNs, are private institutions that possess a specific form of social authority because of their publicly acknowledged track records for solving problems, often acting as disinterested experts in assessing high value transactions and in validating institutional norms and practice.[12] However, rating systems have a relatively short history in Mainland China and are not yet well developed. In fact, the procedures can be divided into the following stages:

Emerging stage

The Interim Regulation on Administration of Corporate Bonds opened a new stage for the Chinese bond market.[13] Although it had not been clearly stated that credit rating was compulsory for the bond issue, there were some rating agencies emerging. Jilin Province Credit Rating Company (Zixin Pinggu Gongsi) was the first established CRA in China. It should be noted that, at that time, most of these credit rating agencies were affiliated with banks.

In 1993, the Regulations on Administration of Corporate Bonds has clearly pointed out that when the corporate entity plans to issue bonds, they may apply for a credit rating from the authorized rating agencies.[14] From this time, credit rating obtained a legal status. In the same year, one of the most important documents with regard to the socialist market economy was published. In the Decision of the Central Committee of CPC on Several Issues Concerning the Establishing the Socialist Market Economy Structure, it stated that: it was important to establish a credit rating system in order to promote the development of a bond market.[15]

After this period, several other legal documents were issued by different authorities. Among them, the Listing Rules of the Corporate Bond Shanghai Stock Exchange (SSE) and Shenzhen Stock Exchange (SZSE) should be noted: for the first time, the credit rating of a company was seen as a compulsory procedure for bond issuing.[16] The Listing Rules of the two Stock Exchanges required respectively that to apply for the listing, the bond issuer must obtain no lower than an A rating grade by the authorized rating agencies.

Early regulatory regime

As stated earlier, CRAs in China have primarily gained recognition via different legal documents. In 1988, the first rating agency independent of a bank, Shanghai Fareast Credit Rating Company (Shanghai Yuandong Zixin Pinggu Gongsi), was established. Following this, several other independent agencies emerged.

Similar to other new emerging financial institutions in China, there were some readjustments procedures required of the CRAs. With the development of the Chinese bond market, the numbers of CRAs increased. However, problems such as massive defaults occurred, the issuers across the country refused or were unable to pay creditors the interest or principal as bonds became due; for instance, in Liaoning and Jilin Provinces, over half the bond obligations went into default.[17] In 1989, in order to avoid continuing mistakes in ratings, with the consciousness of the shortages of this model, the People's Bank of China (hereafter PBOC) issued a notice to stop the business of credit rating agencies that were established by the PBOC and its branches.[18] Moreover, in order to improve the regulatory regime, in 1997, the PBOC issued another notice to set up the regulated licence regime. PBOC authorized nine rating agencies to conduct credit rating business; for instance, Zhongguo Chengxin Securities Rating Co., Ltd (Zhongguo Chengxin Zhengquan Pinggu Youxian Gongsi) and Shanghai Far East Credit Rating Company (Shanghai Yuandong Zixin Pinggu Gongsi).[19] It stated that the ratings from other institutions will not be recognized by the PBOC; when corporations plan to issue bonds, they must obtain the credit rating from these authorized rating agencies.

In 1999, the enforcement of the Securities Law moved the regulation of Chinese CRAs to a new stage.[20] In Chapter 8, Securities Trading Service Organizations stated that professional securities investment consulting organizations and credit rating institutions may be established, where they are needed for securities investment and trading business. It went further in setting out the conditions for the employment of staff of credit rating institutions: they shall be people who have professional knowledge of securities, and have engaged in the securities business for not less than two years.[21]

It should be noted that this law did significantly improve the regulatory regime, although it did not make further specific rules. However, it left room for other detailed regulation in the future. For instance, it stated that the conditions for establishment of rating institutions, the examination and approval procedures and the business rules shall be prescribed by the securities regulatory authority under the State Council.[22] Moreover, in terms of the qualifications of professionals that engage in the securities business, it pointed out that the criteria and administration measures shall be formulated by the securities regulatory authority under the State Council.[23] Finally, it pointed out that the service fees should be charged in accordance with the rates or measures prescribed by the relevant administrative department under the State Council.[24]

One of the most significant improvements in the law, with regard to the information disclosure regime, is that it provided that professional institutions and individuals which produce documents, such as audit reports, asset appraisal reports and legal opinions for the issuance or listing of securities or for securities trading activities shall do so in accordance with the working procedures prescribed in the rules of their profession; these professionals shall check and verify the authenticity, accuracy and entirety of the contents of the reports; otherwise, they shall bear joint liabilities for the parts in the reports for which they are responsible.[25]

This document indicated that the financial regulators in China have realized the function of CRAs in the capital market, especially, in the aspect of information disclosure. Beside generic direction, they also established the groundwork for a future regulatory framework.

Improved regulatory stage

After the first Securities Law came into force; the regulatory regime reached a new level in China. With the development of the Chinese bond market, the business scope of CRAs was broader than before. Various administrative measures or rules confirmed that credit rating as a compulsory procedure for a bond issue. At this time, credit rating agencies had no rules or codes of conduct at a national level that were enforceable. Consequently, the quality and reliability of a rating report became a major issue. The impact of credit rating was also quite limited. The insufficiency of the information supplied had become a bottleneck for the future development of the CRAs. The main questions remaining to be solved were: What are the standards for obtaining the business license and how to conduct the rating business?

In 2003, one important step in the evolution of the credit rating industry was set up: professional employees of CRAs must obtain a qualification from the Securities Association of China (hereafter the SAC).[26] Although the SAC is a self-regulatory body, it should be admitted that it was the first time that there were professional entry requirements for practitioners in the credit rating industry.

Furthermore, the Interim Measures for the Administration of Bonds of Securities Companies stated that: the issuer shall retain credit rating organizations to make credit ratings for the current bonds and make arrangements for tracking the rating; moreover, the rating organizations shall be responsible for the objectiveness, impartiality and punctuality of the rating results.[27]

The contents and the format of the credit rating report has been set down in the corollary regulations: Rules for Credit Rating Agencies on Issuing Rating Report of Bond of Securities Companies (hereafter the Rules).[28] This document has been divided into the following parts: General Requirements, Content and Format of Rating Report, Report of Tracking Rating. Although this document is only concerned with the bonds of securities companies; nonetheless, it has a great impact on subsequent laws and regulations. For instance, it states that the rating report shall be illustrated in a way that is easy to understand.[29] More importantly, the procedures of rating have been established. The rating agencies shall undertake an investigation before issuing the rating report and maintain the authenticity, accuracy and entirety of the contents of the reports.[30] The rating agencies shall establish complete and standardized internal rating criteria and procedures, and the rating report shall be issued according to these criteria and procedures.[31] The rating agencies shall have effective internal control.[32] Moreover, the rating agencies shall establish complete archives for rating entities, including: letter of proxy, original materials provided by the issuer, assessment report, rating report, conclusive views of the rating committee, tracking rating reports.[33] Finally, the content and format of rating report are to be set out with a more detailed approach. The report shall be composed of five different parts; namely, General Information, Statement of Relevant Matters, Rating Report, Tracking Rating Report and Supplementary Provisions.[34]

Importantly, the Statement of Independence can be seen as a significant improvement.[35] The statement shall declare that: besides the client relationship based on this particular rating, the CRA and its rating staffs have no connection that will prejudice the independence, objectiveness and fairness of the rating; if there is any connection, it shall be declared.[36] Independence is crucially important for the CRAs. It may directly impose impacts on the rating result. To examine this issue, it must be analysed from two different layers in China. First of all, the credit rating industry itself shall be independent. As can be seen from earlier analysis in this chapter, the Chinese CRAs were initially affiliated to the banks. For corporate financing, credit rating can help to resolve the problem of information asymmetry. As for direct financing proposed by the banks, the banks could obtain the relevant corporate situation and creditworthiness through the rating report. However, when the CRAs were affiliated with banks, the banks were the lenders and connected with the rating agencies at the same time. Therefore, it resulted in a delicate situation. The function of the CRAs should be as the third party alongside the bond issuers and investors, or the lenders and borrowers.

The Rules also states that the rating report must include the following contents: brief analysis of issuer, for instance, the ownership structure, business scope and unique characteristics; brief analysis of the bond: main articles and measures for debt repayment; brief analysis of the issuer's industry: sufficiently, accurately and detailed disclose the risks; the analysis of the risks in the respect of the issuer; the description and analysis of directors, supervisors, managers and other senior members and whether they have any illicit and criminal record in last three years; the analysis of the financial situation: debt structure, quality of assets, earning situation, cash flow, and related transactions; the analysis of the financing project: possible influences of the raised funds on the financial situation, debt structure and the project itself; the analysis of the security of the debt repayment; the analysis of the issuer's debt repayment abilities, believable degree and anti-risk abilities; establishing the 'special risk reminding' when it is necessary, in order to state the causation and potential losses of the risks.[37] Furthermore, it also requires that the rating report shall clearly state the tracking status of such rating. The tracking report shall focus on the potential influences on the rating result may caused by the internal and external changes of the financial and business situation of the issuer.[38]

For the first time this legal document established a comprehensive regulatory framework for credit rating. The 'independence' requirement was given an important position. It should be noted that the contents and format of a report has been illustrated in depth. Finally the procedures for tracking rating were clearly set down. From this perspective, it can be concluded that the authenticity, accuracy and integrity of credit rating drew more attention from the regulatory bodies. However, the issue of industrial entrance permission still remains unresolved, and the supervisory and regulatory bodies are still to be confirmed.

The year 2003 was very important for the credit rating industry in China. The Decision of the Central Committee of the Communist Party of China on Some Issues concerning the Improvement of the Socialist Market Economy went further than stated, establishing and improving the social credit system and opening the credit services market gradually.[39] This document imposed a significant impact on the Chinese capital market; consequently it had a significant meaning for the validity of a credit rating.

After this ruling, the credit rating agencies developed at a rapid speed. In 2005, Mr Xiaochuan Zhou pointed out a list of serious mistakes committed initially during the late 1980s and mid-1990s in the Chinese Bond Market. Among these mistakes, 'the absence of a credit rating system made it impossible for investors to obtain a clear idea of risks.'[40] He went further stating that:

> we are trying hard to foster the domestic rating agencies necessary for bond market development, although these rating services may grow only slowly over time. The basic policy is to allow international rating agencies to set up joint ventures to provide high quality services.[41]

In fact, the joint venture approach is a safe method for China's emerging capital market, detailed analysis can be found in the later part of this chapter.

Current regulatory regime

The Chinese bond market has developed rapidly in the last few years. From Figure 4.1, it can be seen that, currently, China's bond market comprises of two main markets: the interbank bond market (OTC market) and the exchange

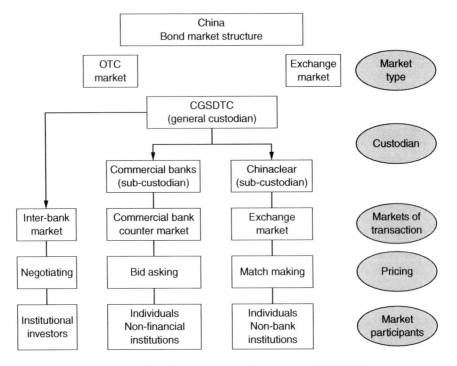

Figure 4.1 The structure of the Chinese bond market (source: CGSDTC[42]).

market. The structure of the bonds has been improved. It can be seen from Figure 4.2, in 2008, the Central Bank paper, Treasury bonds and Policy Bank bonds remained the major products on the primary bond market, which consti-tuted of 88 per cent of the gross amount of bonds issued, 5.42 percentage points lower than the proportion of 93.42 per cent in 2007. Debentures (credit bonds), taking up a small share of the gross volume of issued bonds, enjoyed big increase. The issuance of corporate bonds, commercial paper (CP), and medium term note (MTN) retained a rapid expansion, with RMB236.69 billion of corpo-rate bonds, up by 37.2 per cent over the year of 2007, and RMB597.05 billion of CP and MTN, up by 70.4 per cent.[43]

As for the value of transactions, there was a 60 per cent growth in transaction settlements on the interbank market. In detail, more than 300,000 transaction set-tlements were completed on the interbank bond market in the year 2008, with an aggregate face value exceeding RMB100 trillion. To be more specific, 306,000 settlements were completed throughout the year, a rise of 62.2 per cent over the previous year. Furthermore, on the stock exchange market, there was a 46 per cent growth of transaction volume. A total of 3.382 million bond transactions were completed at the stock exchange market in 2008, with the volume amount-ing to RMB2.54 trillion or 46 per cent higher than that of the previous year. The volume for collateral repo-transactions at the stock exchanges reached RMB2.16

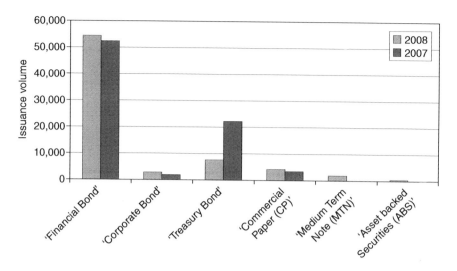

Figure 4.2 The yearly issuance volume of major bonds in 2008 and 2007 (source: Annual Review of China's Bond Market (2008)[44]).

trillion, or 85 per cent of the general volume of bonds transacted on the stock exchange market.[45]

Resulting from the occurrence of the financial crisis and the Euro debt crisis, the global economy has been slowdown. The Chinese economy though, maintained growth with a modest rate. The bond market also gained growth in terms of transaction settlements (see Table 4.1). Without doubt, together with the future improvement of the Chinese financial system, the bond market will be further developed. Therefore, to establish a modern credit rating is crucially important.

Table 4.1 The growth of transaction settlements (2002–2011)

Year	The number of settlements	Year on year growth of the number of settlements (%)	The amount of settlements (trillion RMB)	Year on year growth of the amount of settlements (%)
2002	76,396	103.66	10.63	159.13
2003	97,514	27.64	15.14	42.37
2004	93,034	–4.59	12.79	–15.51
2005	110,604	18.89	22.99	79.75
2006	161,388	45.92	38.39	67.00
2007	188,706	16.93	63.13	64.46
2008	306,638	62.50	101.33	60.5
2009	340,430	11.05	122.08	20.49
2010	518,189	52.22	162.81	33.38
2011	687,749	32.72	180.01	10.56

Source: Annual Review of China's Bond Market (2011).[46]

One of the important steps of the regulatory reform is the enforcement of the Interim Measures for the Administration of the Credit Rating Business Regarding the Securities Market (hereafter Measures).[47] It is a more efficient and complete document on the aspect of regulating the credit rating industry and largely settled the problem of deficiencies of system supply for CRAs.

Under this regulation, the China Securities Regulatory Commission (CSRC) became the chief regulator for CRAs with regard to securities rating. Without the securities rating business licencing of the CSRC, no entity or individual may engage in the securities rating business.[48] This was a landmark step towards a unified set of criteria designed to promote both the efficiency and transparency of China's securities market and bring it into line with international standards. This document clearly stated that the credit rating activities regarding futures business shall refer to these Measures.[49] It indicated that the Measures became the standard for the CRAs in the Chinese securities market.

According to Article 2, the term 'credit rating business regarding the securities market' refers to the credit rating services implemented for the following: the bonds, asset backed securities and other fixed income or debt structured finance securities as issued upon approval of the CSRC; the bonds, asset backed securities and other fixed income or debt structured finance securities listed for trading on a stock exchange, except for national debts; the securities issuers, listed companies, non-listed public companies, securities companies and securities investment fund management companies prescribed in Items 1 and 2.

A credit rating agency that applies for the securities rating business licensing shall meet the following conditions: it has the Chinese legal person qualification, and both its paid in capital and its net assets are no less than RMB20 million; it has at least three senior managers meeting the provisions in these Measures and at least 20 rating professionals having the securities business qualification,[50] with at least ten rating professionals having credit rating experience of three years or more, and at least three rating professionals having the qualification of certified public accountants of China; it has a sound and well operated internal control mechanism and management system; it has complete business rules, including the division and definitions of credit ratings, rating criteria, rating procedures, rating committee system, rating result publication system, tracking rating system, information confidentiality system, and archival management system suitable for a securities rating business; it has never been subjected to criminal punishment for the last five years and never been subjected to administrative punishment due to illegal business operation for the last three years, and has not in any circumstance been investigated due to suspicious illegal operation or crime; it has no bad credit record at the administrative departments for taxation, industry and commerce and finance, etc., self-disciplinary organizations or commercial banks.[51]

Under this regime, it must be noted that it is the first time that a comprehensive licensing system has been established. The Measures went further to set down the criteria for senior managers to obtain the securities business qualification: they must be familiar with professional and legal knowledge regarding the credit rating business, to have the business management ability and the organizational and coordination ability required for performing duties, have passed the senior manager qualification examination of the securities rating business, not fall within any circumstance prescribed by the Company Law or the Securities Law under which one shall not hold a post, not have been banned by the financial regulator from entering the market (unless the ban has expired, in which case this must be disclosed), have not been given an administrative penalty due to illegal operation for the last three years, not be under current investigation due to suspicion of an illegal operation or crime; be honest and sincere, of good conduct, and have no bad credit record at the administrative departments for taxation, industry and commerce or finance, etc., self-disciplinary organizations or commercial banks, etc. for the last three years.[52]

The Measures have further listed the business rules in detail; in particular, the circumstance of conflict of interest. Any securities rating agency which has any of the following interests with an institution or securities issuer being rated shall not accept the entrustment of the assignment for carrying out the securities rating: both the securities rating agency and the institution or securities issuer being rated are controlled by the same actual controller; the same shareholder simultaneously holds 5 per cent or more of the shares of the securities rating agency and the institution or securities issuer being rated; the institution or securities issuer being rated and its actual controller directly or indirectly hold 5 per cent or more of the shares of the credit rating agency; the securities rating agency and its actual controller directly or indirectly hold 5 per cent or more of the shares of the securities issuer or the institution being rated; the securities rating agency or its actual controller has bought or sold the securities being rated within six months before carrying out the securities rating business.[53]

Importantly, the avoidance system has been reaffirmed by the Measures: in case a rating committee member or rating professional in a securities rating agency is under any of the following circumstances when carrying out the securities rating business, he shall withdraw: he himself or any of his lineal relatives holds 5 per cent or more of the shares of the institution or the securities issuer being rated, or is the actual controller of the institution or the securities issuer being rated;[54] he himself or any of his lineal relatives is the director, supervisor or senior manager of the institution or the securities issuer being rated; he himself or any of his lineal relatives is the person in charge or project signer of the accounting firm, law firm, financial consultancy or other securities service agency as hired by institution or the securities issuer being rated; he himself or any of his lineal relatives holds RMB500,000 or more of the securities being rated or the securities issued by the institution being rated; or accumulatively concludes transactions of RMB500,000 or more with the institution or securities issuer being rated.[55]

The Measures primarily focus on the securities rating. As for the interbank bond market, the PBOC issued the Notice on Strengthening the Administration of Credit Rating Practices in the Interbank Bond Market.[56] The notice required the credit rating agencies to carry out onsite interviews with the top management personnel of the issuers, and further refined the regulations on the time required for carrying out such credit rating practices, in order to improve the administration of the practices of the credit rating agencies.

From the above analysis, it can be seen that the information supply system for the CRAs is now more complete. These regulatory measures cover all the basic issues of credit rating regarding the securities market in more detail: the definition of securities rating business, business licensing, senior management and conflict of interests. Furthermore, important issues, for instance the avoidance system and rating report tracking system have been further enhanced. Eventually, the core business of the CRAs, will be to process and analyse previous information, and disseminate new information. Subsequently, the process procedures must be fair and accurate. Although this industry is based on market practices, without a comprehensive legal environment, the CRAs may (driven by the high profits) move away from the correct path. In particular, it is important and wise to establish a legal system before the emergence of any serious scandals.

The questions remaining

From the above analysis, it can be seen that the regulatory and supervisory regime has been significantly improved. However, it must be noted that some questions still remain.

It has been argued that the CRAs should perform as part of the financial regulatory system. In general, CRAs are private institutions that possess a specific form of social authority because of their publicly acknowledged track records for solving problems.[57] Since the establishment of the first credit rating companies owned by the banks, there have not been any major financial scandals. However, one of the reasons might be that compared with any other jurisdictions, the CRAs in mainland China have a short history.

In a general sense, there are some shortfalls in the rating system that may potentially result in negative impacts. The credit culture in China has not been well developed. There is also low public reliance on the credit rating system. The regulatory framework for a credit rating business is not complete. Risk control in the bond market still largely relies on administrative procedures. Moreover, the quality and integrity of rating procedures and reports are relatively low. Finally lack of clarity in bond structures has resulted in confusion in the rating system. In the Chinese bond market, there are so called enterprise bonds (Qiye Zhaiquan), corporate bonds (Gongsi Zhaiquan) and financial bonds of bank debenture (Jinrong Zhaiquan).[58]

The development of CRAs needs contributions from both external and internal aspects. From the external aspect, a transparent system should be sufficient, while for the internal aspect, the capital market should be transparent and therefore healthy. However currently, these two conditions will not be easy to fulfil in China. With only a short history, the environment for credit rating is incomplete: there are still some doubts about the probity of the rating industry. Moreover, the earlier performance of CRAs was not good enough, which deepened the doubts. The financial crisis placed more ongoing criticism on the probity of the financial industry. Therefore, it will be a long road for the Chinese CRAs.

The source of credit information is a major concern. It has been suggested that credit rating in Mainland China is 'mere guesswork'.[59] It has been argued that some information is not publicly available and local credit investigation services tend to be superficial; there is a wide variation in the quality, availability and delivery of credit information from province to province; and company records are only available in Chinese, leaving lots of room for different interpretations.[60] The only official language in China is Chinese, therefore, most of the documents are written in Chinese. Hence, due to the cultural diversity, when being translated into foreign languages, it might be difficult to maintain the precise same meaning. In particular, it can be hard to find the equivalent words in different languages. Also, a number of Chinese words have multiple meanings, which results in additional complexity.

The establishment of the Credit Reference Centre (CRC) of the People's Bank of China (PBOC), established in Shanghai in 2008, can be helpful from this perspective. It is responsible for the construction and operation of the credit information system for Chinese firms and individuals. The CRC, the first national credit centre built upon the Credit Reference Department of the PBC and Shanghai Individual Credit Centre, has formally started its business operations.[61] Although it seems that the CRC is operating a monopoly, in the relatively early stages of a credit culture, this may be helpful. At least, this method can be seen as an efficient tool from the perspective of promoting information sharing.

Even in the mature markets, the information source is an issue to be carefully examined. For instance, as mentioned earlier in this chapter, the ratings are based on information obtained from issuers, underwriters, their experts and other sources that it believes to be reliable. The CRA's role is limited to gathering and analysing a variety of financial, industry, market and economic information, synthesizing that information, and publishing independent, credible assessments of the creditworthiness of securities and issuers, thereby providing a convenient way for investors to judge the credit quality of various alternative investment options.[62] It is not difficult to see that the situation has resulted in certain problems in the recent financial crisis. One step Hong Kong adopted after the crisis is to require the CRAs to disclose to what extent it has examined the quality of information used in the rating process and whether it is satisfied with the quality of information it bases its rating on.[63] Clearly, this is an ongoing discussion around the world.

A further concern is the independence issue. Looking back at the history of CRAs, it is difficult to estimate their degree of independence. Although there are significant improvements in the new regulatory regime, it will still take time to change the situation that is 'apparently separated, but actually connected'. The CRAs have to adjust their attitude: to obtain a better reputation for the market participants, not merely for the government; to rely on the market rules, but not merely on the bond issuers' appetite.

Following this, who will eventually roll up their sleeves as the regulatory bodies? One of the major problems is that there are several regulatory bodies. The National Development and Reform Commission (NDRC),[64] CSRC, China Banking Regulatory Commission (CBRC), China Insurance Regulatory Commission (CIRC) and PBOC all participate in the supervisory procedures. How to obtain cooperation is an issue. The multi-stakeholder management has possibly resulted in the deficiency of CRAs. For instance, when conducting business, the CRAs may need to fulfil different requirements from different regulatory sectors, and this might lead to time wasting. Ideally, there should be a clear structure to the cooperation between different sectors. Currently, for the interbank bond market, the regulatory body is the PBOC; for the exchange bond market the regulatory body is the CSRC. However, there are several other types of bonds upon which the CRAs undertake rating, so who will be the regulator, and who will formulate the business rules?

Last but not least, currently there is a hot topic: beware of the foreign company in charge of a Chinese credit rating business.[65] In fact, the foreign credit rating agencies have already started strategic development in Mainland China. According to Minli Yi, a professor from the Southeast University of Finance and Economics, it is the time to establish our own credit rating industry rapidly, in order to maintain the power of discourse within the Chinese financial intermediaries.[66] Yi's words were echoed by a number of other scholars. These arguments reflect one important issue, what kind of rating agencies' ratings should be followed? In general, the answer is the one most highly recognized by the markets. More commonly, throughout the rest of the world, preference had been given to Moody's, S&P and Fitch. However, this may not be the case today. The financial crisis and the ongoing debate on the value of sovereign ratings have illustrated this situation.

Notably, under the current regulatory regime, foreign credit rating agencies cannot rate locally issued bonds independently, they have to have a partnership or joint venture with one of the local agencies. For instance, the Moody's Corporation acquired 49 per cent of China Cheng Xin International Credit Rating Co. Ltd (hereafter the CCXI) in 2006.[67] These rules can be seen to have derived from consideration given to the character of the Chinese financial markets. As Xiaosan Li, the Executive Vice President of China Executive Leadership Academy, Jinggangshan (CELAJ) mentioned: the credit rating shall not be a mere mathematic model; it must be based on a full understanding of the national conditions, values outlook and local corporate culture.[68] This point of view reflects certain truth, the Chinese securities market was established with a strong Chinese outlook. China's credit rating and its market size, structure and economic characteristics, market behaviour, all represent unique features of the Chinese financial system. As a consequence, the CRAs in China should adopt the most suitable model for the domestic market according to its own market needs, in order to maintain the accuracy of rating. In 2008, the PBOC, CBRC, CSRC and CIRC issued the Several Opinions on Accelerating the Development of the Service Industry with Support from the Financial Sector that stated, it is important to develop the 'native brand' of the CRAs.[69] Of course, on the other hand, China has developed the 'walking out' strategy. In future, the Chinese CRAs may become more active at an international level. The successful rating experiences in other jurisdictions are clearly helpful references for China.

It is too early to draw conclusions; however, it may not be difficult to predict that thinking globally, acting locally is one of the best approaches. For the current situation, it may be suitable to maintain the assessment rights within Chinese CRAs, with reference to the other global reference agencies. The rating results of CRAs may not merely be a financial product but also a political one. Sovereign rating particularly illustrated this argument. In 2010, the rating result issued by the Standard & Poor's made Greece the first euro zone member to have its debt downgraded to junk level.[70] In that event, the controversies around the role of CRAs have been raised as an international issue. Over generous rating and over conservative rating creates doubts in the financial market, which are tightly linked to a state's economic stability. Although there is no similar sovereign rating for China, it has been argued that some of the IPO prices of Chinese companies for overseas listing may be lower than their actual value because of the bias of foreign financial intermediates.[71] Therefore, in fact, CRAs should not judge other's creditworthiness by their own standards. Financial safety should be maintained at a state's own arm's length. Of course, the precondition is that the Chinese CRAs perform in a correct, independent and fair way, reflecting the truth.

Comparative studies with other jurisdictions

Just as for other financial sectors, the CRAs in Mainland China should learn from the current financial crisis. The supervision of CRAs has been placed in an important position recently; the IOSCO, EU, UK and US published new regulatory frameworks.

The IOSCO has published its own Code of Conduct Fundamentals for Credit Rating Agencies (CRAs).[72] It is argued that the regulation of CRAs should be improved according to the new economic situation; in particular, in the structured finance market. Also, following publication of the CRA Principles, a number of commentators, including members of CRAs, suggested that it would be useful if IOSCO were to develop a more specific and detailed code of conduct giving guidance on how the Principles could be implemented in practice.[73] Thus, In May 2008 IOSCO issued a revised Code of Conduct Fundamentals for CRAs. It set out materially enhanced requirements as follows: the quality and integrity of the rating process, the independence and the avoidance of conflicts of interest; and responsibilities to the investing public and issuers.

The EU also adopted the Proposal for a Regulation of the European Parliament and of the Council on Credit Rating Agencies.[74] The failure of the CRAs, according to the EU, can be adequately addressed by measures related to conflicts of interest, the quality of the credit ratings, and the transparency of the rating process, their internal governance, and finally an effective oversight or supervision of the activities of the CRAs.[75] The enactment of the Regulation (EC) No. 1060/2009 of the European Parliament and of the Council on Credit Rating Agencies did improve the regulatory regime from different dimensions.[76] It requires that the credit rating activities are conducted in accordance with the principles of integrity, transparency, responsibility and good governance in order to ensure that the resulting credit ratings used in the Community are independent, objective and of adequate quality.[77] It created a fundamental change in the regulatory landscape. It was aimed at creating a common approach to regulating CRAs throughout the EU, instead of the tradition of industry self-regulation. The common framework has been laid down in relation to the integrity and quality of credit ratings by the individual Member States.[78]

With the establishment of the new EU financial regulatory architecture, the Commission amended the Regulation (EC) No. 1060/2009. The European Securities and Markets Authority (ESMA) will be responsible for the registration and supervision of credit rating agencies, day-to-day supervision and taking appropriate supervisory measures if it has discovered a breach of the CRA Regulation.[79] Furthermore, in January 2013, considering the impacts of the ongoing Euro debt crisis, new rules on when and how credit rating agencies may rate state debts and private firms' financial health were approved by European Parliament, under which the agencies are allowed to issue unsolicited sovereign debt ratings only on set dates, and enable private investors to sue them for negligence.[80]

In order to supplement the Regulation (EC) No 1060/2009, the UK also promulgated the Credit Rating Agencies Regulations 2010.[81] It focuses on the most important issues concerning the CRAs, for example, independence, conflicts of interest, employees and analysts, methodologies and models, outsourcing, and the disclosure and presentation of information.

The US SEC also conducted an examination on credit rating agencies: Fitch Ratings Ltd., Moody's Investor Services Inc., and Standard & Poor's Ratings Services to evaluate whether they are adhering to their published methodologies for determining ratings and managing conflicts of interest.[82] The examinations found: there was a substantial increase in the number and in the complexity of Residential Mortgage-backed Securities (RMBS) and Collateralized Debt Obligation (CDO) deals since 2002, and some of the rating agencies appear to have struggled with the growth; significant aspects of the ratings process were not always disclosed; policies and procedures for rating RMBSs and CDOs could be better documented; the rating agencies are implementing new practices with respect to the information provided; the rating agencies do not always document significant steps in the ratings process, including the rationale for deviations from their models and for the rating committee actions and decisions, and they did not always document significant participants in the ratings process; the surveillance processes used by the rating agencies appear to have been less robust than the processes used for the initial ratings; issues were identified in the management of conflicts of interest and improvements could be made; the rating agencies' internal audit processes varied significantly.[83]

In Hong Kong, the SFC started to license and regulate CRAs and their rating analysts from 1 June 2011. The Code of Conduct for Persons Providing Credit Rating Services sets out the regulatory regime for CRAs.[84] It deals with quality and integrity of the rating process, independence and avoidance of conflicts of interest, responsibilities to the investing public and rated entities, transparency and timeliness of rating disclosure, and disclosure of the Code of Conduct and communication with market participants. In particular, the disclosure requirements for CRAs have been set down. A credit rating agency is required to make the following information available to the public on an annual basis: (a) internal control mechanisms designed to ensure the quality of its credit rating activities; (b) record-keeping policy; and (c) management and rating analyst rotation policy.[85]

The regulation of CRAs is an ongoing issue. It may be too early to draw a conclusion at this stage. However, after comparing the different jurisdictions, it can be seen that most of the documents enhance the regulatory framework; in particular, in the EU, UK and Hong Kong. These regulatory approaches for CRAs mainly emphasize the fair rating procedure, prevention and control of conflict of interest, maintaining business integrity, and transparency. One issue which is particularly interesting is that CRAs in these jurisdictions were not regulated before the recent financial crisis. Lessons learnt from the crisis, pushed the quick development of this regulatory regime.

It could be understood that study and examination of the above models will give the Chinese CRAs experience. Although the Chinese CRAs have been regulated at an early stage, due to the business and technique limitation, there are some issues remaining. With the development of unsecured corporate bonds, the demand for credit rating in China will significantly increase. It should be noted that although there are some qualitative arguments that credit ratings in China do not have enough information, one finding suggests otherwise, when a normally positively biased rating agency gives a low rating, it is valuable news to market participants.[86] From this point of view, the law and regulation will supply a regulatory and supervisory system, while the future of CRAs will be decided by their own performance. Finally, given the various economic structures and individual needs of the different states, there is no 'one size fits all' model for financial development. Therefore, the process of emerging, reforming and development of the Chinese CRAs must primarily focus on the state's needs. Considering the issue of the power of discourse, and further realizing that the capital market itself cannot fully solve the problem of asymmetric information, the CRAs should conduct their business practices targeted on the real requirements of the Chinese market.

The analysis of Chinese securities lawyers

Beside the credit rating agencies, the function of Chinese lawyers in the securities market is interesting to examine. As another major group of securities professionals, this force also stands in the frontline of the capital market.

After the establishment of the securities market, the regulatory regime of securities lawyers has experienced several reforms in China. Among different issues, the qualification for providing securities legal services is central. Securities lawyers, as the gatekeepers, are performing a vitally important function. Subsequently, the admittance of such guardians must be primarily rationalized. In this section, the evolution of securities lawyers will be examined. Further suggestions will be made based on this research.

The provision of securities legal services by law firms and lawyers is subjected to different requirements in China. Currently, the Securities Law, Lawyer's Law[87] and the Measures for the Administration of the Provision of Securities Legal Services by Law Firms are the main sources of the regulatory regime. Accordingly, law firms meeting the following requirements are encouraged to provide securities legal services[88]: having well-established internal management rules, sound risk control rules, a high practice level and a good social reputation; having 20 or more practicing lawyers, of which five or more have experience in providing securities legal services; having purchased valid practice liability insurances; and having no record of administrative penalty due to illegal practice for the last two years.[89]

Moreover, in a general sense, securities lawyer means a lawyer who is providing securities legal services. According to the Lawyer's Law, a lawyer in China refers to a practitioner who has obtained a lawyer's practicing certificate pursuant to the law, and after acceptance of entrustment or appointment, provides legal services to the parties concerned; a lawyer shall safeguard the legitimate rights and interests of the parties concerned, safeguard the correct implementation of the law, and safeguard fairness and justice in society.

At the present time, lawyers that meet any of the following conditions and have no record of any administrative penalty[90] due to illegal practice for the past two years are allowed to provide securities legal services: having experience in providing securities legal services in the last three years; having been practicing during the last consecutive three years, and the lawyer who plans to undertake business together with him has experience of providing securities legal services in the last three years; and having consecutively engaged in the teaching or research in the field of securities law for the last three years, or having accepted training in securities legal services.[91]

From the above provisions, it can be seen that there are no longer any special qualification requirements for securities lawyers. However, initially, there was a unique qualification system which has undergone several reforms in China. In contrast to the UK and Hong Kong, Chinese lawyers used to require an additional license in order to commence securities legal services practice. In 1993, the Ministry of Justice and CSRC established the Qualification System of Securities Lawyers.[92] Under this system, if a lawyer wanted to undertake securities legal services, he had to obtain a separate qualification beside the ordinary qualification of a lawyer. Furthermore, the individual lawyer with such a qualification had to join a law firm before he could provide the services. Finally, within the law firm, there had to be no less than three lawyers with the special qualification for securities legal services. However, the law firm still needed to apply for the qualification for providing securities legal services.[93] It can be seen in legal documents of that period, that all securities legal services had to be provided by law firms and lawyers with these qualifications.

How were these qualifications obtained? In 1993, there were 35 law firms and about 120 lawyers who obtained the qualification.[94] It should be noted that there was no training or exams for the qualification.

Between 1995 and 1996, the local Bureau of Justice selected lawyers for the training course. After that, CSRC took responsibility for the training and examination. In detail, the Ministry of Justice allocated quotas (Zhibiao) for each province; and the provincial Bureau of Justice made a second allocation. However, it had been argued by some legal scholars that there was not only allocation but also designation.[95]

In 1999 there was a significant improvement. The Ministry of Justice and CSRC established an Examination System for the qualification.[96] Under this system, qualified lawyers who had practiced for more than four years and were without a bad record were eligible to apply for the examination. It should be noted that this examination was only held once. It is not difficult to understand that the approach to obtaining the qualification for securities lawyers has been of an inequitable nature. It may be seen as a special qualification system with a Chinese character. The actual power to award the qualification was controlled by the Ministry of Justice, CSRC and Provincial Bureaux of Justice. It seriously jeopardized justice and further resulted in unfair competition. Although, there was an improvement in the exam system, it was a pity that it ended so soon.

Finally, this system led to a monopolized market in the legal services. There were 425 law firms and 1,619 lawyers who obtained the qualification between 1993 and 2002.[97] Moreover, these law firms and lawyers were mainly concentrated in Beijing, Guangdong and Shanghai. This distribution was mainly determined by the economic situation at that time. Beijing, as the capital city of China, attracted various specialists. In the case of Guangdong and Shanghai, they were the two areas where the Shenzhen Stock Exchange and Shanghai Stock Exchange were located. Another possible reason was the regional differences of the listed companies. The nature of the business decided the location of securities lawyers. From Table 4.2, it can be seen that in the year 2002, the numbers of listed companies in Beijing (70), Guangdong (61),[98] Shenzhen (78), and Shanghai (140) were higher than other areas.[99] Although the listed companies in Jiangsu (68), Shandong (68) and Sichuan (61) were more than other areas, the local economy in these provinces cannot compare with Beijing, Guangdong, Shenzhen and Shanghai, therefore there were less securities lawyers and firms.

The unfairness of this system aroused intense controversy between legal scholars and practitioners. Eventually, in 2002, the Ministry of Justice and CSRC abolished the qualification system.[100]

This abolition can be seen as a significant improvement. Lawyers obtained equal entrance to the securities services. In fact, a special license for securities

Table 4.2 Regional distribution of listed companies in 2002

Area	SHSE	SZSE	National
Anhui	17	15	32
Beijing	46	24	70
Fujian	25	16	41
Gansu	10	8	18
Guangdong	19	42	61
Guangxi	7	12	19
Guizhou	8	5	13
Hainan	8	14	22
Hebei	14	16	30
Henan	17	11	28
Heilongjiang	24	9	33
Hubei	30	28	58
Hunan	11	25	36
Inner Mongolia	15	5	20
Jilin	18	15	33
Jiangsu	46	22	68
Jiangxi	14	8	22
Liaoning	28	28	56
Ningxia	3	7	10
Qinghai	6	3	9
Shandong	41	27	68
Shanxi	9	10	19
Shaanxi	13	11	24
Shanghai	140	0	140
Shenzhen	5	73	78
Sichuan	32	29	61
Tianjin	15	7	22
Tibet	6	2	8
Xinjiang	17	6	23
Yunnan	10	8	18
Zhejiang	48	10	58
Chongqing	13	13	26
Sum	715	509	1,224

Source: Shanghai and Shenzhen Stock Exchange.[101]

lawyers should not constitute a problem in itself, particularly in the initial establishment period of the Chinese securities market. Complexity is one of the inherent natures of the securities business. It is not difficult to understand that the
primary aim of this system was to maintain a high level of legal services.

Unfortunately, administrative intervention has resulted in negative effects on
the system. The lack of transparency of the administrative licensing system
added a certain mystery to this procedure. The securities legal service is now a
specialist service. However, this should not be a reason for erecting barriers in
this field.

As can be seen from the above analysis, equal access to qualifications has
been achieved. Although the abolition of the qualification system led to a stop in

the unjust enrichment period in securities legal services, it still left some problems. Typical cases, for instance Lantian Gufen, Qiongminyuan and ST Hongguang, have illustrated the situation.[102]

Ensuring the quality of securities lawyers has become a difficult issue. Compared with some other jurisdictions, the professional training system for lawyers in China is not complete. Based on this rationale, the new Lawyers' Law has again emphasized that the All-China Lawyers Association should organize business training, professional ethics and practice discipline education for lawyers, conducting examination and verification on the practicing activities of lawyers.[103]

In fact, China has already established a continuing training system for lawyers. For instance, according to the plan of the Beijing Association, from August 2005, every lawyer should attend a training course of no less than 40 hours per year.[104] Also, considering the professional needs, training may be conducted by either campus-based or online methods. However, according to the Survey of Management Status of Law Firms in Beijing (2006)[105]: 41.19 per cent of law firms stated that they did not have mature training programmes, particularly for the long term. There were only 4 per cent of firms that could provide the opportunities to study abroad. Although it is not necessary for Chinese lawyers to study abroad in order to maintain their qualification, it is not difficult to see that the knowledge obtained in other, advanced jurisdictions will facilitate the continuing development of Chinese lawyers. Moreover, 50 per cent of law firms could allocate training funds of more than 5 per cent from their annual expenditure budget; while less than 20 per cent of firms could allocate funds of more than 10 per cent of their budget.[106] With the development of a training system, this situation will improve. Nevertheless, the actual outlay on training still needs to be examined.

Considering the nature of their business, securities lawyers need to keep their knowledge updated. Under the current regime, securities legal services refers to the legal services in which the law firms accept the entrustment of clients for the formulation and issuance of written legal opinions and other documents about their securities issuance, listing and trading, etc.[107] In respect of providing securities legal services, a law firm may issue legal opinions about the following matters: initial public offering and listing of stocks; issuance and listing of securities by listed companies; acquisition, important asset restructuring, and repurchase of shares by listed companies; equity incentive plan carried out by the listed company; holding of the general assembly of shareholders by the listed company; directly or indirectly going abroad for the issuance of securities by domestic enterprises, and listing and trading of these securities abroad; establishment, modification, resolution and termination of securities companies, securities investment fund management companies and their branches; raising of securities investment funds, and establishment of integrated asset management plans of securities companies; issuance and listing of securities derivatives; and other matters prescribed by CSRC.[108] It is not difficult to see that performing such functions needs a comprehensive knowledge of financial markets from both a domestic and an international level. The Ministry of Justice and CSRC issued

Rules for the Securities Legal Practices of Law Firms (for Trial Implementation)[109] and Detailed Practicing Rules for the Legal Services of Law Firms for Securities Investment Funds (for Trial Implementation),[110] set out the practicing rules. How should a lawyer's actual professional skills be judged to ensure that these standards can be met? One solution could be that market and competition will evaluate the lawyer's quality, but it still needs some time.

Moreover, lack of an efficient and complete training system is not the only problem. The provision of special practicing lawyers also needs to be examined.[111] A person who has acquired an undergraduate legal education in an institution of higher learning, college or university, in possession of the corresponding professional legal knowledge, engaged in professional work for at least 15 years in the area where legal service personnel are deficient, or had a senior professional title or an equivalent professional level may apply to practice as a lawyer; he shall be permitted to practice as a lawyer once he has passed the examination held by the administrative department in charge of justice under the State Council.[112]

How should openness, fairness and transparency be maintained in this special permission system? At first glance, the provision seems rigorous enough. By contrast, it is not difficult to obtain a LL.B degree under the current educational system in China. Also, whether a legal scholar purely engaged in research for more than 15 years is suitable to practice as a lawyer should be considered carefully. It may be useful in certain situations, for instance, in less developed areas, where there is more need for legal aids. However, this might not be the case for securities lawyers, who need more specialized knowledge. International experience shows that a legal scholar may work as a consultant in a team, without needing to obtain a qualification. Higher respect is given to his knowledge than giving him a title.

Summary

Similarly with other sectors, the regulation for securities intermediaries has experienced different reforms. From a relatively weak starting point up until the current supervisory regime, the issue of reform is ongoing. Research shows that securities professionals constitute an essential part of the market, and facilitate the establishment of a healthy and active securities market. However, they may assist in illegal securities transitions. It was common that professionals took advantage of information which they had obtained directly from their employment. Due to the limitation of scope, historical and current regulatory approaches of the CRAs and securities lawyers have been examined as selected examples. Moreover, some of the international initiatives have also been discussed.

Crediting ratings are not a recommendation or suggestion, directly or indirectly; however, they greatly affect the choices of investors and financial institutions. Moreover, they not only influence the consumer of the information but also the information provider. The market responds to credit rating rapidly, therefore the CRA's behaviour has a significant impact on the financial market.

Overly generous ratings due to various reasons, for instance a conflict of interest, must be banned; meanwhile, to act conservatively with regard to those entities or states in trouble should also be avoided. As a consequence, the self regulatory regime of the CRAs is not enough, efficient and powerful laws and regulations must be enacted. Besides the above general concerns, the Chinese CRAs have their own character. Subsequently, the rating method, regulatory regime and current discourse rights should be established in relation to the real needs of China. Mainland China must work out a suitable model for itself.

In relation to securities lawyers, it can be seen from the above analysis that the regulatory regime for securities lawyers is moving towards a more open and fair approach. However, there are still some problems remaining; in particular in facing the new challenge from financial globalization. How Chinese securities lawyers will meet the demand remains to be studied. Equal access is just the first step, while continuous training is an efficient way to ensure the quality of securities lawyers. Moreover, considering their special nature, the following issues should be taken into account for comprehensive, coherent and continual updating of the training plan: liberalization of capital markets; policy issue; foreign invested risk firms involved in the domestic market; Chinese companies' overseas listing; Chinese companies' cross listing issue; new technology related securities crime; and Chinese securities firms' abilities to address the changes.

Notes

1 Securities Law, promulgation date: 27 October 2005, effective date: 1 January 2006, Article 169.
2 Allen & Overy Global Survey (12 November 2008), The Future Direction of Global Financial Regulation, p. 11.
3 G20 (15 November 2008), Declaration: Summit on Financial Markets and the World Economy www.g20.org/G20/webapp/publicEN/publication/communiques/doc/G20%20Summit%20Declaration.pdf, last accessed: 2 December 2009.
4 Christian Noyer (12 December 2007), 'Possible Ways of Improving the Process of Rating', Speech at the Symposium on Financial Rating, organized by the Cercle France-Amériques, Paris.
5 Thomas Keller (18 November 2005), 'The Role and Function of Rating Agencies', Speech on BIS/Seminar on Developing Corporate Bond Markets in Asia.
6 Timothy J. Sinclair (2001), 'The Infrastructure of Global Governance: Quasi-Regulatory mechanisms and the New Global Finance', *Global Governance*, 7 (4), October–December 2001, p. 441–451.
7 Lawrence J. White (2001), 'The Credit Rating Industry: An Industrial Organization Analysis', paper presented at the Conference on 'The Role of Credit Reporting Systems in the International Economy', The World Bank, Washington, D.C., 1–2 March 2001.
8 David F. Hawkins, Barbara A. Brown and Walter J. Campbell, Rating Industrial Bond (Financial Executives Research Foundation, 1983), p. 38.
9 It should be noted some of the rating procedures are not allowed to be reproduced. Please refer to the individual company.
10 The contents in this paragraph were from: Xinhua Finance and Shanghai Far East Credit Ratings Co., Ltd (2003), Xinhua Far East China Ratings – Pioneering Undertaking to Rank Credit Risks of Enterprises in China, p. 8–10.

11 Timothy J. Sinclair (2001), 'The Infrastructure of Global Governance: Quasi-Regulatory mechanisms and the New Global Finance', *Global Governance*, 7 (4), October–December 2001, pp. 441–451.

12 Ibid.

13 Interim Regulation on Administration of Corporate Bond (Qiye Zhaiquan Guanli Zanxing Tiaoli), promulgation date: 27 March 1987, replaced by the Regulation on Administration of Corporate Bond in 1993.

14 Regulation on Administration of Corporate Bond (Qiye Zhaiquan Guanli Tiaoli), promulgation date: 2 August 1993, effective date: 2 August 1993, Article 15.

15 Central Committee of CPC (14 November 1993), Decision of Central Committee of CPC on Several Issues Concerning the Establishing the Socialist Market Economy Structure, Part 13.

16 Promulgation in 1996, experienced several revisions, recently revised in July 2012.

17 Scott Kennedy (2008). 'China's Emerging Credit Rating Industry: The Official Foundations of Private Authority', *The* China *Quarterly*, 193, p. 65–83.

18 PBOC (19 September 1989), Notice on Revoking the Securities Companies and Credit Rating Companies which have been Established by the People's Bank (Zhongguo Renming Yinhang guanyu Chexiao Renming Yinhang Sheli de Zhengquan Gongsi he Xinyu Pingji Gongsi de Tongzhi), Yinfa 1989 [No. 272].

19 PBOC (16 December 1997), Notice on the Licenses System of the China Chengxin Securities Rating Co., Ltd etc. regarding Corporate Bond Rating Business (Guanyu Zhongguo Chengxin Zhengquan Pinggu Youxian Gongsid deng Jigou Congshi Qiye Zhaiquan Xinyong Pingji Yewu Zige de Tongzhi), Yinfa 1997[No. 574].

20 Promulgation date: 29 December 1998, effective date 1 January 1999.

21 Ibid., Article 158.

22 Ibid., Article 157.

23 Ibid., Article 158.

24 Ibid., Article 160.

25 Ibid., Article 161.

26 SAC (2003), Measure for the Administration on Qualification of Securities Industry Practitioners (Trial), effective date: 1 February 2003, Chapter 2.

27 Interim Measures for the Administration of Bonds of Securities Companies (Zhengquan Gongsi Zhaiquan Guanli Zanxing Banfa), promulgation date: 29 August 2003, effective date: 8 October 2003, revised on 15 October 2004, Article 11.

28 Rules for Credit Rating Agencies on Issuing Rating Report of Bond of Securities Companies (Zixin Pingji Jigou Chuju Zhengquan Gongsi Zhaiquan Xingyong Pingji Baogao Zhunze), promulgation date: 29 August 2003, effective date: 8 October 2003.

29 Ibid., Article 3.

30 Ibid., Article 4.

31 Ibid., Article 5.

32 Ibid., Article 6.

33 Ibid., Article 7.

34 Ibid., Article 8.

35 Ibid., Article 10.

36 Ibid., Article 10 (1).

37 Ibid., Article 13, 16.

38 Ibid., Article 23.

39 Promulgation date: 14 October 2003, Part 5 (16).

40 Xiaochuan Zhou (November 2005), 'China's Corporate Bond Market Development: Lessons Learned', based on the remarks made at the BIS/PBC seminar on 'Developing Corporate Bond Markets in Asia' held in Kunming, China, 17–18 November 2005. www.bis.org/publ/bppdf/bispap26b.pdf, last accessed: 20 May 2010.

41 Ibid.

42 See CGSDTC website, www.chinabond.com.cn/Channel/318702?id=318702, last visit: 3 April 2010. As China's central securities depository (CSD) of bond Market, China Government Securities Depository Trust & Clearing Co. Ltd, (CGSDTC) takes the responsibility of the General Custodian. Registered in State Administration for Industry & Commerce (SAIC) in December 1996, CGSDTC is a nationwide non-bank financial institution. Its main functions are: providing infrastructure service dedicatedly; ensuring the safety of client assets prudentially; supporting financial product innovation actively; conducting financial risk monitoring consciously.

43 The contents in this paragraph were obtained form: Bond Information Department, CGSDTC, Annual Review of China's Bond Market (2008), p. 16–23.

44 Bond Information Department, CGSDTC, Annual Review of China's Bond Market (2008), p. 17.

45 Ibid.

46 Bond Information Department, CGSDTC, Annual Review of China's Bond Market (2011).

47 The Interim Measures for the Administration of the Credit Rating Business Regarding the Securities Market, promulgation date: 24 August 2007, effective date: 1 September 2007.

48 Ibid., Article 2.

49 Ibid., Article 42.

50 The details of the provisions on the senior managers will be discussed in the later part of this chapter.

51 The Interim Measures for the Administration of the Credit Rating Business Regarding the Securities Market, Article 7.

52 Ibid., Article 8.

53 Ibid., Article 12.

54 The scope of 'lineal relatives' has not been defined in this Measure. However, according to the Opinions (I) of the Supreme People's Court on Several Issues concerning the Implementation of the General Principles of the Civil Law of the People's Republic of China (For Trial Implementation), promulgation date: 26 January 1988, effective date: 26 January 1988, Article 12, The near relative stipulated in the General Principles of Civil Law consists of spouse, parents, children, brothers and sisters, grandparents, maternal grandparents, grandchildren and maternal grandchildren.

55 The Interim Measures for the Administration of the Credit Rating Business Regarding the Securities Market ibid., Article 13.

56 PBOC, Notice on Strengthening the Administration of Credit Rating Practices in the Interbank Bond Market, 11 March 2008.

57 Timothy J. Sinclair, 'The Infrastructure of Global Governance: Quasi-regulatory Mechanisms and the New Global Finance', *Global Governance*, 7 (4), p. 441.

58 Contents were from: Zhou Chong (20 March 2007), 'Six Shortages of Rating System in the Chinese Bond Market (Woguo Zhaiquan Xinyong Pingji Zhidu Cunzai Liuda Buzu)', *Shanghai Securities News* www.cnstock.com/paper_new/html/2007–03/20/content_52402983.htm, last accessed: 20 May 2012.

59 'Credit Ratings in China Can Be Mere Guesswork', *Wall Street Journal – Eastern Edition*, 1 May 2004, 243 (2), p C1-C11, 2p.

60 Tim Thomann (April 2008), presentation in FCIB International Credit Executive's Conference, 16–18 April 2008, from 'Credit Management Best Practices and Resources for Business Success in China', *Managing Imports & Exports*, 7 (2008), p. 1–10.

61 See, www.pbccrc.org.cn/zhongxinjieshao1.html, last accessed: 20 May 2013.

62 Fitch (August 2007), Inside the Rating-What Credit Ratings Mean, p. 10.

63 SFC Hong Kong (June 2011), Code of Conduct for Persons providing Credit Rating Services, Section 51.

64 The NDRC is one of the agencies under the State Council. It has been standing at the front of China's economic development and initiative of reform and opening up, in particular with the transition from the planned economy to socialist market economy. It keeps strengthening and improving macroeconomic management, forcefully promoting the sustained, rapid and sound development of the national economy. See NDRC website: http://en.ndrc.gov.cn/mfczp/default.htm, last accessed: 20 November 2010.

65 Xiaomei Mao, Xiaohui Zhao and Yu Wang (3 March 2009), 'Beware of the Foreign Company in Charge of Chinese Credit Rating Business (Jingti Jingrong Huayuquan Pangluo)', http://news.xinhuanet.com/mrdx/2009–03/04/content_10940789.htm, last accessed: 20 May 2010.

66 Ibid.

67 See CCXI website, www.ccxi.com.cn/CompanyInfo.aspx?cid=261, last visit: 3 April 2010.

68 Xiaomei Mao, Xiaohui Zhao and Yu Wang, see note 65.

69 19 March 2008, Yinfa [2008] No. 90, Part 5.

70 'BBC News – Greek credit status downgraded to "junk"', 27 April 2010, http://news.bbc.co.uk/2/hi/business/8647903.stm, last accessed: 2 September 2010. In 2010, several states were involved in the fears of a sovereign debt crisis, including European Union members Greece, Spain and Portugal. This led to a crisis of confidence between these countries and other EU members. Junk bonds (high-yield bonds), are lower than investment-grade securities; these bonds are considered to be 'speculative' because the issuing company's ability to meet the debt obligations is less certain. See Glossary of London Stock Exchange, at www.londonstockexchange.com/global/glossary/h.htm, last accessed: 2 November 2010.

71 Interview No. 8.

72 IOSCO, 2004.

73 IOSCO (May 2008), Code of Conduct Fundamentals for Credit Rating Agencies, p. 2.

74 European Commission (November 2008), http://ec.europa.eu/internal_market/securities/docs/agencies/proposal_en.pdf, last accessed: 20 May 2010.

75 Ibid.

76 Promulgation date, 16 September 2009.

77 Ibid., preamble (1).

78 Ibid., Preamble (75).

79 European Commission (2 June 2010), 'Commission Proposes Improved EU Supervision of Credit Rating Agencies and Launches Debate on Corporate Governance in Financial Institutions', http://europa.eu/rapid/press-release_IP-10–656_en.htm?locale=en, last accessed: 20 May 2013.

80 European Parliament News (16 January 2013), 'Tougher Credit Rating Rules Confirmed by Parliament's Vote', www.europarl.europa.eu/news/en/pressroom/content/20130114IPR05310/html/Tougher-credit-rating-rules-confirmed-by-Parliament%27s-vote, last accessed: 20 May 2013.

81 Made: 22 March 2010, laid before Parliament: 23March 2010, came into force: 7 June 2010.

82 SEC (July 2008), 'SEC Examinations Find Shortcomings in Credit Rating Agencies' Practices and Disclosure to Investors', www.sec.gov/news/press/2008/2008–135.htm, last accessed 20 May 2010.

83 Ibid.

84 SFC, effective date: 1 June 2011.

85 Ibid., Section 71.

86 Winnie P.H. Poon & Kam C. Chan (2008). 'An Empirical Examination of the Informational Content of Credit Ratings in China', *Journal of Business Research*, Elsevier, 61 (7), pp. 790–797.

87 Lawyer's Law, promulgation date: 15 May 1996, revised: 28 October 2007, effective date: 1 June 2008, revised date: 26 October 2012.

88 The CSRC and Ministry of Justice had opened the barrier for every lawyer. The term 'encouraged' suggested that the market demands for a group of high quality securities lawyer. On the other hand, the Measures for the Administration of the Provision of Securities Legal Services by Law Firms itself showed the cautious attitude as well: there are not many regulations merely for supervising the lawyer's services.

89 Measures for the Administration of the Provision of Securities Legal Services by Law Firms, promulgation date: 9 March 2007, effective date: 1 May 2007, Article 8.

90 As for the administrative penalty for lawyers, the administrative department of Justice can impose a warning, fine, confiscation of illegal gains or suspension of practice. See: The Measures for Punishing Lawyers and Law Firms for Their Illegal Acts, promulgation date: 7 April 2010, effective date: 1 June 2010.

91 Measures for the Administration of the Provision of Securities Legal Services by Law Firms, Article 9.

92 Provisional Regulation of the Qualification for Provision of Securities Legal Services by Lawyers and law Firms, promulgation date: 12 January 1993, Article 4.

93 Ibid., Article 5.

94 XianZhou Wei (2003): 'Who can be a Securities Lawyer? (Shuineng Shenren Zhengquan Falü Yewu)', *The Journal of Chinese Lawyer*, 6, p. 20.

95 Liufang Fang, Peng Jiang, Haixia Cheng, 'Securities Lawyers and Informstion Disclsoure of the Listed Companies (Zhengquan Lüshi yu Shangshi Gongsi Xinxi Pilu)', http://news3.xinhuanet.com/fortune/2002–08/05/content_510364.htm, last accessed: 20 May 2010.

96 http://old.csrc.gov.cn/n575458/n575667/n642011/2005470.html, last accessed: 20 May 2010.

97 XianZhou Wei, see note 94.

98 Here, the data for Shenzhen is listed separately from Guangdong province because the Shenzhen Stock Exchange is located in Shenzhen city, and Shenzhen is a designated Special Economic Zone, separate from the rest of Guangdong Province.

99 The CSRC, www.csrc.gov.cn/n575458/n4239016/n4239073/n8148622/n8148706/8171969.html, last accessed: on 6 June 2009.

100 Notice of Cancellation of Approval of the Qualification for Provision of Securities Legal Services by Lawyers and law Firms (23 December 2002).

101 Available at: www.csrc.gov.cn/pub/newsite/scb/tjnj/2003/ssgs_7389/, last accessed: 15 September 2010.

102 For the details of the cases see Chapter 1.

103 Lawyer's Law, Article 46.

104 Lawyers Association of Beijing (10 August 2005), 'Notice of Training for Lawyers', www.bmla.org.cn/bjlawyers2/news/bulletinmore.jsp, last accessed: 19 May 2010.

105 Lawyers Association of Beijing (16 October 2006), www.acla.org.cn/pages/2006–10–20/s36846.htm, last accessed: 19 May 2010.

106 Ibid.

107 Measures for the Administration of the Provision of Securities Legal Services by Law Firms, Article 2.

108 Ibid., Article 6.

109 Issued date: 20 October 2010, effective date: 1 January 2011.

110 Issued date: 20 October 2010, effective date: 1 January 2011.

111 They are lawyers who have qualified via an alternative route.

112 Lawyer's Law, Article 8.

5 The role and function of the China Securities Regulatory Commission

Introduction

Information disclosure is one of the core regimes in the capital market that needs to be further enhanced. A weak regulatory and supervisory framework for information disclosure may result in a market failure. Scandals such as Enron and the current financial crisis amplify this point. China's securities market has developed substantially in past decades. An information disclosure regime has been gradually established and continuous regulatory measures are being taken to enhance this system. The China Securities Regulatory Commission (hereafter the CSRC) has been playing an important role in regulation and supervision of China's developing capital market. However, questions are being raised, among other issues, about whether the CSRC has suitable powers in relation to the supervision and regulation of the information disclosure regime, and about the effectiveness of the supervision and regulation of information disclosure in China. Is the CSRC a weak regulator? With a comparitive study of the function and role of the Financial Services Authority (hereafter FSA)[1] and today's Financial Conduct Authority (hereafter FCA) in the UK and the Securities and Futures Commission of Hong Kong (SFC), this research offers an analysis of the regulatory behaviour of the CSRC regarding the information disclosure regime in China.

Basic function of the CSRC

The establishment of Shanghai Stock Exchange (hereafter the SSE) and Shenzhen Stock Exchange (hereafter the SZSE), boosted the quick development of the Chinese securities market. Nevertheless, the regulation of the securities market needed to be further enhanced. There was some disorder and chaos happening at that time; for instance, the 'Shenzhen 8.10 event'.[2] According to Hongru Liu, former chairman of the CSRC, the 'Shenzhen 8.10 event' produced the need for the establishment of the CSRC.[3] In order to regulate and supervise the Chinese securities market, the CRSC was founded in 1992.[4] Together with the Securities Committee of the State Council (hereafter SCSC),[5] the CSRC played an important role in the initial formation of the Chinese capital market.

Since 1998, the CSRC has become the central regulatory body supervising the Chinese securities market. In the past two decades, it continued to develop supervisory capabilities. Table 5.1 shows the organizational structure of the CSRC. Compared with before, it has established a more comprehensive internal structure. Together with its regional offices, Securities Supervision Offices at SSE and SZSE, the CSRC aims to better fulfil its regulatory function.

The Securities Law stated that the principle of this law is to standardize the issuing and trading of securities, protect the lawful rights and interests of investors, safeguard economic order and the interests of society and promote the development of the socialist market economy.[6] Moreover, it is stated on the website of CSRC that 'Investors' protection is our top priority.'[7] These can be seen as the basic regulatory objectives.

According to the Securities Law, the basic functions of the CSRC are to regulate the securities market according to law, maintain order of the securities market and ensure lawful operation.[8]

Moreover, it should perform the following detailed functions: to formulate rules and regulations concerning regulation of the securities market and to lawfully exercise its power of examination and approval or verification; to regulate the offering, trading, registration, custody and clearing of securities; to regulate the securities business activities of the organizations that are engaged in securities business; to formulate the qualification criteria and code of conduct for persons engaged in securities business; to supervise and inspect the disclosure of information in connection with securities offering and trading; to guide and supervise the activities of the Securities Industry Association according to law; to investigate and deal with violations of laws and administrative regulations concerning the regulation of the securities market.[9]

Table 5.1 Organizational structure of the CSRC

General Office
Department of Public Offering Supervision
Department of Unlisted Public Company Supervision
Department of Market Supervision
Department of Intermediary Supervision
Office of Risk Management
Department of Listed Company Supervision
Department of Fund Supervision
Department of Futures Supervision
Enforcement Bureau (Office of Chief Enforcement Officer)
Department of Legal Affairs (Office of Chief Counsel)
Office of Administrative Sanction Committee
Department of Accounting (Office of Chief Accountant)
Department of International Affairs
Department of Personnel & Education
Department of Regional Offices Coordination
Disciplinary Bureau

Source: CSRC.[10]

As can be seen from the above, the CSRC has a series of functions that cover the basic aspects of the securities market. According to law, the CSRC may adopt the following measures to perform its duties and functions: carrying out an on-the-spot examination; investigating and collecting evidence when suspected irregularity has happened; consulting the parties under investigation and requiring explanations; referring to and photocopying materials relating to the case under investigation; referring to and photocopying the securities trading records and other relevant documents; sealing up any document or material that may be transferred, concealed or damaged; consulting the capital account, security account or bank account of any relevant party relating to a case under investigation; in the case of any evidence certifying that any property involved in a case such as illegal proceeds or securities that has been or may be transferred or concealed or where any important evidence has been or may be concealed, forged or damaged, freezing or sealing up of the foregoing properties or evidence upon the approval of the principal of the securities regulatory authority under the State Council; when investigating into any major securities irregularity such as market manipulation or insider trading, restricting the securities transactions of the parties concerned.[11]

The issue of regulatory measures, as the weapon of supervisory bodies, is a delicate topic in China. The controversy is targeted on whether the CSRC has sufficient powers. In fact, there was an evolutionary progress before reaching the current regime. This progress involved the different judicial, public and industrial sectors; details will be explained in the latter part of this chapter.

Besides the basic functions, it is important to examine what indeed the CSRC is dealing with. In principle, the aspects can be summarized as: permitting market entrance; supervising business operation; managing corporation exit; investigating and punishing law violation. Among the different functions, an important part is supervising the compliance of information disclosure.

The CSRC has played a vitally important role in the development of the Chinese securities market. More detailed work of the CSRC will be examined.

Establishing and refining regulatory framework

The CSRC has been working on establishing a regulatory framework for the Chinese securities market. Starting from a relatively weak base, the CSRC is continuing to seek to enhance the legal framework. For China, the economy under transition itself may not directly create problems. However, this situation presents certain challenges for the regulatory bodies. Conflicts between maintaining the legal certainty and meeting new challenges can be found in various places.

Thus, participating in drafting the laws, regulations and rules of the securities and futures market as well as detailed rules for implementation, reviewing and verifying the regulations and rules drafted by the departments became one of the primary functions of the CSRC. In fact, the CSRC did fill in the gaps between different legal documents. These documents have covered different aspects of the securities markets; for instance, IPO, continuing disclosure, corporate governance, overseas listing, mergers and takeovers, payment and settlement system.

With regard to the information disclosure system, one of the central concerns in the securities market, the CSRC has paid intensive attention to this issue. It developed a series of disclosure rules which are important to the regime. Furthermore, it has also stipulated and revised detailed requirements according to the latest markets changes. For instance in 2008, the Content and Format for Annual Report of Securities Companies is revised in order to promote the quality of financial information.[12] This guideline was first published in 1999, and revised in 2002 before being revised again in 2008. In comparing it with the older versions, the new edition is more complete. It is clear that the updated version is more consistent with the current situation.

The Compilation Rules for Information Disclosure by Companies that Offer Securities to the Public: Special Provisions for Information Disclosure of Commercial Banks is one of the important documents which regulate disclosure behaviour.[13] The main focus of this document is the commercial banks. For instance, it requires that: commercial banks shall disclose in regular reports the major financial indicators in the last three years before the end of the current reporting period, including the loan ratio of the single largest customer.[14]

Regulating the non-tradable shares in the Chinese stock market is a typical example. A feature of the Chinese securities market is the distinction of tradable and non-tradable shares. China introduced a special mechanism, the creation of state shares and legal person shares, which both carry significant constraints on tradability, generally either state-owned or state-controlled; on the other hand, tradable shares are composed of A, B and H shares;[15] a typical public company had about one-third of its shares in each category of state, legal person and tradable shares.[16] The share structure reform is aiming to release the constraints on tradability in order to facilitate long-term development. According to Article 2 of the Guiding Opinions of the China Securities Regulatory Commission, State-owned Assets Supervision and Administration Commission, Ministry of Finance, People's Bank of China, and the Ministry of Commerce on Share Trading Reform of Listed Companies: share splitting refers to the shares of listed companies in the A shares market and are divided into non-tradable and tradable shares according to whether they can be listed for trading on the stock exchange; this is a special problem during the transition of economic situation in China; the different disposal of shares has distorted the pricing mechanism of the capital market, and restricted the effective play of resource allocation functions thereof; the price of the stocks of listed companies cannot work as a market based incentive and restriction for majority shareholders and the management team so that there is no common basis of interest in corporate governance; for such stocks there are two kinds of prices in capital flow: the negotiated price for the transfer of non-tradable shares and the competitive transaction price of tradable shares, so there is no market operating basis for capital operations; the different disposal of stocks in this context cannot meet the need for the reform, opening up and stable development of the capital market, so the difference between tradable shares and non-tradable shares will be eliminated through share trading reform.[17]

China's stock market has changed from an equity divided market to an all floating one: both with non-tradable shares (hereafter NTS) and other shares with a sales limit, became transferable stocks, only with different sales limit periods.[18] Due to this circumstance, the transparency of substantive share transferring became a new issue. Clearly, the shareholder who has more than 5 per cent of the shares was in a better position.[19] If these shareholders were to reduce the shares substantially over a short period, there would be a significant impact on the securities market. Thus, to establish a special regulatory and disclosure regime for reducing NTS is very necessary.

In 2008, the CSRC improved the relevant systems. First, the Guiding Opinions on the Listed Companies' Transfer of Original Shares Released from Trading Restrictions has been issued.[20] This Guidance is targeted to regulate the substantive sale of excessive stock shares without sales limit by shareholders of listed companies. It stated that such sales must be conducted according to the disclosure requirements for the particular shareholders.[21] Moreover, if the shareholder plans to sell such shares, which are more than 1 per cent of the company's total shares publicly in the coming month, he should operate through the Massive Trading System.[22] Most importantly, the controlling shareholder must not transfer such shares within 30 days before publishing the annual or half year report.[23] Whoever is holding or controlling more than 5 per cent of the company's total shares, plans to sell NTS, shall disclose the information promptly and accurately according to law.[24]

Furthermore, the Shanghai Stock Exchange (SSE) and the Shenzhen Stock Exchange (SZSE) issued detailed guidance, notices and rules to regulate this behaviour.[25] In these documents, the two stock exchanges stated they would expose to public criticism, and also impose trading restriction on, shareholders who misconducted sales of NTS; moreover, the two stock exchanges will require such shareholders to repurchase the shares within a certain limited time.

Finally, the China Securities Depository and Clearing Corporation Limited (CSDCC) began to disclose relevant information about reducing the holding of non-tradable shares every month since July 2008.[26] This approach has improved the transparency of the securities market, and allowed the regulatory body and general public to obtain up dated information. Table 5.2 is the relevant data on share reform.

It can be seen from the above analysis: the CSRC has paid more attention to the information disclosure issue. The reform of this regime will be continuing along with the development of the securities market. Taking the disclosure regime for NTS as an example, effective measures have been taken to closely monitor the transaction of shares released for trading; in particular, together with the stock exchanges, establishment of timely control against abnormal transactions, can effectively prevent and reduce unusual circumstances.

Table 3.2 The share reform (ban-lifting & lessening holding) (Unit: 0.1 billion)

	Ban-lift			Lessening holding		
	Accounts holding non-tradable shares ≥5%	Accounts holding non-tradable shares <5%	Total	Accounts holding non-tradable shares ≥5%	Accounts holding non-tradable shares <5%	Total
June 2006	0.00	0.11	0.11	0.00	0.00	0.00
July 2006	0.00	0.00	0.00	0.00	0.00	0.00
August 2006	9.40	23.42	32.82	0.10	2.10	2.20
September 2006	0.83	0.52	1.36	0.10	1.57	1.67
October 2006	0.88	22.85	23.73	0.19	2.07	2.25
November 2006	7.87	10.56	18.44	1.09	5.79	6.88
December 2006	11.22	14.01	25.24	1.80	7.40	9.20
January 2007	10.07	12.52	22.59	3.68	8.68	12.35
February 2007	9.76	13.08	22.84	2.00	5.24	7.23
March 2007	14.58	22.40	36.98	3.75	9.95	13.69
April 2007	27.32	56.40	83.72	5.92	20.33	26.25
May 2007	18.53	38.49	57.02	6.61	18.84	25.46
June 2007	14.37	16.86	31.22	3.51	11.49	15.01
July 2007	15.41	20.96	36.37	2.67	8.68	11.35
August 2007	34.67	16.39	51.05	5.36	13.24	18.60
September 2007	12.33	9.81	22.14	6.11	9.89	16.00
October 2007	75.20	48.81	124.01	3.54	4.43	7.96
November 2007	29.90	10.10	40.00	3.83	4.50	8.33
December 2007	16.25	5.64	21.89	7.71	7.95	15.66
January 2008	16.18	9.08	25.27	6.68	9.74	16.43
February 2008	11.24	35.82	47.06	2.56	4.89	7.45
March 2008	17.20	6.34	23.54	3.13	5.83	8.96
April 2008	25.32	6.35	31.68	1.60	4.38	5.98
May 2008	30.05	4.22	34.27	1.96	4.69	6.65
June 2008	23.58	6.03	29.61	1.39	3.11	4.51
July 2008	21.68	3.66	25.34	2.93	5.56	8.49
August 2008	210.37	5.10	215.47	0.94	3.87	4.80
September 2008	9.05	1.58	10.62	1.47	3.05	4.53
October 2008	79.44	10.61	90.05	1.42	2.62	4.04
November 2008	47.70	6.14	53.85	2.50	4.44	6.94
December 2008	110.01	16.02	126.03	3.63	4.60	8.23
Total	910.41	453.88	1,364.32	88.18	198.93	287.10

Source: CSDCC.[27]

Conducting investigations

Besides the normative function, in order to maintain an open, fair and orderly financial market, the CSRC has been endowed with investigative and evidence taking powers. It may be argued that, from this point of view, the CSRC is similar to an 'economic police'.

Currently, the Enforcement Bureau (Office of Chief Enforcement Officer) is in charge of investigations relating to the securities market.[28] In recent years, the CSRC has continuously sought to improve the efficiency of investigation. At the same time, traditional criminal methods have changed in the financial market. For instance, in some internet securities crimes, the lawbreakers set network servers in remote regions or even in other jurisdictions, which may increase the difficulties and costs of investigation. In order to meet these challenges, the CSRC reorganized the investigation system. It also established the Enforcement General Team (Jicha Zongdui) in 2007.[29] It mainly deals with cases of insider dealing, market manipulation, false and misleading statements, and some serious or sensitive cases.

It should be noted that the investigative power itself has evolved during the last two decades. In particular, the question of what powers shall be given to the CSRC is a central issue. Notably, the CSRC did not have the authority to examine bank accounts, company registration documents, to freeze fund accounts and securities accounts until 2006.[30] This phenomenon led to the inefficiency of the CSRC, in particular, when dealing with securities crimes. In the case of Yi'an Technology Co., Ltd, the CSRC issued the administrative sanction decision to confiscate illegal income of RMB0.449 billion and imposed a penalty of RMB0.449 billion.[31] However, the account was not in funds.[32] In 2006, the Securities Law endowed the CSRC with the above powers. Furthermore, besides the Securities Law, the Measures of Freezing and Sealing up Accounts by the CSRC (hereafter Measures) stated the powers in detail.[33]

Considering the special features of securities crimes, it is quite necessary to confer such powers on the CSRC. In some other jurisdictions, similar situations can be found; for instance, the Securities and Exchange Commission (SEC) in the United States. This is based on the consideration of prevention and controlling illicit securities transactions. In general, illicit securities transactions relating to information disclosure have the following characteristics: fast spreading; the evidence is easily destroyed; the proceeds of crime are easily transferred and concealed; the case itself may cause systemic risks for the whole securities market. A further consideration will be that in certain jurisdictions, such as the United Kingdom, the financial regulator has the power to bring criminal prosecutions in relation to crimes against the securities markets. Nevertheless, such powers must be established on a balanced base with other financial regulators, and be exercised in a rational style.

In the Measures, two core issues have been addressed: first, they established the working framework for investigation; second, they set down the content and format of legal enforcement documents, which will improve the efficiency of investigation. Furthermore, they can help to prevent the abuse of power. The measures stated that if the CSRC found the following situations, it could apply for a freezing and sealing up order: there is a evidence showing that any illegal funds and securities involved have been or may be transferred or concealed, or important evidence has been or may be concealed, forged or damaged.[34] According to the Measures, the following evidence can be deemed as important: it may affect the magnitude of the investigation; it has key functions for judging the case; it cannot be substituted.[35]

Thus, investigation powers have been enhanced through the enactment of the Measures. The CSRC has been better armed through using freezing and sealing up measures to control and prevent illegal securities transactions. It may significantly reduce the delay in dealing with cases and subsequently protect the assets of investors. Compared with before, the efficiency of investigation has been improved, enhancing the regulatory aims of the CSRC.

ST Weida Medical Applied Technology Co., Ltd (hereafter ST Weida) was one of the cases under investigation. The CSRC conducted an on-site examination of ST Weida from 23 to 27 July 2007.[36] Four major incidents of lawbreaking were found: false and misleading statements in the financial report, the business transaction, the property rights of a subsidiary and misappropriating funds by related parties.[37] The Shenzhen Securities Regulatory Bureau had issued a notice to require ST Weida to rectify and reform the situation; on 25 September, the company agreed to conduct the rectification and reform.[38] It can be seen from this case, the CSRC played an important role in preventing further illegal behaviour.

Today, the reaction time to financial crime by the CSRC is shorter than before. From January to November 2012, the CSRC handled 363 cases, an increase of 25 per cent over the last year. Among them, there were 185 cases reported by the stock exchanges, which accounted for 51 per cent; 102 cases were reported by petition, which accounted for 28 per cent; 76 cases were from other sources, including dispatched offices of the CSRC, which accounted for 21 per cent.[39]

In 2012, Wanfu Biotechnology (Hunan) Agricultural Development Co. Ltd (Wanfu) was investigated by the CSRC for its behaviour concerning false disclosure. In May 2013, the CSRC announced an administrative penalty, under which Wanfu is required to rectify its inflated revenues posted over the past four years, and is fined RMB300,000. A number of executives are fined, and two of them have been delivered to the public security for fraud and false disclosure. Notably, in this case, the financial intermediaries also are punished. Ping An Securities Company will have its sponsorship qualifications suspended for three months, due to the failure on conducting adequate due diligence. Documents conceding securities listing issued by Huannan Bo'ao Law Firm will not be accepted in the next 12 months. The Securities Service Licence of Zhonglei Accounting Firm will be revoked.[40]

Nevertheless, there is an issue that should not be ignored: most of these investigations are *ex post facto*, there is no advanced pre-warning management system.[41] A pre-warning system needs to be enhanced based on a comprehensive online monitoring system. From this point of view, it is important that the CSRC conducts its normal functions and other roles consistently, because this will play an important part in preventing illegal behaviour.

Executing administrative decisions

Law and regulation has given administrative powers to the CSRC. In the first half year of 2008, the CSRC registered 66 cases, informally investigated 83 cases, concluded 73 cases, and delivered 11 cases to the Public Security sector,[42] furthermore, it delivered 47 administrative punishments and market entrance prohibitions.[43]

It is interesting to note that although the Chinese securities market has not been well developed, the known amount of securities crime is relatively small. It has been argued that in China, the 'causes of action are many but the actions are few'.[44] However, there is common awareness that the actual amount of law breaching behaviour is higher. There are two reasons resulting from this situation: first, at the initial stage of the development of the Chinese securities market, the legal framework was incomplete; second, as discussed in the previous chapter, in the past, there may be a local protection philosophy in Mainland China, which indicates that some of the local governments are not willing to see enterprises in their region be charged for criminal offences.[45] In general, the listed companies are very important for the local economy. Some of them are so called 'star' or 'pillar' enterprises. Thus, putting them on trial may directly affect the local economic environment.

A prosecutor explained that: currently, for securities crimes, it is very difficult to put defendants in front of the courts. In most cases, one of the main reasons leading to this situation is the lack of information ... unless such behaviour had serious results.[46] Moreover, examining existing cases, it is not even easy to prove the results are serious.[47] It is common that once one shareholder files an action, other shareholders tend to pile in, with large numbers.[48] This may lead to postponement of the case. The lack of operational guidance and judicial explanations related to class actions in China further enlarge the problem.

In these circumstances, the administrative powers of the CSRC have become very significant. It effectively exercises control over illicit securities transactions. Together with continuous monitoring of the market, this power can control securities crime at an early stage. During the performance of its supervisory function, the CSRC has more resources than other judicial departments, which may assist it to disclose illegal securities transactions. This method is less time consuming, and is also important for control of financial crime. Overall, it is crucially important that the CSRC is enforcing its own rules and imposing sanctions in appropriate cases.[49]

Promoting investor protection

Protection of investors is one of the major tasks of the CSRC. The Chinese investors, in particular retail investors, have lacked legal awareness for some time. By different methods, the CSRC makes efforts to safeguard the legal rights and interests of investors and to promote a consistent education system. Such an education system should target the retail investors, based on the latest development and reforms of the Chinese securities market.[50]

With regard to the information disclosure regime, among different issues, the CSRC also emphasizes the disclosure of risks to investors. For instance, the CSRC required that the education of investors and disclosure of risks shall be specifically reflected in every section of the customer service system. The securities companies shall commence the work of disclosure of risks at the time of opening of accounts for their clients, they shall explain the contents of the relevant business affairs contracts and agreements to clients, clearly display the risks associated with the investment in securities, and make sure that the clients have signed their signatures to the risk disclosure letters of acknowledgement.[51]

The importance of risk disclosure is decided by the features of the Chinese securities market, continuing reform and development. Therefore, for investors, along with the establishment of the multi-level capital market system, the requirements of enhancing full understanding of the market with its different risk factors have been advised. In this context, as the chief regulator, the CSRC has placed attention on risk disclosure. The disclosure regime of the Growth Enterprises Board (hereafter GEB) can be seen as a typical example.

The GEB formally started its operation on 30 October 2009.[52] Compared with those on the main board market, the standard of issuance and listing on the GEB market is lower; the GEB firms are usually characterized by their small scale and changeable business performance, with higher investment risks.[53] With regard to investor protection, the information disclosure system for the GEB is a front line issue. The CSRC issued the Interim Measures on Administration of Initial Public Offerings and Listings on the Growth Enterprise Board (hereafter Measures).[54] It requires that the admittance system for investors that fits their risk bearing capacities, should be established on the GEB market and the investment risks should be disclosed to the investors.[55] Furthermore, the Measures also require that the issuer shall note in a prominent place of its prospectus that: the stocks have a relatively high investment risk; companies listed on the GEB may have characteristics such as instability in performance and high risk in business operations, investors may face relatively big market fluctuations; investors should know the investment risks and the risk factors disclosed by the company, and make investment decisions in a prudent manner.[56]

These laws and regulations provide solid support for investor protection. Moreover, the CSRC also place relevant disclosure requirements on investors. Investors are required to cooperate in the securities company's investor eligibility management scheme when applying to activate GEB transactions, and honestly provide the obligatory information, and shall not evade the relevant requirements by making false statements or by any other means; when an investor does not cooperate or provides any false information, the securities company may refuse to provide the GEB transaction activation service to the investor.[57] Establishment of an appropriate management system in the GEB is an important step for the safety of the new market model; in particular, the number of retail investors is significantly large in China. Furthermore, to impose suitable information disclosure requirements according to the nature and characters of the market can further facilitate the healthy growth of the GEB. It shall be noted, that with the development of the GEB, the information disclosure regime for the GEB will be reformed and further enhanced.[58]

From the example of the GEB, it can be seen that compared to other mature markets, in the Chinese securities market, the retail investors are occupying a significant portion. Therefore, to enhance the education; in particular to address the transition nature of the Chinese market is a crucial task for the CSRC.

Participating in international cooperation

The CSRC is continuingly seeking a more sophisticated method to regulate the securities market. The combination of advanced models from external mature markets with Chinese domestic regulation itself can be seen as a 'Chineselized' approach, which helped the development in the last few years in other sectors of China.

The CSRC has joined a number of international and regional organizations; for instance, the International Organization of Securities Commissions (hereafter the IOSCO) has published numbers of documents and facilitates the promotion of good regulation in different countries. However, it should be noted that the majority of these legal documents only provide basic principles and guidance for the regulatory framework. International Disclosure Principles for Cross-border Offerings and Listings of Debt Securities by Foreign Issuers (hereafter Principles) can be seen as one of the typical examples.[59] In the introduction, this was pointed out amongst other things:

> The purpose of these Principles is not to override existing requirements, but rather to facilitate a better understanding of issues ... the International Debt Disclosure Principles should provide useful guidance to securities regulators who are developing or reviewing their regulatory disclosure regimes for cross-border offerings and listings of debt securities...[60]

Further examples can be found in the Principles. For instance, when dealing with the Significant Changes in Part XIII (Financial Information), it stated that:

> The principles discussed in this section assume that the Issuer will be required under national laws and regulations to provide consolidated financial statements according to high quality internationally accepted accounting standards.[61]

Moreover, after examining the contents, it is not difficult to discover that the Principles are more concerned with helping to establish a fundamental framework in the securities market. Detailed rules may not be suitable for all countries, however, in some circumstances, what the new emerging markets need may be the rules with more technical support.

There is another layer to these documents, namely, more detailed international standards. Typical examples can be found in the industrial groups or associations; for instance, auditing standards or accounting standards. However, for a developing country, whether the high standards are suitable for the domestic infrastructure should be considered very carefully. Since the majority of such standards are designed and spread according to the needs of developed countries, how will China meet these standards? There is a long way to go.

Multilateral team work may bring broad benefits for the CSRC. Also, bilateral cooperation may directly result in a win-win situation. By the end of January 2013, the CSRC had signed 53 Memoranda of Understanding (MOUs) with securities and futures regulators in different jurisdictions around the world.[62] The MOUs signed between the regulators can enhance the information exchange and cooperation between securities and futures supervision and promote sound development of capital markets in both countries.

It can be seen from the above analysis that China keeps on finding the efficient approach to regulate the securities market, through bilateral, multilateral or international cooperation. China's approach may be decided by the emerging and transitional feature of the market.[63] Internationally cooperated supervision should be based on common recognition. However, national interests and domestic capability need to be put in a prime position. Historically, China has had similar experiences in reforms to those of other sectors. Hence, it is important to adopt a similar approach, pursuing international cooperation whilst simultaneously maintaining the 'Chineseness' in securities regulation. 'Everything with good preparation can be successful.'[64] Facing the new opportunities and challenges, how experiences from other markets should be merged into the local environment, is still an ongoing topic for Chinese financial regulators.

Through establishing and refining regulatory framework, conducting investigation, executing administrative decisions, promoting investor protection, and actively participating in the international cooperation, the CSRC oversees the Chinese securities market. The CSRC in exercising these functions plays a vital role in leading the market modernisation and establishing a transparent, safe and robust system.[65]

Issues for future consideration

From the above analysis, it can be seen that the basic regulatory framework has been established in China. However, there are some issues that need to be examined. As an emerging market in a transitional economy, the development of China's capital markets is still constrained by some structural and institutional problems, for instance, the supervisory capacity should be further enhanced.[66]

Current regulatory features

For a good regulator, one of the most import duties is to identify the latest situation. For China, the situation of a strong economy under transition itself may not directly create difficulties. However, this feature can lead to certain challenges for the regulators. According to the China Capital Markets Development Report, the regulatory regime in China has the following features:[67]

1   The legal system and regulatory framework is developing. Adjustments, revisions of the existing law, rules and regulations will be an ongoing issue.
2   Securities regulation and supervision largely relies on administrative measures. The regulatory framework and its capacity are not well matched with market developments. Compared with before, complexity has increased which leads to higher uncertainty. These difficulties require the CSRC to enhance its work. Furthermore, demands for qualified professionals in regulatory agencies are fast increasing.
3   The impact of self-regulatory organizations is limited. The Securities Association of China (SAC) has yet not become fully functional. It lacks the ability to work independently from regulatory agencies.[68]
4   A strong culture of equality is being established. To set up an open, fair market, requires cooperation from different sectors. For instance, professional integrity needs to be further improved. Also currently, the rating agencies need to be better regulated in China.[69]

In fact, these features decided the regulatory style of the CSRC, which emphasizes 'development' and 'improvement'. Therefore, another issue needs to be noted, the CSRC shall maintain the legality and fairness of its administrative powers. Legality requires the CSRC to perform its function according to the relevant law and regulation, and should not go beyond its vested powers and original legislative purpose;[70] fairness requires the CSRC to execute its role without any bias. These two elements are internally linked. It also has been suggested that when an administrative agency exercises its power, it should be done in conformity with the principle of reasonableness; this means that an administrative agency should take into consideration many related factors, conduct and implement discretion reasonably and without bias, while ensuring the establishment of corresponding legal supervision and relief mechanisms.[71] It should be noted that, as a modern regulator, it is necessary to achieve a high level of accountability and credibility. The financial regulator should be publicly accountable through its own functional behaviour. The problem of inconsistency between different legal documents should not become the excuse for lack of credibility. Pre-commitments and market responses should not create big conflicts.

Bringing incentives to the market

Traditionally in China, the investors, issuers and other financial intermediaries have relied more on administrative management. Other sanction measures are not fully developed. For instance, there are very few securities crimes that have reached a final judgement. Furthermore, civil compensation is not easy to achieve. A class action by investors, in particular retail investors, is still a controversial issue.[72]

It should be admitted that market regulation and supervision that simply relies on administrative measures can no longer meet the growing needs of the securities market. One old issue in Chinese securities market was the puzzle of administration procedures. Actually the permission system of the CSRC has been reformed. There are some reductions in the procedures for the administrative permission, and the entire attitude towards the administrative permission tends to be more simplified.[73] Most significantly, the working process of the CSRC has become more transparent than before. From the flow chart for the administrative permission approval, it can be seen that the working process of the CSRC has been clearly set out. This largely reduces the regulatory puzzle, and brings further incentives to the securities market. Now, relevant working procedures can be found on the official website of the CSRC (see Figure 5.2).[74] Bureaucracy should be avoided, particularly for a financial regulator. In this circumstance, achieving a dynamic balance between the regulating behaviour and bringing incentives to the market should be considered more by the CSRC. As a modern financial regulator, avoiding bureaucracy is an important step. Moreover,

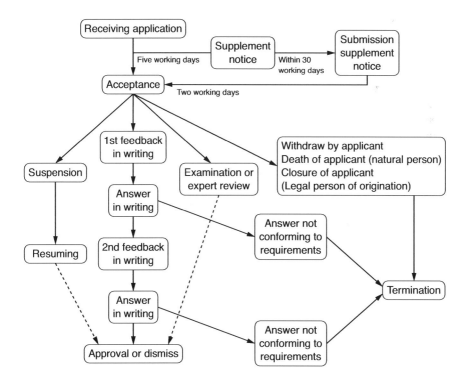

Figure 5.1 Flow chart of the administrative permission approval (source: CSRC[75]).

boosting financial innovation and market development is another central issue. There should be no contradiction between enhancing regulation and bringing incentives to the securities market. Enhancing the regulatory regime should not simply become an excuse for enlarging its power.[76]

Maintaining market confidence

Experiences obtained from other jurisdictions have demonstrated that market confidence is crucially important for the financial order, and the whole country's economy. For instance, the Financial Services and Markets Act 2000 clearly stated the importance of this issue.[77] However, it should be noted that this function should be better addressed in Mainland China.

It must be accepted that compared with previously, the maintenance of market confidence is more complex today; in particular, after the global financial crisis, weak regulatory regimes have been questioned again and again. It should be admitted that, in a transitional economy, the financial regulators have been expected to perform more functions than in the developed countries. This is reflected in the following: the larger demand for complete regulation; the more important external rules and ratios; the greater need for effective monitoring and supervision.[78] This is because, in developing and transitional countries, regulation may be at a more fundamental level and hence in need of improvement. However, it should be borne in mind that, in some developed countries, the financial services sector is much larger (i.e. there are many more institutions), for instance the US, UK, Hong Kong. Therefore, many more monitoring institutions may also mean a greater need for monitoring and supervision. The main differences are the financial regulators in developing countries put the improvement of legal frameworks at a prime, while those in the developed countries pay more heed to the efficiency issue.

Besides this, the financial regulators may be expected to undertake the task of maintaining market confidence, in particular, when market performance itself cannot give investors confidence. In this context, as stated in a previous paragraph, the regulator is required to perform an enhanced function in this aspect. The CSRC, as the securities regulator of a new and emerging market, may pay more heed to investor confidence, in order to facilitate the healthy growth of the Chinese securities market.

Keeping up with the latest situation

In 2008, following the decline of the Chinese securities market, the CSRC held a press conference. The conference focused on market performance, reducing the non-tradable shares, improving the relationship between market supply and demand, increasing listed company repurchase and combating securities crime.[79] According to the conference, the information disclosure regime is facing new challenges. The next step for the CSRC would be to target the following aspects: insider dealing, in particular using information relating to takeovers and mergers;

market manipulation, in particular fabricating and disseminating false information in order to manipulate the stock market; breach of trust, especially embezzling public funds by majority shareholders, actual controllers and board directors; securities fraud, in particular use of the internet to operate illegal securities consultant and investment businesses.

The CSRC enhanced the work in combating securities crime. Recent cases illustrated this; in particular, when dealing with the government officials and executives involved in insider dealing case. In 2011, Qihong Li, the former mayor of the Zhongshan City, Guangzhou was sentenced to 11 years in jail after being convicted of insider trading, disclosing private information and taking bribes. Moreover, from 2005 to the end of August 2012, the relevant department in CSRC primarily investigated 458 cases concerning insider dealing, filed 219 insider dealing cases, delivered to the public security department 58 insider dealing cases.[80] From 2007 to the end of the year 2011, there were 22 cases concluded concerning insider dealing in China (one case in 2007, one case in 2008, four cases in 2009, five cases in 2010, 11 cases in 2011).[81]

It is not difficult to see that new types of lawbreaking behaviour and securities crime will emerge from time to time. Therefore, as a regulator, the CSRC's ability to address these new challenges is very important. Adjustment and amendment shall be conducted in a timely manner. One more issue to be considered is that the standard starting point for prosecution of securities crimes shall be adjusted according to the latest circumstances. Currently, the starting point has been questioned as lower than is actually happening in the securities market. However, the starting point must be consistent with other economic crimes.[82] Therefore, the law enforcement agencies and CSRC shall establish a suitable standard for the Chinese market.

Completing the database

The ability to monitor ongoing illegal transactions is one of the central concerns for the CSRC. Compared with other jurisdictions, real time adjustments need to be improved in Mainland China. From this point of view, developing an advanced online monitoring system would be an efficient approach to this problem.

Moreover, inter-agency and inter-market information sharing can be further strengthened. The prevention and control of securities crimes should start from an early stage. It is becoming increasingly difficult for any single regulator to function on its own. The Chinese financial regulators must establish a comprehensive database for better supervision. On the other hand, preventing and controlling illicit securities behaviour is a systemic project. It is not enough to just rely on the particular power of some regulators. It needs wide cooperation from the whole of society.

During the research fieldwork, it was interesting for the author to notice that the library of the University of Hong Kong holds a collection of listed company papers. These documents included the issue of new shares, mergers and takeovers which were released by Hong Kong listed companies. The papers are available in either print or electronic formats since the Stock Exchange of Hong Kong began to provide company documents in CD-ROMs in 1997. Also, the 'Listed Companies: Balance Sheet Data 1968–1988' is worth examination.[83]

Another database example is Disclosure(R) Online Database – US Public Company Profiles.[84] It contains business and financial information extracted from annual and periodic reports filed with the Securities and Exchange Commission (SEC) for over 10,000 publicly owned companies. These companies are listed on the US Stock Exchange, New York Stock Exchange and Over the Counter stocks. Collected information can be used for analysing a company's financial strengths and weaknesses or company trends and future directions.

Although these two examples are primarily for academic or business research, it is reflected in mature markets that the database information issue has been placed in an important position. There are now similar business databases developed for commercial usage in China. The financial regulators in China may look at the international best practices to develop new monitoring methods for information disclosure, based on a cooperative approach. In fact, this issue has been raised already.[85] Also, the People's Bank of China raised this issue in the 10th China Financial Development Forum.[86] The financial regulators may quicken their steps in order to achieve better results.

The comparative studies

As with other sectors, Chinese legal reform has come an 'extraordinary distance – further than anyone could have foreseen',[87] and has demonstrated great achievements. The unique approach, which combines domestic need and international experiences, has played an important role. To establish a stable and sound securities market, the experiences obtained from other mature markets are helpful. The roles of financial regulators are similar in a broad sense; however, the working procedures and styles may be different. In this part, the UK and Hong Kong aspects will be introduced.

The UK perspective

The current securities regulatory regime in the UK has evolved in April 2013. The Financial Conduct Authority (FCA) and Prudential Regulatory Authority (PRA) began supervising the market. To evaluate the working process of this new regime may need a longer observation time, since the formal establishment of the FCA and PRA was on 1 April 2013. Therefore, beside the current structure, the FSA regime is being examined in this part.

FSA regime

Before April 2013, as an independent government body, the Financial Services Authority (FSA) had been endowed with four statutory objectives by the

Financial Services and Markets Act 2000 (hereafter the FSMA 2000): market confidence, maintaining confidence in the financial system; public awareness, promoting public understanding of the financial system; consumer protection, securing the appropriate degree of protection for consumers; reduction of financial crime, reducing the extent to which it is possible for a business to be used for a purpose connected with financial crime.[88]

The FSA set out its aims under three broad headings, which include: promoting efficient orderly and fair markets, helping retail consumers achieve a fair deal, and improving business capability and effectiveness.[89] Furthermore, according to the law, based on the above aims and regulatory objectives, the general function of the FSA were: making rules under the FSMA 2000; preparing and issuing codes under the Act; giving of general guidance; determining the general policy and principles by reference to which it performs particular functions.[90]

In order to regulate the financial market, besides the rule-making power, the FSA also has power to authorize, regulate, investigate and discipline authorized persons. For instance, it can require information and conduct investigations.[91] Furthermore, the FSA could impose disciplinary punishments, public censure and financial penalties[92] and bring criminal prosecutions for crimes against the securities markets (e.g. insider dealing, market manipulation, engaging in financial services business without authorization) as well as money laundering.[93] The authority of a financial regulator largely depends on its disciplinary approaches on monitoring and supervising financial transactions. The necessity of disciplinary measures has been illustrated from past experiences, without these measures, a financial regulator can be seen as 'the tiger without teeth'.

Moreover, the FSA introduced the Advanced Risk-Responsive Operating Framework (ARROW), which has been enhanced into ARROW II in 2006.[94] The FSA used the term 'risk' in the sense: 'the risk that the objectives set out in the legislation will not be met'.[95] Within ARROW II, there were two basic approaches that can be used to supervise firms: the ARROW Firms approach – used when assessing risks in individual firms ('vertical' supervision); and the ARROW Themes approach – used when assessing cross-cutting risks (those involving several firms or relating to the market as a whole ('horizontal' work), one or a mixture of the two approaches will be used to deal with risks in the most efficient way. Moreover, according to the regulatory aims and objectives, the FSA structured the risk assessment based on two factors: the impact on the FSA's objectives if the particular risk actually materialized, and the probability that the particular risk will materialize. Thus, the impact and probability scores of a firm (or group of firms) help to determine the nature of the risk. Finally, the score will be matched with a particular risk category. With these assessments, the FSA will decide the regulatory relationship with the firm, which can best address potential problems.

Another issue to be noted is that promoting the best practice in the UK has been given an important position by the financial regulators. They continue to search for the best approaches and apply these approaches to the financial industry. In 2007, the FSA published Good and Poor Practices in Key Features Documents.[96] In this paper, the FSA disclosed that only around 15 per cent of the sample KFDs met both COBS requirements and their view of the standard necessary to meet both Principle 7 and TCF Outcome 3.[97] Moreover, the paper listed samples of good and poor practices respectively. The good practice contained a clear and simple statement to the effect that the investments are stock market based, the implications of which most customers would understand.[98] Furthermore, the good practice also contained a specific risk statement relating to different financial products.[99]

In contrast, the important section in poor practice was set out in a way that was unhelpful to customers, for example: some entries are not risks, but matters of fact or policy conditions (e.g. 'If you cash in your bond within five years of making an investment, you will be subject to an early withdrawal charge.'); long lists of risk factors which read like disclaimers and may make it difficult for customers to distinguish between these and more general policy conditions; one KFD disclaimed responsibility for postal delays.[100]

Another very helpful approach was that the FSA also suggested how to improve these poor practices. For instance:

> Your investments, and any return from them, are only as secure as the selected range of assets purchased by the funds you choose. Your investments are only at risk if any of these financial instruments fail to meet their obligations.
>
> (FSA: Consumers, if they understand this, will want to know the risk of the instruments failing to meet their obligations.)

> If large numbers of Plans are encashed at the same time, the funds may incur costs in selling assets prior to their selected maturity date to meet these encashments, and these costs may cause a fall in unit price and therefore the return on your Plan. The named Firm may alternatively defer encashments for up to three months if it considers that this would be more beneficial to Planholders generally. This would only happen in very exceptional circumstances.
>
> (FSA: As this is an exceptional risk it may be more appropriate to show the three month condition under a heading such as 'Can I take my money out?')[101]

Finally, the FSA used a clear-cut approach to illustrate good and poor practices. Figure 5.2 is an example of the practice of using language. Thus, the examples laid out, together with the suggestions from the FSA, this method can provide the financial institutions with a straightforward way to improve the quality of their services. Financial information is often published with complex contents which require professional knowledge to understand. Therefore, for the general investors, plain and simple language is essentially helpful.

Poor practice	Good practice
Can I change my mind?	**Can I change my mind?**
If you change your mind you have a legal right to cancel your contract. When we accept your application we'll send you a Cancellation Notice that confirms the actual steps that must be taken in order to cancel the contract. The Cancellation Notice confirms that you have a 30 day period to consider if you want to change your mind. This 30 day period starts from the date you receive the Policy Provisions and Policy Schedule (Terms and conditions of the bond). If you decide to cancel, during this period, you should send your cancellation instruction to the address provided in the Cancellation Notice. We'll then return any payments you have made. If you cancel during the 30 day period, you may get back less than you paid in. This is because we may deduct from the amount you get back any fall in the investment value during this period.	After you've invested, you'll receive a notice telling you of your right to change your mind and how to cancel. You'll then have 30 days to cancel your investment. If you decide to cancel, we'll give you your money back. If, however, in the meantime the value of the underlying investment has fallen, you may not get back the full amount you paid in.
Please ensure that you include your bond number in any correspondence with us. At the end of the 30 day period you will be bound by the terms and conditions of the bond and any money received by Firm Name will not be refundable.	*The example above tells consumers all they need to know at this stage in the buying process without any sense of 'dumbing down' or of appearing patronizing.* *The example on the left illustrates:*
Where believe we may be unable to encash assets readily, note that we may defer the purchase of certain investments until after the 30 day cancellation notice period.	*· what can happen if the KFD's objective is forgotten; and* *· how a bureaucratic style can obscure simple messages.*

Figure 5.2 Examples of poor and good practice (source: FSA[102]).

Current regime

Currently, the 'twin peaks' financial regulatory structure is operating in the UK. The Financial Services Act 2012 created two new bodies, the FCA and PRA, which have replaced the FSA. Beside them, the other bodies involved in the financial regulatory regime are the Bank of England (BOE), The Financial Policy Committee (FPC) and Her Majesty's Treasury (the Treasury).

Funded by the financial services firms regulated, the FCA is operationally independent of Government, accountable to the Treasury and Parliament. The aim of the FCA is to protect consumers, ensure the financial industry remains stable and promote healthy competition between financial services providers.[103] Furthermore, the FCA has been endowed with rule-making, investigative and enforcement powers, in order to regulate the financial services industry.[104]

Having formally taken up the responsibility in April 2013, the FCA's objectives for the period of 2013/2014 are to secure an appropriate degree of protection for consumers; to protect and enhance the integrity of the UK financial system; to promote effective competition in the interests of consumers.[105] As for the regulatory method, the FCA will take a risk-based, proportionate approach to supervision, recognizing the diversity among firms and markets, and focus on the bigger issues, either in individual firms or within and across sectors.[106] Furthermore, the FCA has designed a Firm Systematic Framework (FSF) to focus the supervision on the key conduct risks in firms.[107]

As the result of financial regulatory reform, the PRA has been established under the BOE, is currently responsible for the prudential regulation and supervision of banks, building societies, credit unions, insurers and major investment firms. It aims to promote the safety and soundness of these firms, seeking to minimize the adverse effects that they can have on the stability of the UK financial system; and contribute to ensuring that insurance policyholders are appropriately protected.[108]

As prudential regulator, the PRA has two statutory objectives: to promote the safety and soundness of the firms it regulates, and particularly for insurers, to contribute to the securing of an appropriate degree of protection for the policyholders.[109] Furthermore, the PRA takes a judgement-based, forward-looking and focused regulatory approach, in order to fulfil its objectives.[110]

As mentioned earlier, this current regulatory approach is a result of the reform after the recent global financial crisis. Based on the lessons learnt, the new UK regime should be able to address the regulatory problems likely to be encountered.

The Hong Kong perspective

In Hong Kong, Securities and Futures Ordinance and its subsidiary legislation endowed the Securities and Futures Commission with a broad range of investigative, remedial and disciplinary powers.[111] Inside the regulatory system of the SFC, there are some important points of principles of regulation that need to be examined. Besides firmness and fairness, the SFC also focuses on the following principles: consistency, which tries to ensure that SFC is consistent in its decisions or actions whilst having regard to the specific circumstances of each case; proportionality, which tries to ensure that decisions or actions are proportionate, or balanced; negotiate and not dictate, which tries to act in open dialogue and negotiation.[112]

Similar to other financial regulators, the SFC has a range of regulatory tools, policy projects and compensation schemes. In general, these tools are diagnostic, monitoring, preventative or remedial in nature. Diagnostic tools, aim to identify and assess risks; monitoring tools, aim to monitor and track identified risks; preventative tools, aim to prevent and limit risks; remedial tools, aim to respond to risks that have arisen: for instance, the investor compensation scheme is an example of a remedial tool used as a response when an intermediary fails and causes loss to investors.[113]

Together, these tools have facilitated the fulfilment of the function of the SFC. A financial regulator must adopt multiple measures to ensure effective supervision. Therefore, suitable regulatory powers shall be given to the regulators. In order to achieve its regulatory aims, the SFC has the following powers: to set licensing standards to ensure the practitioners are fit and proper; approve licences and maintain a public register of licensees; issue codes and guidelines to inform the industry of its expected standard of conduct; monitor licensees, financial soundness and compliance with ordinance, codes, guidelines, rules and regulations; handle misconduct complaints against licensees; and investigate and take action against misconduct.[114]

Moreover, among others, the SFC takes a risk-based approach to regulating the market. The SFC conducted 252 risk-based inspections of licensed corporations at their premises during 2011 to 2012.[115] In terms of enforcement, the SFC successfully prosecuted 37 entities (25 persons and 12 corporations), two of whom were convicted of market manipulation and one was convicted of insider dealing; six company directors were disqualified for failing to perform their duties properly.[116] In the aspect of information disclosure, the Court of First Instance gave orders to disqualify Li Xinggui, Zheng Yingsheng and Zhou Li Yang, former executive directors of Pearl Oriental Innovation Ltd, from being directors or being involved in the management of any corporation, without the leave of the court, for one year, based on the failure of disclosing material information to shareholders.[117]

Last but not least, the SFC also promotes the best practices to the securities industry. As for the information disclosure, taking the post sale continuing obligations as an example, it has been required by the SFC that the issuer of unlisted structured investment products shall make available to investors, in a timely manner, any information, notice or document that it is required to provide to them with pursuant to the law or regulations; and in addition to provision of information through intermediaries, issuers should consider also making information available by means of their own websites as a matter of best practice.[118] In fact, the concept of best practice has been widely adopted in Hong Kong. The requirement and recommendation from the SFC may facilitate financial institutions in Hong Kong to reach a high level of the best international practices of accounting, auditing, disclosure and governance.

Regulatory philosophy

It can be seen from the comparative studies that the basic regulatory rules and approaches among the three jurisdictions are quite similar. However, the 'regulatory philosophy' is different.

Partnership model

The relationship between regulator and regulated is a sensitive topic. Historically, the two parties are seen as opposed to each other in Mainland China.

Obviously, the regulatory body should be firm and strict enough in order to fulfil its supervisory function; especially in a developing market. By contrast, it can be seen from some mature markets that the relationship between regulator and regulated tends more to emphasize a 'partnership' element. Although this approach has been questioned during and after the financial crisis, for the lack of strict regulation; the partnership approach may facilitate a cooperative attitude from the regulated firms as well. The SFC pointed out that, 'A robust and vibrant market can be achieved through relationships built upon trust and cooperation among regulators, intermediaries and investors'.[119]

To be a modern financial regulator, it is difficult to achieve the regulatory objectives without cooperation from the financial industry. A mutual benefit culture should be enhanced in the supervisory framework in Mainland China. Regulation, supervision and monitoring should not be merely against the financial industry. Supposing that there is a partnership in the future between the CSRC and listed companies besides the general regulatory relationship, the regulatory situation may be smoother. Although the financial crisis suggested that the regulatory regime should be enhanced immediately, this philosophy should not be left aside. Strict financial regulation should aim to create an effective supervisory regime, but not necessarily result in confrontation.

Risk-based approach

Risk-based approach supervision is an important regulatory method in other jurisdictions with mature securities markets. From the earlier analysis, it can be seen that although the understanding of the term of risk-based approaches is slightly different between the UK and Hong Kong, the basic functions are similar. This approach may be enhanced in Mainland China. When regulatory responses are based on the assessment of different factors, it can be imagined that these responses will be more focused, efficient and cost effective. This is important for the CSRC, particularly under current circumstances, which means in a developing stage. Taking the UK's experience as an example, the FCA will carry out a risk-based, proportionate approach to supervision. A Firm Systematic Framework (FSF), which focuses the supervision on the key conduct risks in firms, is designed. Following this approach, the financial regulator can organize recourses so as to keep a high level of supervision. Targeting the individual firm's potential problems could save time and economic costs.

Financial crises always lead to the proposal of regulatory reform. Although the Chinese financial system has not been affected deeply, the efficiency and effectiveness of the supervisory system still needs to be improved. With the development and reform of the market, increasing complexity also requires regular review and upgrading of the supervisory and monitoring system. The CSRC has already started the risk-based approach, for instance, the supervising and regulating of securities companies.[120] Learning from other jurisdictions may facilitate the CSRC to improve its regulatory capabilities.

Promoting best practice

Promoting best practice has been placed in an important position by the financial regulators in both the UK and Hong Kong. As stated in an earlier section, this approach is quite straightforward. In regard to information disclosure, to set up a series of complex rules is not the final aim. Eventually, that the relevant information can be understood by every party in a clear, fair and accurate manner is the most important task. To maintain integrity and to function fairly and efficiently, the market needs high quality information, timely disclosures and efficient access to this information. Investors need this information to make investment decisions and to trade. When relevant information is properly disclosed in a clear and simple fashion, it will facilitate the reaching of the above aim.

As discussed earlier, some of the Chinese investors, in particular the retail investors, are in a sense lacking adequate knowledge of financial information; thus, this approach may be more suitable for Mainland China. Compared with other jurisdictions, the CSRC may need to develop this regulatory approach, promoting best practice. From this point of view, it may be argued that the approach of the CSRC could become more 'positive' in the future. Moreover, detailed rules and regulations take time to draft and implement. In contrast, to promote good or best practice is less time consuming and cost effective and can be better addressed to specific issues.

Summary

'It is never an easy job to be a regulator in China, and even more difficult to be a good regulator', stated Mingkang Liu, the former Chairman of banking regulation in China.[121] It is a similar case for the securities regulator in Mainland China. The financial crisis also called attention to the enhancement of the regulatory regime in the financial industry. Facilitating innovation and competition is one of the required tasks for the financial regulators. However, to achieve a balance between financial innovation and supervision is also crucially important.

Traditionally, the supervisory bodies in emerging markets prefer a strict regulatory framework. But it should be noted that an over regulated style may constrain the development of capital markets. It may also create some 'side effects', for instance, abusing regulatory power, increasing regulatory cost and reducing market efficiency. A well balanced regulatory value is needed.

The CSRC, as can be seen from the analysis above, has been endowed with various regulatory powers and tools, similar to other jurisdictions. It has placed emphasis on the regulatory and supervisory regime for the securities market and information disclosure. On the other hand, there are some regulatory actions that need to be improved for the CSRC. Suggestions have been made in the early part of this chapter. Also, the regulatory philosophy of the CSRC may be adjusted according to the updated situation. From this point of view, to promote a rational attitude for every financial regulator is very important.

The global financial crisis has driven international awareness to focus on enhancing the regulatory and supervisory regime. Arguments and suggestions are arising from different countries, and in fact, for the financial regulators in Mainland China, this is a unique period to experience, to practice and to develop. It may be concluded in the Chinese way that some opportunities are coming out of the crisis.

Notes

1 The FSA has now become to two regulatory authorities, the FCA and Prudential Regulatory Authority (PRA). The materials cited in this chapter are mainly based on the FSA regime, because the FCA and PRA were only formally established on 1 April 2013. However, the current regime will also be examined.

2 Chang Liu, Nan Zhou, Na Wang, Wenjuan Bao (18 August 2007), '80 Old Photos Showing the Storms in Chinese Securities Market (80zhang Laozhaopian Zaixian Xinzhongguo Zhengquan Fengyun)', *Guangzhou Daily (Guangzhou Ribao)*, http://gzdaily.dayoo.com/html/2007-08/18/content_29455.htm, last accessed: 9 January 2013. The 'Shenzhen 8.10 event' is one of the important events in the history of the Chinese capital market. In 1992, after receiving the news of the selling of new stocks subscription form (Xingu Rengou Chouqian Biao), about 1,200,000 people rushed to Shenzhen City from July. From 7 August, investors were waiting on the street. The forms had been sold out within three hours on 9 August 1992. However, without sufficient purchasing chances, some of the people were unsatisfied and chaos happened.

3 Yan Nan (27 September 2009), 'In front of the Stage and behind of the Scene – the Birth of the CSRC (Zhengjianhui Dansheng de Taiqian Muhou)', *China Economic Weekly (Zhongguo Jingji Zhoukan)*, www.ceweekly.cn/Html/magazine/200992741 671604345.html, last accessed: 9 January 2010. The article was based on the interview of Daojiu Zhou, former chairman of the CSRC.

4 See CSRC website, www.csrc.gov.cn/, last accessed: 6 January 2013.

5 According to the scheme of institutional reforming of the State Council, the SCSC was dissolved in 1998. The CSRC is the central national securities regulator. See PBC website, www.pbc.gov.cn/jinrongyexiangguan/zhengquanyexiangguan/zheng-quanyejianguan.asp, last accessed: 9 January 2010.

6 Securities Law, Article 1.

7 See CSRC website, www.csrc.gov.cn/n575458/index.html, last accessed: 24 August 2009.

8 Securities Law, Article 178.

9 Ibid., Article 179.

10 See CSRC website, www.csrc.gov.cn/pub/csrc_en/about/organ/, last accessed: 6 May 2013.

11 Securities Law Article 180.

12 Promulgation date: 19 November 1999, revised: 4 February 2002, revised: 14 January 2008.

13 CSRC, promulgation date: 25 July 2008, effective date: 1 September 2008.

14 Ibid., Article 4.

15 In China, A share is denominated in Chinese currency, the RMB. B share refers to a foreign invested share issued domestically by Chinese companies. B share is denominated in RMB but traded in foreign currencies.

16 Wai Ho Yeung (2009), 'Non-tradable Share Reform in China: A Review of Progress', *The Company Lawyer*, 30(11), p. 340–346.

17 Promulgation date: 23 August 2005, effective date: 23 August 2005, Article 2.

18 CSRC (August 2008), 'Q&A by CSRC Spokesman on Hot Issue', www.csrc.gov.cn/n575458/n4001948/n4002030/10801369.html, last accessed: 24 August 2012.

19 Generally, the NTS are tradable depending on lock up rules. Shareholders owning NTS less than 5 per cent of a company's total share capital is called: 'small NTS (Xiaofei)', greater than 5 per cent is called 'large NTS (Dafei)'. When the NTS can be transferred, if without a steady control, may lead to the price fluctuations in securities market.

20 Guiding Opinions on the Listed Companies' Transfer of Original Shares Released from Trading Restrictions, CSRC [2008] No. 15, promulgation date: 20 April 2008, effective date: 20 April 2008.

21 Ibid., Article 2.

22 Ibid., Article 3.

23 Ibid., Article 5.

24 Ibid., Article 8.

25 SSE (24 April 2008), Guidance on the Block Trading of Stock Trading without Sales Limit, www.sse.com.cn/ps/zhs/sjs/hotspot/hotspot20080424b.html and SZSE (8 May 2008), 'Taking Multi-measures, the SZSE Controls the Illegal Shares Reducing', www.szse.cn/main/aboutus/bsyw/2008050912487.shtml, last accessed: 24 August 2012.

26 CSDCC, China Securities Registration and Settlement Statistical Yearbook (2008). CSDCC is China's central securities depository and clearing institution. CSDCC is under the supervision of CSRC, and provides centralized registration, depository and clearing services for securities transaction. See www.sipf.com.cn/en/chinassecuritiesmarketoverview/organisations/index.shtml#a, last accessed: 20 November 2012.

27 CSDCC, China Securities Registration and Settlement Statistical Yearbook (2008), p. 105.

28 CSRC, www.csrc.gov.cn/pub/csrc_en/about/organ/FunctionalDepartments/200811/t20081121_68659.htm, last accessed: 30 May 2013. The main functions are: to set out the laws, regulations and rules for securities and futures enforcement; handling clues to various violations; to organize informal investigations; to put on records and rescind cases; to organize investigation and punishment of important cases; to coordinate, guide and supervise cases investigation and relevant work; to recheck cases investigation reports; to disclose the details of cases; to coordinate the handling of cross-country cases; to organize industry anti-money laundering; to handle compulsive procedures such as border control for enforcement, attachment and freezing; to organize and coordinate the execution of administrative sanction; to organize evaluation and rewarding for enforcement; to conduct cases statistics and training.

29 CSRC, www.csrc.gov.cn/n575458/n776436/n805025/n825092/index.html, last accessed: 24 August 2012.

30 Hongming Cheng (2008), Insider Trading in China: the Case for the Chinese Securities Regulatory Commission, *Journal of Financial Crime*, 2008, 15(2), p. 165–178.

31 CSRC (23 April 2001), [2001] No. 7. The CSRC investigated the Guangzhou Xinsheng Investment Consultant Co., Ltd, Guangzhou Zhongbai Investment Consultant Co., Ltd, Guangzhou Baiyuan Investment Consultant Co., Ltd and Guangzhou Jinyi Investment Consultant Co., Ltd, and found the four companies illegally manipulated the stock of Yi'an Technology Co., Ltd from 1998 to 2001.

32 Jian Xu (2007), 'The Significant Issues in the Revising of Chinese Securities Law (Woguo Zhengquanfa Xiugai de Ruogan Zhongda Wenti)', in *The Legal Frontier of the Chinese Capital Market (Zhongguo Ziben Shichang Qianyan)*, ed. Feng Guo, Beijing: China Intellectual Property Publishing House, p. 199. Jian Xu was the one of the leading draftsmen of the Securities Law, he looked back to the revising procedure of the Securities Law and stated that, without effective power, the CSRC could not perform its function duly and promptly; it occurred that, in some significant cases, when the CSRC investigated the case, the companies had closed up, the

relevant personnel had left, and the bank account had been closed. After consulting foreign experts, the CSRC has been endowed with the necessary investigating power, for instance, freezing and sealing up bank accounts; furthermore, relevant limitations on these powers had been introduced, for example, the signature of the person in charge in CSRC and its regional office was required.

33 Measures of Freezing and Sealing up Account of the CSRC, promulgated date: 30 December 2005, effective date: 1 January 2006, revised date: 23 May 2011, effective date: 1 October 2011.
34 Ibid., Article 4.
35 Ibid., Article 6.
36 CSRC (March 2008), 'CSRC is Investigating ST Weida's Four Lawbreaking Behaviours (Zhengjianhui Li'an Checha STWeida Sizong Zui)', www.csrc.gov.cn/n575458/n870654/n4243666/10104653.html, last accessed: 24 August 2009.
37 Ibid.
38 Ibid.
39 CSRC (20 December 2012), 'The Detective Ability for the Securities Crime has been Enhanced'.
40 Source: CSRC.
41 Ibid.
42 Securities Law, Article 186: Where the CSRC finds any securities irregularity involved in a suspected crime when performing its functions and duties according to law, it shall transfer the case to the judicial organ for handling.
43 CSRC (August 2008), 'Q&A by CSRC Spokesman on Hot Issue', www.csrc.gov.cn/n575458/n4001948/n4002030/10801369.html, last accessed: 24 August 2009.
44 Robert Lewis, 'Shareholders in Action – Causes of Action are Many but the Action are Few', *Intentional Financial Law Review*, 53 2007, p. 52. The author argued that if the CSRC and other regulatory authorities are not vigilant or if (as has been the case in some cases) the CSRC simply grants listed companies a form of corporate amnesty, shareholder remedies are more limited.
45 Interview No. 1.
46 Interview No. 2.
47 Interview No. 3.
48 Robert Lewis (2007), 'Shareholders in Action – Causes of Action are Many but the Actions are Few', *International Financial Law Review*. 53, p. 53.
49 Ibid.
50 Further details can be found in Chapter 6.
51 CSRC (May 2007), Notice of the China Securities Regulatory Commission on the Compliance of Business Operations by the Securities Companies According to Law and the Relevant Work of Further Strengthening the Education of Investors.
52 For an explanation of GEB and ChiNext, see Chapter 2.
53 CSRC (22 August 2009), 'CSRC News Spokesman Answers Reporters' Questions on Promulgating the "Interim Provisions on Appropriate Management of Investors on the Growth Enterprise Board Market (Draft for Comment)" and Relevant Supporting Documents', www.csrc.gov.cn/pub/csrc_en/newsfacts/release/200908/t20090822_121166.htm, last accessed: 9 January 2010.
54 Interim Measures on Administration of Initial Public Offerings and Listings on the Growth Enterprise Board, promulgation date: 31 March 2009, effective date: 1 May 2009.
55 Ibid., Article 7.
56 Ibid., Article 40.
57 Interim Provisions on the Eligibility Management of Investors in the Growth Enterprise Market, promulgation date: 30 June 2009, effective date: 15 July 2009, Article 6.
58 Xia Li (7 November 2009), 'Gang Yao: The Information Disclosure Rules for the

GEB will be Adjusted and Complemented (Yao Gang: Chuangyeban Xinxi Pilu Guize jiang Jinxing Tiaozheng he Buchong)', *Financial News (Jinrong Shibao)*, www.financialnews.com.cn/zq/txt/2009–11/07/content_240089.htm, last accessed: 8 January 2010. Gang Yao stated that the stability of the GEB is relatively weak and the price of securities will be easy to fluctuate; information shall be authentic, accurate and integrate, and promptly, therefore, the supervision of information disclosure must be enhanced.

59 Technical Committee of the IOSCO (March 2007): Final Report of International Disclosure Principles for Cross-border Offerings and Listings of Debt Securities by Foreign Issuers.
60 Ibid., p. 1.
61 Ibid., Part XIII (Financial Information), p. 25.
62 CSRC, www.csrc.gov.cn/pub/newsite/gjb/jghz/201303/t20130314_222203.htm, last accessed: 24 May 2013.
63 Fulin Shang: Preface to 'Report on China's Capital Market Development', www.csrc.gov.cn/n575458/n4001948/n4002030/10128373.html, last accessed: 24 August 2009.
64 Ibid.
65 CSRC (2008), 'The Challenges Facing China's Capital Markets', in China Capital Markets Development Report, Beijing: China Financial Publishing House, p. 277.
66 CSRC (2008), 'The Challenges Facing China's Capital Markets', in China Capital Markets Development Report, Beijing: China Financial Publishing House, p. 277.
67 CSRC (2008), China Capital Markets Development Report, Beijing: China Financial Publishing House.
68 For details of the SAC, see Chapter 3.
69 See China Capital Markets Development Report, Chapter 4.
70 Zhongle Zhan, Fengying Li (April 2004), 'Securities Supervision and Judicial Review (in China)', *13 Pacific Rim Law and Policy Journal 329*, translated by Inseon Paik, p. 5.
71 Ibid.
72 See Chapter 6.
73 Interview No. 4.
74 See CSRC website, www.csrc.gov.cn, last accessed: 9 January 2010.
75 CSRC, www.csrc.gov.cn/pub/zjhpublic/G00306205/201001/P020100105691792506 860.doc, last accessed: 7 January 2013.
76 Interview No. 5.
77 Details can be found in the later part of this chapter.
78 Charles Goodhart, Philipp Hartmann, David Llewellyn, Liliana Rojas-Suarez, Steven Weisbrod (1998), Financial Regulation: Why, how and where now? Routledge: London and New York, p. 104.
79 CSRC (August 2008), 'Q&A by CSRC Spokesman on Hot Issues', www.csrc.gov.cn/n575458/n575667/n818795/10768746.html, last accessed: 25 August 2012.
80 According to the CSRC Insider Dealing Warning and Education Exhibition.
81 Ibid.
82 Interview No. 6.
83 Elim Chan, George W.L. Hui, Wai-kee Lau, working paper.
84 See http://w3.nexis.com/sources/scripts/info.pl?3723, last accessed: 25 August 2009.
85 See CSRC, 'Why the Need to Establish an Information Sharing System between Financial Regulators', http://hubei.csrc.gov.cn/n575458/n870586/n1335340/n82001 34/10642077.html, last accessed: 25 August 2009.
86 Yan Miao (3 September 2009), 'Central Bank: Maintaining Financial Stabilities shall Establish the Unified Supervisory Information Platform (Yanghang: Weihu Jinrong Wending ying Jianli Tongyi Jianguan Xinxi Pingtai)', www.cnstock.com/08index/2009–09/02/content_4555553.htm, last accessed: 8 January 2010.

87 Donald. C. Clarke, 'Legislating for a Market Economy in China', (2007) No. 191 *China Quarterly*, p. 567–585.
88 Date of Royal Assent: 14 June 2000, Section 3,4,5,6.
89 FSA, www.fsa.gov.uk/Pages/About/Aims/index.shtml, last accessed: 25 August 2009.
90 FSMA, Section 2.
91 Ibid., Part XI.
92 Ibid., Part XIV, and also, for market abuse, Part VIII.
93 Ibid. Sections 401 and 402.
94 The contents in this paragraph were summarized from: FSA (November 2006), The FSA's Risk-Based Approach – A Guide for Non-executive Directors.
95 FSA (December 2000), Building the New Regulator: Progress Report 1, p. 4, www.fsa.gov.uk/pubs/policy/bnr_progress1.pdf, last accessed: 25 August 2009.
96 FSA (September 2007), Good and Poor Practices in Key Features Documents, www.fsa.gov.uk/pubs/other/key_features.pdf, last accessed: 25 August 2009. The FSA reviewed 200 samples of the Key Features Documents (KFDs) according to the following legal and practical requirements: FSA Principle 7, a firm must pay due regard to the information needs of its clients, and communicate information to them in a way that is clear, fair and not misleading; FSA Conduct of Business Sourcebook (COBS) rules; FSA Treating Customers Fairly (TCF) Outcome 3, consumers are provided with clear information and are kept appropriately informed before, during and after the point of sale, and accept good practice for clear design and language. Also, all Key Features Documents must include key headings outlining the product, its aims, the investor's commitment, risks, general questions and answers (Q&As) and charges. See p. 5–6.
97 Ibid., p. 6.
98 Ibid., p. 24. For instance: 'the value of your investment can go up and down and you may get back less than you invested; what you get back will depend on investment performance, nothing is guaranteed, past performance is no guarantee of future performance; when you cash in your plan you may get back less than you invested because your investments grew less than illustrated or you took money out; our charges may increase; inflation will reduce what you could buy in the future; tax rules could change; if you use your right to cancel your Collective Investment Plan within the first 30 days, and the value of your investment has fallen by the time we receive your instructions at our administration unit, the amount you get will be less than the amount you have paid in.'
99 Ibid., p. 25. Taking the risks that apply to a Corporate Bond Fund as a reference:

> changes in interest rates and inflation could affect the value of the investments that make up the Corporate Bond Fund; the value of the income payable can go up and down and is not guaranteed; the fund focuses on income, so you should not expect the value of your investment to increase; the Corporate Bond Fund invests in loans to companies, if companies are not able to pay the interest they promised or repay the bonds they have issued, the value of the fund would go down; the value of these investments can go down as well as up because of market changes, but any changes in value are likely to be less marked than those of investments in shares.

100 Ibid., p. 23.
101 Ibid., p. 25.
102 Ibid., p. 19.
103 FCA website, www.fca.org.uk/about, last accessed: 20 May 2013.
104 Ibid.
105 FCA, FCA Business Plan 2013/14.
106 Ibid.

107 Ibid. FSF is forward-looking and focuses on highlighting the areas of greatest potential risk. Under FSF, the FCA will examine key conduct risks in a firm and identify the causes of those risks. This method will cover all types of firms, considering potential harm to consumers and the impact on market integrity.
108 Andrew Bailey (2012), The Prudential Regulation Authority.
109 Ibid.
110 Ibid.
111 The SFC is established by the Securities and Futures Commission Ordinance (SFCO). The SFCO and nine other securities and futures related ordinances were consolidated into the Securities and Futures Ordinance (SFO), which came into operation on 1 April 2003. See www.sfc.hk/sfc/html/EN/aboutsfc/objectives/objectives.html, last accessed: 25 August 2012.
112 SFC, www.sfc.hk/sfc/html/EN/legislation/regulatory/regulatory/vol. 1_ch2.html, last accessed: 25 August 2012.
113 Ibid. And, further information of the investor compensation scheme can be found in the Chapter 6.
114 SFC, www.sfc.hk/sfc/html/EN/aboutsfc/regulate/regulate.html, last accessed: 25 August 2012.
115 SFC, 2011–2012 Annual Report, p. 32.
116 Ibid., p. 40.
117 Ibid., p. 41.
118 Code on Unlisted Structured Investment Products, June 2010, Part III.
119 SFC, www.sfc.hk/web/EN/about-the-sfc/our-role/how-we-function/regulatory-philosophy.html, last accessed: 25 August 2012.
120 More details can be found in Chapters 3 and 6.
121 MingKang Liu (28 June 2009), 'Basic Rules Helped China Sidestep Bank Crisis', *Financial Times*.

6 Investor protection

Problems and progress

Introduction

Investors are the essential part of an active capital market. Without their contribution, a market cannot operate. Whether investors can obtain sufficient protection may affect the efficiency of a market. In this context, financial regulators place this issue in a vitally important position. The Chinese securities market, as an emerging and transitional market, needs to pay attention to this topic, and improvements to the regime are required. In the last two decades, some cases and scandals caused economic losses to investors, and had further negative social impacts.

The reasons that led to these social consequences were various. What are the processes and problems for the protection of investors in the Chinese securities market? In this chapter, the main aim is to examine the protection methods for investors; in particular when retail investors suffer losses arising from imperfect information disclosure. Starting from the unique structure of Chinese investors, the basic legal method for investor protection will be examined. Second, the Securities Investor Protection Fund will be analysed in detail. Moreover, the role of corporate governance and investor education will be illustrated.

The analysis of Chinese investors

Chinese investors are slightly different from those in mature markets and have certain unique characteristics. These characteristics are reflected by their compositional structure, trading behaviour and perception of the market. Under the current regime, Chinese investors include individual investors, institutional investors, Qualified Domestic Institutional Investors (QDIIs) and Qualified Foreign Institutional Investors (QFIIs).

From the table, it can be seen that although there is a significant increase in institutional investors, individuals still form the majority of investors in the Chinese securities market. The Chinese individual investors are more mature than before; however, there are still some aspects that need to be improved. Contradictory behaviour exists among retail investors. Disrespecting and ignoring the scientific nature of the capital market is still not rare. On one hand,

Table 6.1 Total number of accounts by the end of each year (2000–2011) (Unit: 10,000)

Year	Total	Individual (A share)	Institution (A share)	Individual (B share)	Institution (B share)
2000	5,904.64	5,851.76	25.66	25.73	1.49
2001	6,679.27	6,500.98	30.45	146.26	1.58
2002	6,823.09	6,638.31	30.83	152.37	1.58
2003	6,961.02	6,771.35	32.18	155.89	1.60
2004	7,106.11	6,912.65	33.22	158.55	1.69
2005	7,189.44	6,994.12	34.01	159.60	1.71
2006	7,482.11	7,281.29	36.26	162.67	1.89
2007	11,286.43	11,005.22	46.90	232.19	2.12
2008	12,363.89	12,074.93	48.61	238.02	2.33
2009	14,027.88	13,727.72	54.06	243.72	2.38
2010	15,454.02	15,146.04	58.02	247.44	2.52
2011	16,546.90	16,233.42	61.32	249.46	2.70

Source: China Securities Depository and Clearing Corporation Limited.[1]

suspicions exist in the securities market; on the other hand, these investors believe that the Chinese government will not allow the securities market to collapse. The market philosophy in trading behaviour of Chinese investors is still not mature enough. This situation has resulted in various problems; details will be discussed later in this chapter.

Institutional investors are necessary elements in a capital market. During the last two decades, institutional investors have experienced reforms: from domestic to international, and from international to domestic. The Qualified Domestic Institutional Investors (QDIIs) and Qualified Foreign Institutional Investors (QFIIs) are special systems in the Chinese securities market. The numbers of these specially qualified investors are still increasing.

QDIIs are domestic fund management institutions, securities companies or other securities business companies that have been approved by the CSRC to raise funds within the territory of the People's Republic of China and use part or all of the funds in a portfolio format to engage in overseas securities investment management.[2] At the end of the May 2013, there were 111 companies that had been approved, for instance, The Industrial and Commercial Bank of China Ltd (ICBC), The People's Insurance Company (Group) of China (PICC) and China Asset Management Company, Ltd.[3]

QFIIs are overseas fund management institutions, insurance companies, securities companies and other asset management institutions which have been approved by the CSRC to invest in China's securities market and granted investment quotas by State Administration of Foreign Exchange (hereafter SAFE).[4] At the end of May 2013, there were 202 QFIIs approved by the CSRC, for instance: UBS Limited (approved on 23 May 2003), Credit Suisse AG (approved on 14 October 2008) and Mitsubishi UFJ Securities Co., Ltd (approved on 29 December 2008).[5]

The basic structure of Chinese investors indicates that the market itself is not mature enough. Notably, individual investors are the major component.

Institutional investors are still expected to perform more important roles in the stability of the capital markets. Furthermore, the special components, QDIIs and QFIIs, are facing the situation that system supplies are not sufficient. Last but not least, the securities market itself is still under reform, resulting in uncertainty. One example is the pending of the 'Through Train Scheme'. The proposed 'Through Train Scheme', aimed to allow individual Mainland investors to invest in Hong Kong, and led to a rapid rise in stock prices and equity related derivative issuance in 2007. However, prices reversed sharply when the Mainland announced in November 2007 that progress on the scheme would take more time than envisaged, as the model still needed to be worked out.[6] This uncertainty created fluctuation in the securities market.

The sophisticated level of the Chinese individual investors is lower than those in mature markets. It can be seen from Figure 6.1 that the turnover rate by Chinese investors, representing the percentage change in a security's holding, is significantly higher than those from the mature markets. It indicates that during that period, Chinese individual investors tended to chose short-term investments. Other evidence can be found in various empirical studies.

It is worth taking a closer look at the retail investors in China. According to international practice, an individual investor is often referred to as the retail investor or small investor. There are a considerable number of retail investors in China. They are in a relatively weaker position than the institutional investors. There are various issues that have resulted in this situation. One reason for making the protection of retail investors difficult is the lack of an open and fair information disclosure system. Existing studies have illustrated the economic reasons for this issue. Information asymmetry puts retail investors in a less favourable position. Moreover, compared with other mature markets, the situation may be even more serious in the Chinese market. Second, inefficient legal

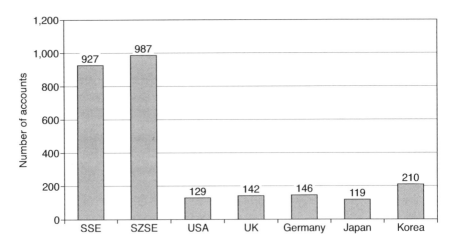

Figure 6.1 Comparison of turnover rate (source: China Capital Markets Development Report[7]).

frameworks aggravate the weakness. As with the other sectors in China, the protection of investors has experienced several reforms; details will be examined later in this chapter. Third, the imbalance inside listed companies leaves retail investors with an inferior status. Corporate governance is essentially important for investors. However, the significance of corporate governance as an issue, has only been considered important in the last few years. Last but not least, the lack of self-protection awareness further worsens the situation. As discussed before, the investors, in particular the individual investors, may ignore the scientific theories in the Chinese capital market. The demand for information is less significant than in the mature markets.

All these conditions have led to a complex situation. As for the information disclosure regime, Figure 6.2 shows the information sources which determine the decision making of retail investors. The survey was conducted by the Securities Association of China (hereafter to SAC) and China Securities Investor Protection Fund Companies Limited (hereafter the SIPF) in 2007.[8] It can be seen that the main sources came from self analysis (37.6 per cent), from TV and radio and newspapers were not far behind (36.2 per cent and 35.4 per cent respectively). The impact of the institutional analysis report (20.8 per cent) and the information from trading services providers (16.9 per cent) were relatively limited.

Also, the retail investors' incomes were quite limited. Figure 6.3 illustrates this situation. The survey showed that 35.2 per cent of the investors received an average monthly income of less than RMB2,000, 33.4 per cent of the investors received a monthly income of between RMB2,000 and RMB5,000, and only about 20 per cent of the investors received more than RMB5,000 as a monthly income. On average, the personal monthly incomes were RMB3,813; while family monthly incomes were RMB5,599. It can be seen that medium and low income investors were the main participants of the securities market in 2007.

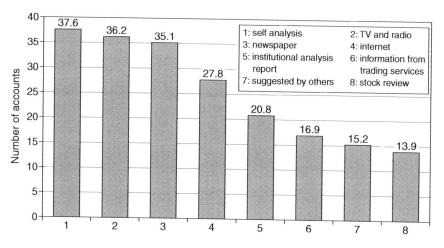

Figure 6.2 Information source for decision making by retail investors (source: SAC & SIPF[9]).

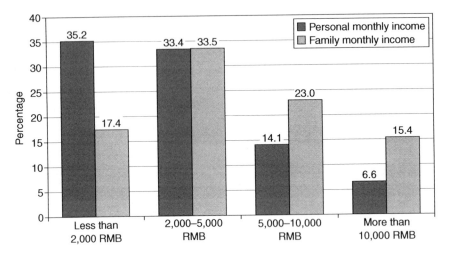

Figure 6.3 Income distribution of retail investors (source: SAC & SIPF[10]).

Therefore, the protection of investors is in a very crucial situation. It is not diffi-cult to understand that with such low incomes, some of the investors may take excessive risks and invest all their savings in the capital market.

Moreover, according to the survey, the majority of retail investors believed their rights had been violated. Figure 6.4 gives an analysis of the reasons. It can be seen that the main reasons were imperfect disclosure (56.1 per cent), market manipulation (44.2 per cent), imperfect governmental behaviour (37.6 per cent), violations by majority shareholders (31.3 per cent), and the quality of trading services (8.4 per cent). Notably, there were only 5.5 per cent of investors who believed that their rights had not been violated. These results suggested that the protection regime for investors must be further enhanced and improved.

It is not fair to state that these phenomena can only be found in the Chinese market. In fact, they are also common in mature markets. The problems of imperfect disclosure, market manipulation, majority shareholders encroaching, and imperfect governmental behaviour, may also be difficult to settle in other jurisdictions. However, if China can address these problems at an early stage, it will definitely boost the prosperity of the Chinese market.

One issue that needs to be noted is, that with the development of the Chinese financial market since 2008, although there have been some fluctuations, the confidence index of Chinese investors has increased, as shown in Figure 6.5. It can be seen from this survey that currently, investors are taking a positive atti-tude to the market. The SIPF has developed three different surveys, i.e. a com-prehensive survey focusing on the investor psychology and behaviour pattern, a special survey focusing on hot topics in the market, and the confidence survey focusing on investor anticipation. The SIPF developed independently the 'China Securities Investors' Confidence Index Preparation Plan', on the basis of learning

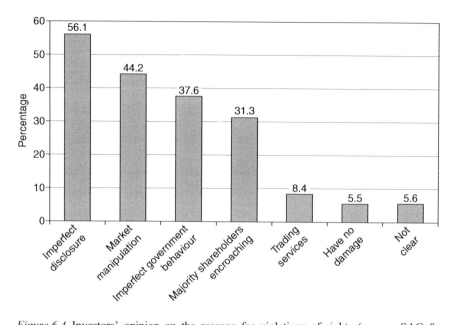

Figure 6.4 Investors' opinion on the reasons for violations of rights (source: SAC & SIPF[11]).

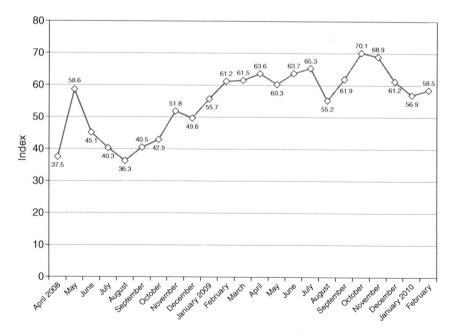

Figure 6.5 Securities investors' confidence index (source: SIPF[12]).

from the working experiences of the overseas confidence survey in March 2009. From January 2009 to February 2010, the index has remained above 50.[13] This result suggested the investors stayed optimistic. One of the reasons which led to this result is the improvement of the investor protection regime.

Legal methods of investor protection

The general legal methods of investor protection have been established through different laws and regulations. Figure 6.6 is the list of the basic rights of Chinese

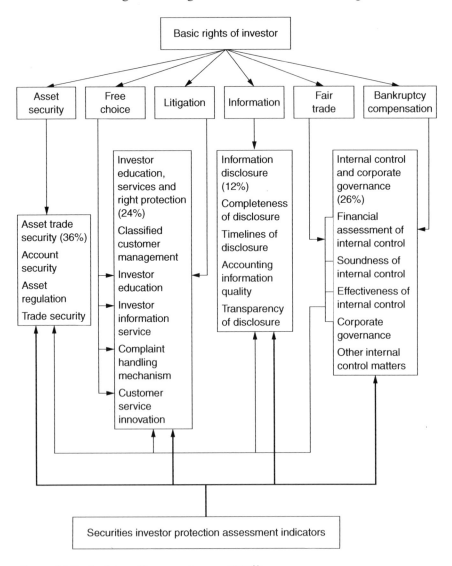

Figure 6.6 Basic rights of investors (source: SIPF[14]).

investors. It can be seen from the figure that the basic protection regime has been established.

At the inception of the Securities Law, it was stated that one of the purposes of this law is to protect the lawful rights and interests of investors.[15] Various sections of the Company Law have also emphasized the importance of the protection of investors.[16] The Criminal Law has enhanced the regulatory regime on insider dealing, market manipulation and other securities crimes, in particular Amendment VI to the Criminal Law.[17] For instance, the Amendment revised Article 161, enlarged the scope of crime and added 'failing to disclose other important information' as a new crime. Another example is the revision of Article 182, the manipulating futures market is added as a type of crime, and the punishment under this Article increased to ten years imprisonment, when the circumstances are extraordinarily serious.[18]

Notably, the Property Law has made a clear statement on the protection of investors.[19] Article 65 states that the legal savings, investments and the corresponding proceeds of an individual shall be under the protection of law. It further states that the state, any collective or individual may contribute funds to establish a limited liability company, a company limited by shares or any other enterprise. Where the real properties or movable properties owned by the state, a collective or an individual are invested in an enterprise, the contributor shall enjoy such rights as obtaining asset returns, making important decisions and selecting operators and managers and perform their duties in accordance with the agreement or on the basis of his proportion of investment.[20]

The Property Law's statements on the protection of investments have far reaching effects on the capital market. In the last few years, the complexity of investment rights has led to controversies regarding its nature. Is this a property right, a creditor's right or even an independent right? The protection of investors' rights was a vague concept. In addition, compared with other legal rights, the protection of the private property right has been slightly ignored in the past. Obviously, the enactment of the Property Law has established a new level of fundamental principles. One of the significant impacts of the Property Law is that it has defined different rights. The Securities Law may take Property Law as a reference, in particular, in the aspects of affirmation, publicity and transferring of securities.[21] It is not difficult to imagine that there will be more detailed rules and implementation in the near future based on the general principles of Property Law.

The CSRC also established different methods to address investor protection. As one of the central regulatory bodies of the capital market, the work the CSRC has conducted is crucially important to the stability of the Chinese securities market. Investor protection is one of the major tasks for the CSRC, and it has promoted the establishment of an open, fair and just environment for investors.[22]

The laws and regulations have played a significant role in the process of Chinese legal reform. In the aspect of investor protection, the function of the People's Court should not be ignored. The importance of the People's Court in the regulation of China's securities market has increased in past decades. This is evidenced by the People's Court's engagement in the resolution of disputes, arising from the commodity and financial futures market and securities related to false statements.[23] Typical cases are the Guangxia (Yinchuan) Industrial Co., Ltd, Guangdong Kelong Electrical Holding Co., Ltd, Shangdong Jiufa Edible Fungus Co., Ltd and Hangxiao Steel Structure.[24] Among different legal documents, the Notice of the Supreme People's Court on Temporary Refusal of Filings of Securities-Related Civil Compensation Cases,[25] the Notice of the Supreme People's Court on Relevant Issues of Filing of Civil Tort Dispute Cases Arising from False Statement on the Securities Market,[26] and Several Provisions of the Supreme People's Court on Hearing Civil Compensation Cases Arising from False Statements on the Securities Market[27] are the most important components in relation to the information disclosure regime.

The notices of the Supreme People's Court (hereafter SPC) reflect the gradual evolution process. In the first Notice, the SPC instructed the local people's courts not to accept civil compensation claims arising from insider dealing, fraud and market manipulation. It stated in the Notice: these behaviours must be regulated; these new issues have already emerged in local court practices; however, currently, the People's Courts are limited by the legislation and other judicial conditions and are therefore not ready to accept and hear such cases. One of the major reasons was that the People's Court required a period of time in order to conduct the necessary research and preparation; in particular, in a situation that was not a complete legal environment.[28]

The Second Notice has significantly improved the regulatory regime in respect of imperfect information disclosure. It stated that the People's Courts can accept and hear cases arising from false statements. However, there were some limitations in the document. For instance, there was a precondition for the acceptance of the claim: the false statement must have been investigated by the China Securities Regulatory Commission or its dispatched office, and they made an effective penalty decision.[29]

Another limit was the form of litigation. It stated that with respect to a case of civil compensation arising from false statement, the People's Court shall accept it in the form of a single or joint lawsuit, not in the form of a class action.[30]

It should be noted that there were some controversies surrounding the procedures. According to Mr Guoguang Li, Vice-President of the SPC at that time, the precondition was quite necessary: it could help to reduce the claimants' difficulties of obtaining evidence.[31] As for the format of litigation he went further to state that: due to the large number of claimants, allowing class actions would increase complexity; in particular, the time, amount and price of transactions may vary, and a class action could influence the process of the trial.[32] Therefore, investors' class actions remain a questionable issue in the Chinese legal system.

The third document is of significant importance. The basic framework for acceptance and hearing of civil compensation cases, arising from false statements on the Chinese securities market, has been established. From the acceptance of cases, jurisdiction of the courts, litigation procedures, ascertainment of false statement, and exemption from liabilities to the calculation of losses of investors; the SPC has provided investors with a more powerful arm, which has had significant impacts on the litigation history of the Chinese securities market.

However, the approaches provided in the Provisions have certain limitations. Most importantly, they maintained the precondition system for litigation.[33] The litigation must be based on an administrative decision or a criminal order or judgement. These preconditions may prevent an excessive case load. On the other hand, they play a limited role in assisting the prevention of market abuse in the Chinese securities market.[34] Under the emerging and transitional nature of the market, the failure to prevent further illegal securities transactions is detrimental and will further result in negative impacts on investors.

Civil compensation, as one of the components of the remedy system, plays an important role in the investor protection regime, in particular for retail investors. Without an open and fair compensation system, it is senseless to talk about the protection method. From the above analysis, it can be seen that in Mainland China, the legal framework for protection of investors has been established. Currently, the regime is based on the Company Law and Securities Law, supplemented by other administrative measures. Moreover, the Criminal Law, Civil law and Property Law provide effective support. Through establishing an efficient civil compensation system, illegal and illicit securities transactions may be reduced and limited to a certain degree. Investors are the essential component of the capital markets; their confidence in a particular market may influence its further development. Therefore, continuing reforms and improvement of the civil compensation system are required for the Chinese securities market. This will not only help in the protecting of securities investors after suffering economic losses, but also eventually, can promote the healthy growth of the Chinese capital market.

The investor protection fund

Protection of retail investors is a complex issue, influenced by many different factors. As a result of information asymmetry, when dealing with securities transactions, the retail investors are in a relatively weaker position than the securities companies. Also, because of the business nature, securities companies may have potential conflicts of interest with the investors, when the latter are clients of the former.[35] Although there are different rules and regulations in this field, this regime is under reform.[36] Therefore, the law and regulations have stated the importance of the establishment of the securities investor protection fund. Accordingly, China Securities Investor Protection Fund Companies Limited (SIPF) was registered in August 2005 and started to practice in September 2005.[37]

The company was funded by the State Council, with a registered capital of RMB6.3 billion.[38] At the start, the board comprised seven nonexecutive members, respectively coming from the China Securities Regulatory Commission, Ministry of Finance, Shanghai Stock Exchange, China Securities Clearing and Depository Corporation and People's Bank of China. The SIPF aims to manage the investor protection fund, and to reimburse investors in line with the statutory process, in the event that securities companies are closed, become insolvent, or have imposed upon them mandatory administrative measures by the CSRC; for instance, takeover or operation on a depository basis.[39]

Administrative Measures of Securities Investor Protection Fund

According to the Administrative Measures of Securities Investor Protection Fund (hereafter Measures), the primary aims of the investor protection fund (hereafter protection fund) are to prevent and deal with risks associated with securities companies, to maintain the social economic order and public interests, to protect the lawful rights of investors, and to promote a healthy securities market.[40]

As for the funding source of the protection fund, it is mainly collected from the securities companies and securities exchanges based on a taking from the market and returning to the market philosophy.[41]

The Measures went further to state that when a securities company is in a certain condition; namely, its licence being cancelled, closure, insolvency, or under an administrative custodian or other compulsory supervisory management, it shall pay compensation to the investors from the protection fund according to the law and regulations.[42] However, the fund required that the investors themselves shall be responsible for losses in their securities investment activities arising from fluctuations in the securities market or changes in the value of their invested products.[43]

The Measures aimed to establish a primary framework for the use of the protection fund, but more detailed rules and their application will be required; in particular, the compensation scope has not been addressed in the Measures. On the other hand, the Measures are a significant improvement in the process of investor protection.

Measures for Applying for the Use of Securities Investor Protection Fund (Trial)

The continuing reform of the Chinese securities market requires corresponding development in the legal sector. In order to regulate the applications for the use of the securities investor protection fund and ensure the lawful use and the security of the securities investor protection fund, the Measures for Applying for the Use of Securities Investor Protection Fund (Trial) came into force.[44]

According to the Measures, when securities companies are under the disposal, which means the companies have been ordered by the CSRC to suspend their business operations for rectification, have been designated to other institutions for custody, have been taken over, or have been abrogated, they shall be governed by the present Measures when they apply for using their protection fund to purchase the credits of individuals or the settlement funds of their clients' securities.[45]

Basically, the operation system is as follows: the institution that is responsible for exercising the legal person duties and functions of a securities company under disposal shall be responsible for filing applications for using the protection funds. The SIPF shall exercise the duties and functions of issuing and managing the protection funds. Moreover, the CSRC shall be responsible for inspecting and supervising the applications and use of protection funds.[46]

Chapter II of the Measures detailed the setting up of the procedures of the application of the protection fund: SIPF shall enter into a 'Loan Agreement on Securities Investor Protection Fund' with the custodian settlement institutions and the institutions authorized by the CSRC, according to the approved risk deposition schemes of the securities companies and the protection fund use schemes, so as clarify the quotas, purposes of use and procedures.[47] The custodian or the groups of relevant local governments for purchasing the credits of individuals shall make recognition of the settlement funds of the clients' securities and the credits of individuals, and shall be responsible for the authenticity, accuracy and lawfulness of the recognitions.[48]

The custodian settlement institution shall file an application to the institution authorized by the CSRC. The application materials shall include the following: an application report form; the outline details of the credit of the individuals that need to be purchased by the head office or branches of the securities company under disposal, which have been recognized by the custodian settlement institution; a special audit report on the credits of individuals; a confirmation report made by the relevant group of the local government, or a confirmation report made by the custodian settlement institution; and an implementation scheme for purchasing the credits of individuals.[49]

Besides the above, the granting of protection funds has been set out in detail in Chapter III of the Measures.[50] First of all, the SIPF shall open a special account for the deposit of securities investor protection funds with the Business Department of the People's Bank of China. Second, when the SIPF grants the custodian settlement institution any protection funds, it shall enter into a loan agreement with the custodian settlement institution and the institution authorized by the CSRC and shall designate a commercial bank (the entrusted bank) to grant the loan on its behalf. Third, when the custodian settlement institution uses the protection fund to purchase the credits of the individuals and the settlement funds of clients' securities, it shall open a deposit account for the protection funds with the entrusted bank, and shall report its opening of the bank accounts to the institution authorized by the CSRC, the local branch of the People's Bank of China, and the SIPF for archival filing. Following this, the purchasing of the credits of individuals shall be based on the principle of 'purchasing a batch after confirming a batch'. The custodian settlement institution shall open a protection fund deposit account with each of the branches of the entrusted bank in all the places where the purchases are carried out, and shall report this to the relevant institutions for archival filing. Finally, the branch or sub-branch of the entrusted bank shall grant the purchase funds to the creditors after examining the purchase checklist of the credits of individuals.

It can be seen from the above provisions: the procedures for the application and granting of the protection funds are very comprehensive. It is not difficult to understand that such a strict regime is designed to prevent misuse and abuse of the protection fund.

Implementation Measures for the Payment of Securities Investor Protection Funds by Securities Companies (Trial)

In order to regulate the payment of securities investor protection funds by securities companies, the Implementation Measures for the Payment of Securities Investor Protection Funds by Securities Companies (Trial) have been enacted.[51]

It requires that all securities companies registered within the territory of China shall pay the protection funds.[52] As for the payment ratio, a securities company shall pay into protection funds at a rate between 0.5 per cent and 5 per cent of its business income.[53]

With regard to payment methods, Chapter III set up the detailed requirements.[54] The securities company shall pay into the protection fund by way of an advance payment in the current year and the settlement and payment in the following year. Moreover, a securities company shall pay into the protection fund by two instalments per annum, and shall transfer the protection fund that shall be paid in the first half of a year prior to 15 July, and make up the whole year prior to 15 January of the following year. Furthermore, when a securities company pays into the protection fund in advance, it shall calculate the amount of protection fund it should pay according to the business income in the first half of the current year or the whole current year according to the determined payment ratio, and report the Declaration Form for the Advance Payment of Protection Fund as well as the interim or annual financial statements to the SIPF.

In the same chapter the Measures further states the requirements for the documents to be submitted when a securities company applies for settlement and payment as the following: a Declaration Form for the Settlement and Payment of Protection Funds, the annual audit report or special audit report for business incomes as issued by the accounting firm, and audit reports on the annual net capital figure and the supervisory statements for risk monitoring indicators.[55] Moreover, the documents submitted by a securities company shall be signed by its legal representative, accountant in charge and person in charge, and be affixed with its seal; the persons shall be responsible for the authenticity and integrity of the documents submitted.[56]

Notably, for investors in the futures market, a similar fund has been set up according to the Provisional Measures on Futures Investor Protection Funds.[57]

Moreover, the CSRC introduced the classification regulatory system for securities companies. The classification of securities companies refers to the evaluation and determination of the classes of securities companies, on the basis of the risk management capabilities and in combination with their market competitiveness and continuous regulatory compliance.[58] The risk management capability of a securities company shall be evaluated by virtue of six indicators: capital adequacy, corporate governance and regulatory compliance management, dynamic risk control, information system safety, protection of clients' rights and interests and information disclosure. The classification shall reflect the company's capability to manage liquidity risks, regulatory compliance risks, market risks, credit risks, technical risks and operational risks.[59] Based on the evaluation scores of securities companies, the CSRC shall divide securities companies into 11 subclasses in five classes, including Class A (AAA, AA, A), Class B (BBB, BB, B), Class C (CCC, CC, C), Class D and Class E. A securities company that receives a risk disposal measure, such as being legally ordered to stop business for rectification, being in the custody of or taken over by other designated institutions or being subject to administrative reorganization, if the evaluation score is zero, it shall be of Class E; and if the evaluation score is below 60, it shall be of Class D.[60]

Based on this classification method and rating of securities companies, uniform standards, dynamic management, differential charging and a fund raising mechanism were implemented.[61] Table 6.2 illustrates the payment proportion for the protection fund.[62] Notably, in April 2013, the CSRC revised the payment requirement. The ten types of securities companies are required to pay 0.5, 0.75, 1, 1.5, 1.75, 2, 2.5, 2.75, 3 and 3.5 per cent of their operating revenue to the SIPF when the size of SIPF exceeds RMB20 billion; moreover, securities brokers that have been rated A for three consecutive years and been granted AA or A rating during the latest reporting period need to pay 0.5 to 0.75 per cent of their operating revenue to the SIPF.[63] From Table 6.2 it can be seen that when the securities companies are ranked higher, the payment proportion will be lower; when they are ranked lower, the payment proportion will be higher. This system may help to improve the internal management of securities companies by the design set out above. Furthermore, the awareness of promoting a sound risk management mechanism within a securities company has been raised. This can benefit the investors through the method of 'the higher the risk, the higher the payment proportion by securities companies'. When investors suffer losses from a securities company, they may obtain the economic compensation that has been pre-paid by the company.

Table 6.2 Type of securities companies and comparison of proportion

Type of regulation and supervision	Payment proportion (%)
A AAA	0.5
AA	1
A	1.5
B BBB	2
BB	2.5
B	3
C CCC	3.5
CC	4
C	4.5
D D	5

Sources: SIPF.[64]

The SIPF has raised funds on a market-oriented basis for investor protection mechanisms. From Table 6.3, it can be seen that a fundamental system has been established. It replaced the previous practice of special financing from the People's Bank of China.[65] Similarly with other sectors in China, the continuing reforms will improve the operation of this regime.

The UK perspective

In the UK, similar protection methods can be found. The Financial Services Compensation Scheme (hereafter FSCS), set up under the Financial Services and Markets Act 2000 (FSMA), is the UK's statutory fund of last resort for customers of authorized financial services firms.[66] The FSCS can pay compensation if a firm is unable or likely to be unable to pay claims against it. In general, the FSCS protects: deposits; insurance policies; insurance broking (for business on or after 14 January 2005), including connected travel insurance where the policy is sold alongside a holiday or other related travel, e.g. by travel firms and holiday providers, (for business on or after 1 January 2009); investment business, and for advice and arranging home finance (for business on or after 31 October 2004).

The funding sources are the firms authorized by the Financial Conduct Authority (hereafter the FCA) and the Prudential Regulation Authority (hereafter the PRA). Under the current funding system which started on 1 April 2008, the FSCS levy is split into five classes: deposits, life and pensions, general insurance, investments, and home finance. Furthermore, each class is divided into two subclasses based on providers or intermediation activities. The subclasses are based on the activities a firm undertakes. Therefore, a firm's contribution is calculated on the tariff base applicable to the relevant subclass. A threshold for each subclass is set by the FCA and PRA by reference to what a particular subclass or class can be expected to afford in a year. The threshold sets the maximum that

Table 6.3 Statistics of the raising of protection fund (Unit: RMB100 million)

Year	Protection funds raising				
	Brokerage cost	*Handed-in funds of securities company*	*Interest of frozen purchasing fund*	*Donation accepted*	*Purchasing income and liquidation of bankruptcy assets of the related responsible party*
2006	3.467	0.000	13.270	0.026	0.000
2007	20.339	28.403	56.593	0.005	1.348
2008	15.783	44.025	44.258	0.000	3.949
2009	28.518	40.810	13.490	0.038	5.900
2010	16.681	12.390	26.211	0.000	9.112
2011	25.441	28.681	13.078	0.000	5.870
2012	13.813	14.187	4.070	0.000	2.811
Total	124.042	168.496	170.970	0.069	28.990

Source: SIPF.[67]

the FSCS can levy for compensation in any one year. Currently, the total levy on all classes under the general retail pool provides an annual capacity of about £4.03 billion to the FSCS.[68]

As for compensation, there are some limitations under the FCA rules and guidance; for instance, currently, under the deposits category, the amount to be paid is up to £85,000 per person (for claims against firms declared in default from 31 December 2010); under investment category, the amount to be paid is up to £50,000 per person per firm (for claims against firms declared in default from 1 January 2010).[69] The scheme was set up mainly to assist private individuals, although claims by smaller businesses are also covered. The FSCS can pay compensation only when an authorized firm is unable, or likely to be unable, to pay claims made against it. Finally, the FSCS will carry out an investigation before determining the financial position of the firm.

Upon the claim made by the investor, the FSCS will investigate the firm in question, finding that the firm is unable, or likely to be unable, to pay such claims. Following this, the FSCS will declare the firm in default and contact the claimant with an application form. After receiving the application form, the FSCS will review and process the claim, and inform the claimant in writing.[70]

One issue must be noted is that the FSCS website has maintained a database for the firms declared in default.[71] Therefore, potential claimants can search for the firm by themselves. In addition, the website interface is quite friendly and easy to use. It is helpful in reducing the administrative cost and increases efficiency.

The Hong Kong perspective

The Investor Compensation Company Limited (ICC) is a wholly owned subsidiary of the Securities and Futures Commission (SFC), established for the purpose of administration of claims against the Investor Compensation Fund (Fund).[72] In details, the ICC is responsible for receipt, determination and payment of valid claims against the Fund, making payments to claimants and pursuing recoveries against defaulting licensed intermediaries or authorized financial institutions. The Fund is established to pay compensation to investors who suffer pecuniary losses as a result of a default of a licensed intermediary or authorized financial institution, in relation to exchange traded products in Hong Kong. There is no nationality requirement for the claimants. It aims to provide a certain level of security to retail investors.

As for the source of money, it mainly comes from the Investor Compensation Levy (Levy) on exchange traded product transactions. Currently, the Levy on securities transactions is 0.002 per cent payable by buyers and sellers. For futures contracts, it is HK$0.5 per side of a contract or HK$0.1 per side of a mini contract or stock futures contract. In other words, for every 50,000 HK$ securities traded, the buyer and seller need to pay an Investor Compensation Levy of HK$1 each.[73]

The amount of compensation in relation to a securities transaction payable to the claimants will not exceed HK$150,000. If the claimants sustained losses in relation to a futures contract, the upper limit of the compensation is similarly

HK$150,000. Moreover, for joint accounts, each of the account holders will be subject to a maximum payment limit of HK$150,000.[74]

Compared with other jurisdictions, and compared with its earlier stages, the protection fund in Mainland China has experienced many different reforms. These changes are aimed at establishing the primary framework for the use of the protection fund. With the development and innovation of the Chinese securities market, more updated rules and policies will be required. For example, the compensation limit has not been addressed in Mainland China. Another issue to be noted is that the protection fund can only be used in circumstances where the securities companies have their licence cancelled, are closed, insolvent, or under an administrative mandate or other compulsory supervisory management. As for losses arising from bad investment advice, poor investment management, misrepresentation, false and misleading statements, insider dealing, and market manipulation, the investors must resort to other methods. For a new emerging market, the use of a comprehensive approach to cover the economic losses of the investors is important. However, the lack of a fully developed system may lead to difficulties in obtaining compensation. From a practical perspective, in mature markets, the compensation system has been introduced when firms are providing services. For instance, in the UK, a description of the circumstances and the extent to which a firm is covered by the compensation scheme, and where the retail client will be entitled to compensation from the compensation scheme, must be disclosed.[75] Table 6.4 is a typical example under FCA regime, similar approaches can be found in Hong Kong.[76] The Chinese financial institution may enhance such trading services, in order to improve efficiency.

Furthermore, examining the SIPF itself as a corporate body, it may be argued that the governance structure should be improved. Its board of directors should not only be responsible to the financial regulators and government, but also to the general public and financial industry. Internal risk control should be enhanced in order to prevent moral hazard and power abuse.[77] Moreover, the actual working procedures could be more transparent and less complex. The victims are not always professional enough to understand and make claims.

Overall, besides the above deficiencies, the establishment of the protection fund is a significant improvement in the process of investor protection, and an important step towards a mature capital market.

Table 6.4 Example of FSCS disclosure

Are we covered by the Financial Services Compensation Scheme (FSCS)? We are covered by the FSCS. You may be entitled to compensation from the scheme if we cannot meet our obligations. This depends on the type of business and the circumstances of the claim.
Most types of investment business are eligible, for up to a maximum limit of £50,000.
Further information about the compensation scheme arrangements is available from the FSCS.

Source: FCA.[78]

The function of corporate governance

As stated earlier, information asymmetry leaves the retail investors in an inferior position. From the above analysis, it can be seen that external control via legal methods is important. Compensation methods such as the SIPF also play an important role. The law and regulation focuses on enhancing the supervisory and regulatory regime of listed companies in order to protect investors. On the other hand, good corporate governance within listed companies or securities companies should also be established.[79]

As one of the key elements in improving market efficiency and enhancing investor confidence, corporate governance involves a set of relationships between a company's management, its board, its shareholders and other stakeholders. Corporate governance provides the structure through which the objectives of the company are set and the approaches of attaining the objectives and monitoring performance are determined.[80] Good corporate governance can provide an efficient approach for the protection of shareholders and investors.

This is a relatively new topic in China. The discord in corporate governance has resulted in various negative impacts on the Chinese securities market. For listed companies of whatever sector and for securities companies alike, corporate governance must be fully addressed. The governance of securities companies is an important aspect to be noted for a number of reasons. First of all, the nature of the business has determined that securities companies are in a more advantaged position than the general public. Moreover, they are responsible for huge amounts of clients' funds. In addition, some of the securities companies are themselves listed companies. Therefore, a good corporate governance structure, for instance, a transparent and efficient disclosure system, can prevent the misappropriation of the clients' funds and further enhance the protection of investors.[81]

The system of corporate governance depends on a group of institutions and how corporate governance is implemented.[82] The Company Law, Securities Law and the relevant regulatory regime have focused on this issue. Without doubt, the further continuing reform of this regime will enhance the protection of investors.

The role of investor education

Investor education is very important and an effective approach for investor protection, particularly in a developing market. As stated earlier, retail investors have lacked awareness of self protection for some time. Therefore, the primary task of investor education is to enhance the understanding of legal rights. The absence of legal knowledge and, in particular, the lack of a specific understanding of the securities market may lead to serious negative results.

Another point is to develop a multi-directional education system. Education targeted at the Chinese market, and the 'Right to Know', should be in a central position. Through education the investors become informed of their rights and the protection available to them.

Risk education must not be ignored. It can be seen from earlier chapters that Chinese investors are not as mature as those in other markets. Therefore the risk factors in the capital market must be highlighted to allow full understanding. Given the background of the global financial crisis, education is of vital importance.

Updating knowledge should be an essential part of investor education. Currently, the Chinese securities market is under reform. The combination of a new trading system, innovative financial products, and the historical problems, for instance false or misleading information, requires education to focus on the latest situation. From this point of view, investor education should not be conducted solely by the supervisory bodies; close cooperation with academics, practitioners and the media is needed.

A case study: the road of 'right-defending'

Recalling the case study of Zhejiang Hangxiao Steel Structure Co., Ltd (hereafter Hangxiao Steel Structure), after two years, a final decision was made in May 2009. The company committed to pay compensation of about RMB4,000,000 to the 118 claimants.[83] Compared with other earlier cases, all of the victims employed lawyers, which indicated a new step on the road of 'right-defending'. 'Right-defending' is an expression used in China, referring to the phenomenon that victims protect their lawful rights through various methods. Although it is operated according to the Constitution and laws, right-defending may, however, face difficulties in China.

Among various issues, one particular dilemma is the high operational cost of right-defending.[84] It has been argued that the reasons for the high cost of right-defending are: inefficiency of related departments; high charges by intermediaries; excessive charges by the related departments; inappropriate behaviour of victims; costs intentionally increased by the wrongdoers and delay caused by undue enforcement of judgements.[85] These reasons are not isolated. From the aspect of governance, a lack of experience and an incomplete legal framework or codes of conducts are the major reasons. For the victims themselves, weak awareness of self protection is one of the chief elements. Moreover, it has been argued that according to the parties concerned, rights-defending can be divided into two groups in China: equal and unequal. The former arises from a civil legal relationship, while the latter arises from any of the following: civil, criminal and administrative legal relationships. The incomplete legal framework has resulted in high costs for equal types of right-defending, while the social and economic imbalance has led to the high cost of unequal types.[86] Securities transactions themselves are complex; therefore, the right-defending relating to it may face various situations which lead to high costs. It may be difficult to fix retail investors within the two categories. When dealing with the listed companies or securities companies, the investors will enter a civil legal relationship; while dealing with the administrative departments or regulatory bodies, the retail investors will enter a administrative legal relationship; and when retail investors suffer losses from insider dealing or market manipulation, they may enter the criminal legal relationship, since criminal offences have been involved. Therefore, the incomplete and inefficient legal environment leads to difficulties; and information asymmetry has aggravated the situation.

Earlier in the Chinese securities market, there were many claims made by Complaint Letters and Visits; this method has a Chinese background.[87] The 2nd Conference of the Securities and Futures Regulatory System on Complaint Letters and Visits has emphasized the important relationship between this approach and investor protection.[88] Also, the Rules of the CSRC on Complaint Letters and Visits Work (Trial) set up the basic working guidance for the system.[89] The cases that will be accepted for petition include the following: disclosing institutional and/or personal unlawful behaviour; disclosing unlawful behaviour and other misconducts by the personnel of the CSRC and its local branches; making suggestions in relation to the work of the CSRC and other policies.

Although the Complaint Letters and Visits system has been established, the actual income recovered needs to be examined. This should be brought to the attention of the financial regulators. However, their ability to prevent and control securities crime and illicit transactions is quite limited.

Another issue concerning right-defending is that in last few years, some lawyers, scholars, brokers and other people lobbied to establish the special forum for investor protection; for example, Weixing Zhang, a leading financial analyst, has suggested the establishment of a non-governmental organization, the Association of Chinese Investors, in order to operate in a 'professional' way, for instance involving more lawyers, economists and scholars in the actions of investor protection and delivering and lobbying for suitable compensation proposals for retail investors; these activities will be conducted under a constitution.[90] For unknown reasons, this proposal had not been completed. In fact, such an approach could be helpful to a certain degree. An organization established by the investors themselves could address the needs of investors more directly.

With the development of the whole Chinese financial system, the atmosphere has improved. In the Hangxiao Steel Structure case, one of the significant improvements was that all the 118 claimants employed lawyers as their representatives. Earlier in China, some of the investors did not tend to employ lawyers for litigation. There were various reasons for this. Some investors may have thought that they could deal with the case by themselves. Some investors did not want to incur any more costs. One important consideration, among others, was that the investors were lacking in confidence in the whole legal environment, in particular in the regulation of the capital market. Another issue that cannot be ignored was that some lawyers in general did not fulfil their responsibilities. In fact some may even have facilitated illegal transactions and crimes in the capital market themselves. Therefore investors lack of confidence in lawyers.

Securities litigation itself is quite complex. These considerations further resulted in a vicious circle. On one hand, it is very difficult for the investors to obtain compensation, on the other hand, it is also difficult for the financial regulators to control and regulate illicit and illegal behaviour. Lawyers who deal with securities business, have been expected to perform as the 'gatekeepers' in China. Therefore, their illegal behaviour seriously damaged investors' confidence in the market. Another reason leading to this was the lack of confidence in the legal system.[91]

The situation changed with the Hangxiao Steel Structure case. The positive function of lawyers was fully reflected in this case. Most of these lawyers had also participated in other earlier securities litigations in China and gained lots of experience. From their point of view, this case is a milestone in the litigation history of the Chinese securities market. The case has also had a revelatory function, from the perspectives of timescale, attitude of the company concerned, and the legal environment.[92]

Compared with before, the improvements are perceptible. According to Yushen Tao, the lawyer who participated in several securities litigations, including the Guangxia (Yinchuan) Industrial Co., Ltd Case (hereafter Yingunagxia), Guangdong Kelong Electrical Holding Co., Ltd case, Shandong Jiufa Edible Fungus Co., Ltd case and Hangxiao Steel case, the Yinguangxia era has become history, the legislative and judicial environment for investor protection has improved significantly.[93] According to his experiences, these improvements can be reflected by:

1   Result: There are still some claims that have not been settled in the Yinguangxia case; the mediation rate is nearly 100 per cent in the Hangxiao Steel Structure case.
2   Time: It took about five years to reach the judgement in the Yinguangxia case; it took two years to reach the current result in the Hangxiao Steel Structure case and it took only two days to reach the mediation agreement.
3   Attitude of the Company: Yingguangxia had an inflexible attitude which resulted in negative effects; Hangxiao Steel Structure had a flexible and cooperative attitude which significantly smoothed the procedures.
4   Legal environment: The Yinguangxia case experienced different legal reforms, in particular the three Notices from the SPC which were analysed in an earlier part of this chapter. The case was not accepted by the Yinchuan Intermediate People's Court until April 2004. The Hangxiao Steel Structure case was conducted under a more comprehensive and mature legal framework, which meant there were applicable laws and regulations.
5   Investors: At the time of the Yinguangxia case, there were some investors who did not appoint lawyers; in the Hangxiao Steel Structure case, all the claimants appointed lawyers which led to a more professional and efficient resolution.

Another issue that needs to be noted is that in the Hangxiao Steel Structure case, there was the application of mediation to settle securities disputes. In 2003, the Several Provisions of the Supreme People's Court on Hearing Civil Compensation Cases Arising from False Statement on the Securities Market has already stated that the People's Courts shall, when trying cases of civil compensation arising from false statements in the securities market, emphasize mediation and encourage the parties concerned to reconcile with each other.[94]

However, the application of this method has suffered for a long period. For instance, the Dongfang Electronic Co., Ltd case (hereafter Dongfang case) was the case with the biggest litigation claim arising from a false statement at that time. For a case which involved 6,970 claimants and lasted from 2003 to 2007, it was not easy to reach a satisfying result; in fact, mediation played an important role in this case.[95] It provided many useful models for the mediation method.

It may be argued that the Hangxiao Steel Structure case indicated the end of an era. In one ongoing case, Ping An Securities Company also set compensation fund for investors for false disclosure made by Wanfu Biotechnology (Hunan) Agricultural Development Co., Ltd.[96] However, the good sign may not be the end of the dark story. Investors, in particular the retail investors, have experienced a different evolution of the Chinese capital market. It is now a time for the investor protection regime to face a period of systemic upgrading. Under the fast financial innovation, investors may face new types of risks. Overseas or cross listing has brought great benefits for China. However, one issue that needs to be considered is how to protect investors when they suffer losses from cross-border transactions. The case of Mainland investors' claims against the Minibond of Lehmans' Brothers in 2008 is a typical example.[97] How to establish that effective protection is a new topic.[98]

Summary

From the above study, it can be seen that a primary regime for investor protection has been established in Mainland China. The continuing reform shall guarantee that the regulatory method can target the latest situation. In fact, this is the primary task for the supervision and regulation of the Chinese securities market. It has been argued that it is the time to introduce a new attitude to the investor protection regime – a people-oriented approach. The protection should be aimed at investors, supported by investors and the positive results will be shared by the investors.[99]

The issue of investor protection is a multi-faceted concept. Considering the complexity of investor protection, some people argued for the establishment of a special comprehensive Investor Protection Law.[100] Currently, the law and regulation tend more to the fundamental system of supply in China. Detailed rules and their applications are required.

It should not be ignored that financial innovation is playing an important role in the Chinese securities market. The emerging and transitional nature of the market determined that new issues will continue to arise. Therefore, the establishment of a basic framework and to adjust and amend the regulatory regime according to the new situation is equally important. And, the most central issue is to enforce the law and regulation fairly, duly and correctly.

Enhancing information disclosure has had a substantial positive impact on investor protection. Compared with securities companies, investors, especially retail investors, are in a weaker position. They may require more corporate information in order to protect themselves. From an early stage, Chinese law and regulation has paid great attention to promoting an open, fair and just information disclosure regime. The continuing improvements will be beneficial to all investors.

A common way for investors to protect themselves is through litigation. However, mediation may be a fast and effective settlement mechanism. For the courts, it may reduce the amount of litigation, for the investors, it may reduce the litigation cost, and for the defendant, it may reduce negative impacts, which is crucially important for the listed companies. Therefore, mediation can be seen as a 'win-win-win' approach. Again, the precondition is that the mediation is to be conducted in a fair way.

The investor protection fund has played important role in the protection of investors. However, as discussed earlier, comparing with other jurisdiction, the application scope, procedure, and the governance of fund should be further enhanced in China. Furthermore, as a general observation, the fund management should consider the needs of the claimants and design a more user-friendly system to facilitate the actual application of the fund.

From a broad view, another consideration is to promote a credit culture in China. The market will recognize the importance of investors, in particular retail investors. It has been argued that in the UK the investors have been endowed with more power; in contrast in Mainland China, the financial institutions have been favoured.[101] From this point of view, Chinese investors, in particular retail investors, are clearly the weaker party in the capital market. Although the law and regulation have empowered retail investors with more tools and weapons, there is still a long way to go.

Notes

1 China Securities Depository and Clearing Corporation Limited, 2011 China Securities Registration and Settlement Statistical Yearbook, www.chinaclear.cn/main/03/0305/0305_1.html, last accessed: 23 May 2013. A shares are denominated in Chinese currency, the RMB. B shares refer to foreign-invested shares issued domestically by Chinese companies. B shares are denominated in RMB but traded in foreign currencies.
2 Trial Measures for the Administration of Overseas Securities Investment by Qualified Domestic Institutional Investors, promulgation date: 18 June 2007, effective date: 5 July 2007, Article 2.
3 State Administration of Foreign Exchange, www.safe.gov.cn, last accessed: 31 May 2013.
4 Measures on Administration of Domestic Securities Investments of Qualified Foreign Institutional Investors (QFII), promulgation date: 24 August 2006, effective date: 1 September 2006, Article 2.
5 State Administration of Foreign Exchange, www.safe.gov.cn, last accessed: 31 May 2013.
6 IMF (February 2008), People's Republic of China – Hong Kong Special Administrative Region: 2007 Article IV Consultation – Staff Report; and Public Information Notice on the Executive Board Discussion, IMF Country Report No. 08/44, p. 5.

7 CSRC (2008), China Capital Markets Development Report, Chapter 3, Beijing: China Financial Publishing House. The data for China was based on 2007, while other jurisdictions were based on 2005.

8 CSA, SIPF (July 2007), Survey of Investors of Chinese Securities Market – Analysis Report. With the approval of the State Council, the CSRC, Ministry of Finance (MOF) and the PBOC promulgated the Measures for the Administration of Securities Investor Protection Funds in June 2005 and agreed to set up a wholly state-owned protection fund co. On 30 August, 2005, the SIPF was registered with the State Administration for Industry and Commerce with a registered capital of RMB6.3 billion injected by the State Council via the MOF. The SIPF is under the regulation of the CSRC. See SIPF website, www.sipf.com.cn/en/AboutSIPF/introductionandcorporatefunctions/index.shtml, last accessed: 1 November 2012.

9 Ibid.

10 Ibid.

11 Ibid.

12 SIPF, Investors' Confidence Index.

13 The contents here were quoted from: www.sipf.com.cn/en/investorservices/investorsurvey/index.shtml, and www.sipf.com.cn/en/investorservices/investorsurvey/investorconfidenceindex/2010/8416.shtml, last accessed: 10 December 2012. This Plan measures investors' confidence from four dimensions, including: Economic Fundamentals; Economic Policies; International Environment; and the Stock Exchange Index. The first three dimensions are portrayed respectively by three indicators and the fourth dimension is portrayed by five aspects, including stock valuation, an optimistic securities market, securities market rebound, securities market anti-tumble and buy in. The questionnaire consists of a total of 12 questions. From April, the SIPF started to conduct monthly surveys on confidence of securities investors via the website, www.sipf.com.cn, and compiled an investors' confidence index at the beginning of every month, in which about 10,000 investors participate. The confidence index should lie between 0 and 100, with 50 being neutral. When the index is over 50, it indicates that more investors are of optimistic and positive opinions than those of pessimistic and negative opinions and the overall confidence level of investors inclines to be optimistic. The higher the index is, the more confident the investors are. And when the index is below 50, it indicates that more investors are of a pessimistic and negative opinion than those of optimistic and positive opinions and the overall confidence level of investors inclines to be pessimistic.

14 SIPF (12 November 2009), 'Mr. Chen Gongyan: Securities Investor Protection in the Context of Financial Crisis', www.sipf.com.cn/en/newsupdate/updates/11/4954.shtml, last accessed: 27 December 2012.

15 Revised date: 27 October 2005, effective date: 1 January 2006, Article 1.

16 Revised date: 27 October 2005, effective date: 1 January 2006.

17 Amendment VI, promulgation date: 29 June 2006, effective date: 29 June 2006. The Amendment revised Article 161, where a company or enterprise furnishes to shareholders and the general public false financial and accounting reports or the reports conceal important facts, or fail to disclose other important information, and seriously damaged the interests of shareholders, or other serious circumstances are caused thereby. The persons who are directly in charge, and other persons who are directly responsible for the crime, shall be sentenced to a fixed term of imprisonment of not more than three years or criminal detention, and shall be fined not less than RMB20,000 but not more than RMB200,000.

18 The revision to Article 182 states that persons manipulating the securities or futures market, if causing serious consequences, shall be sentenced to a fixed term of imprisonment of not more than five years or criminal detention; moreover, a fine shall also be imposed instead of the aforesaid sentence or on top of the aforesaid sentence; if the circumstance is extraordinarily serious, the person shall be sentenced to a fixed

term of imprisonment of not less than five years but not more than ten years and shall also be fined.

19 Promulgation date: 16 March 2007, effective date: 1 October 2007.

20 Ibid., Article 67.

21 Liming Wang (16 July 2009), 'The Impacts of the Property Law on the Chinese Securities Market (Lun Wuqunfa dui Woguo Zhengquan Shichang de Yingxiang)', www.yadian.cc/paper/63734/, last visited: 21 March 2013.

22 For a more detailed analysis of the CSRC, see Chapter 5.

23 Sanzhu Zhu (2009), The Role of Law and Governance in Financial market: The Case of Emerging Chinese Securities Market, working paper.

24 For further details of these cases, see Chapter 1, as well as the latter part of this chapter.

25 Notice of the Supreme People's Court on Temporary Refusal of Filings of Securities-Related Civil Compensation Cases (Zuigao Renmin Fayuan guanyu she Zhengquan Minshi Peichang Anjian Zan bu yu Shouli de Tongzhi), 21 September 2001, Famingchuan [2001] No. 406.

26 Notice of the Supreme People's Court on Relevant Issues of Filing of Civil Tort Dispute Cases Arising From False Statement on the Securities Market (Zuigao Renmin Fayuan guanyu Shouli Zhengquan Shichang yin Xujia Chenshu Yinfa de Minshi Qingquan Jiufen Anjian Youguan Wenti de Tongzhi), 15 January 2002.

27 Several Provisions of the Supreme People's Court on Hearing Civil Compensation Cases Arising from False Statement on the Securities Market (Zuigao Renmin Fayuan guanyu Shenli Zhengquan Shichang yin Xujia Chenshu Yinfa de Minshi Peichang Anjian de Ruogan Guiding), 9 January 2003.

28 Vice-president of SPC Li Guoguang's Answers about the The Notice of the Supreme People's Court on Relevant Issues of Filing of Civil Tort Dispute Cases Arising From False Statement on the Securities Market (Zuigao Renmin Fayuan Fuyuanzhang Li Guoguang jiu Zuigao Renmin Fayuan guanyu Shouli Zhengquan Shichang yin Xujia Chenshu Yinfa de Minshi Qingquan Jiufen Anjian youguan Wenti de Tongzhi), 15 January 2002.

29 Notice of the Supreme People's Court on Relevant Issues of Filing of Civil Tort Dispute Cases Arising From False Statement on the Securities Market (Zuigao Renmin Fayuan guanyu Shouli Zhengquan Shichang yin Xujia Chenshu Yinfa de Minshi Qingquan Jiufen Anjian Youguan Wenti de Tongzhi), 15 January 2002, Article 2.

30 Ibid., Article 4.

31 Vice-president of SPC Li Guoguang's Answers about the The Notice of the Supreme People's Court on Relevant Issues of Filing of Civil Tort Dispute Cases Arising From False Statement on the Securities Market, 15 January 2002.

32 Ibid.

33 Several Provisions of the Supreme People's Court on Hearing Civil Compensation Cases Arising from False Statement on the Securities Market, 9 January 2003, Article 6. Where a lawsuit for civil compensation brought by an investor against the false statement maker, in accordance with a decision on administrative penalty by a relevant organ, or in accordance with a criminal order or judgement by the people's court, for the reason that his rights have been infringed by the false statement, conforming with Article 108 of the Civil Litigation Law, the People's Court shall entertain the lawsuit.

34 Sanzhu Zhu (2007), Securities Resolution in China, Ashgate Publishing: Aldershot, p. 195.

35 Further details can be found in Chapter 3.

36 Ibid.

37 See SIPF website, www.sipf.com.cn/bin/FrontPage?m=s&channelFlag=GREATEV ENT&articleId=AB6BF2A09C9911DCB8F4DFC06FD9CD92, last visited 26 June 2012.

38 Ibid.

39 Ibid.
40 Administrative Measures of Securities Investor Protection Fund, promulgation date: 30 June 2005, effective date: 1 July 2005, Article 1.
41 Ibid., Article 12. This philosophy, as a Chinese expression, refers to a levy imposed on the securities companies, from which payments are made to investors.
42 Ibid., Article 17.
43 Ibid., Article 4.
44 Measures for Applying for the Use of Securities Investor Protection Fund (Trial), promulgation date: 7 March 2006, effective date: 7 March 2006.
45 Ibid., Article 2.
46 Ibid., Article 3.
47 Ibid., Article 5.
48 Ibid., Article 6.
49 Ibid., Article 7.
50 Ibid., Article 17, 18, 19, 20, 21, 22, 23, 24 and 25.
51 Implementation Measures for the Payment of Securities Investor Protection Funds by Securities Companies (Trial), promulgation date: 28 March 2007, effective date: 1 January 2007.
52 Ibid., Article 3.
53 Ibid., Article 6. The percentage will depend on the risk category of the securities company in question; further details can be found in the latter part of this chapter.
54 Ibid., Article 8, 9 and 10.
55 Ibid., Article 12.
56 Ibid., Article 13.
57 Provisional Measures on Futures Investor Protection Funds, promulgation date: 19 April 2007, effective date: 1 August 2007.
58 Provisions on the Classified Supervision and Administration of Securities Companies, promulgation date: 26 May 2009, effective date: 26 May 2009, revised date: 14 May 2010, Article 2.
59 Ibid., Article 5.
60 Ibid., Article 17. For details of the risk disposal measures, see Chapter 3.
61 SIPF (12 November 2009), 'Mr. Chen Gongyan: Securities Investor Protection in the Context of Financial Crisis', www.sipf.com.cn/en/newsupdate/updates/11/4954.shtml, last accessed: 27 December 2012.
62 For a company under the Class E, its potential risks have become reality and it has received a risk disposal measure.
63 CSRC (19 April 2013), 'The CSRC Reduced the Ratio for SIPF Payment Requirement'.
64 Ibid.
65 Ibid.
66 All the information about the FSCS was obtained from its official website: www.fscs.org.uk, last accessed: 15 May 2013.
67 SIPF, Monthly Statistical Report of China Securities Investor Protection Fund (November 2012), Data for year 2012 is the accumulative statistics from January to October 2012.
68 Ibid.
69 See www.fscs.org.uk/what-we-cover/eligibility-rules/compensation-limits/, last accessed: 30 May 2013.
70 The information here was obtained from: www.fscs.org.uk/your-claim/, last accessed: 10 December 2012.
71 See www.fscs.org.uk/what-we-cover/search-for-companies-in-default/, last accessed: 15 September 2012.
72 All information obtained from the ICC's website, www.hkicc.org.hk/about_us/introduction_e.htm, last accessed: 15 September 2012.

73 ICC website, www.hkicc.org.hk/investor/source_e.htm, last accessed: 10 December 2012.

74 ICC website, www.hkicc.org.hk/investor/fund_limit_e.htm, last accessed: 10 December 2012.

75 FCA, Conduct of Business Sourcebook, 9 Annex 1.

76 SFC (April 2001), Code of Conduct for Persons Registered with the Securities and Futures Commission, Schedule 4.

77 Gongyan Chen, Suyi Liu, Mingwei Wang (April 2007), 'The Characters of the FSCS and its Impact on China (Yingguo Touzizhe Baohu Jiuji Zhidu Tedian ji dui Women de Qishi)', p. 51, www.sipf.com.cn/en/index.shtml, last accessed: 30 December 2009.

78 FCA, Conduct of Business Sourcebook 6 Annex 1G: Services and Costs Disclosure Document Described in COBS 6.3.7G (1).

79 More details analysis of the function of corporate governance please refers to the Chapter 3.

80 OECD (2004), OECD Principle of Corporate Governance, Preamble.

81 Further details can be found in the Chapter 3.

82 Donald C. Clarke (15 July 2003), 'Corporate Governance in China: an Overview', working paper, http://papers.ssrn.com/sol3/papers.cfm?abstract_id=424885, last accessed; 30 December 2009.

83 Yuping Hu, Wenke Zhu, Jing Yan (21 May 2009), 'The Closure of Hangxiao Steel Structure Case, 118 Claimants will Receive about 4,000,000 RMB Compensation (HangXiao Ganggou Xujia Chenshu An Jiben Jie'an, 118 Wei Touzizhe Gonghuopei yue 400 Wanyuan)', http://hzdaily.hangzhou.com.cn/dskb/page/3/2009–05/21/34/2009052134_pdf.pdf, last accessed: 15 September 2013.

84 Bixin Jiang (2006), 'Multiple Measures shall be Applied to Resolving the High Cost Problem of Right-defending (Pojie Gaochengben Weiquan xuyao Duoguan Qixia)', *People's Tribunal*, 10 (2006), p. 36.

85 Ibid.

86 Yuqing Li (2006), 'The Strange Phenomenon of High Cost Right-Defending (Gaochengben Weiquan zhi Guai Xianxiang)', *People's Tribunal*, 10 (2006), p. 33.

87 The term Complaint Letters and Visits refers to the activities that a citizen, legal person or any other organization who, by way of letter, e-mail, telephone or visit, etc., reports facts, submits proposals or opinions, or files a complaint to the people's government at various levels or working departments of the people's government at or above the county level, which shall be dealt with by the relevant administrative organs according to law. See Regulation on Complaint Letters and Visits, promulgation date: 10 January 2005, effective date: 1 May 2005, Article 2.

88 CSRC (27 August 2007), The CSRC Held the 2nd Conference of the Securities and Futures Regulatory System on Petition Method, http://old.csrc.gov.cn/n575458/n575667/n818795/4217682.html, last accessed: 15 September 2012.

89 Effective date, 14 July 2005.

90 Baoqiang Liu (August 2004), 'Weixing Zhang: The Association of Chinese Investors is a Weapon (Zhang Weixiang: Zhengquan Touzizhe Xiehui shi Gumin Weiquan de Gongqi)', http://finance.sina.com.cn/t/20040819/1345960936.shtml, last accessed: 15 September 2012.

91 Interview No. 8.

92 Guangyun Fu, Hua Huang (21 May 2009), 'Closure of the Mediation of Hangxiao Steel Structure Case (Hangxiao Ganggou An Tiaojie zhong Poju)', *International Finance News (Guoji Jinrong Bao)*, http://paper.people.com.cn/gjjrb/html/2009–05/21/content_257767.htm, last accessed: 14 September 2012.

93 Yuan Lu (14 July 2009), 'Yinguangxia Era Became History, Legislative and Judicial Environment of Securities Right-Defending has been Improved ('Yinguangxia' Shidai cheng Lishi, Zhengquan Weiquan Lifa Sifa Huanjing Dada Gaishan)', *First*

Finance   Daily   Newspaper   (Diyi   Caijing   Ribao),   www.china-cbn.com/s/n/
001002000/20090714/000000120523.shtml, last accessed: 15 September 2012.

94 Promulgation date: 9 January 2003, Article 4.

95 www. Secutimes.com (Zhengquan Shibao, Shibao Zaixian), Transcript from the
Video: Investor Protection Series (5), 28 July 2009, www.secutimes.com/general-
Subject.do?method=getShow&subjectId=61, last accessed: 15 September 2009.
Yixin Song, one of the lawyers in the case, stated that lawyers have played an
important role in the mediation. Minwei Zheng, another lawyer in this case, stated:
the majority of the claimants were satisfied with the mediation results, although initially, the expectation of claimants for winning the case was not high. The Dongfang
case was named the 'Ist case of the Chinese securities market'. In 2002, Yantai
Intermediate People' Court held that the company provided a false financial statement. Since 2003, the investors had brought litigation against Dongfang Electronic
Co., Ltd in order to obtain compensation.

96 For more detail, see Chapter 5.

97 Minibond is one type of the structured financial products related to Lehman Brothers. Other types are Pyxis Notes, ProFund Notes, Octave Notes, etc. 'Structured
products' in Hong Kong generally refer to products which, in addition to an exposure to the credit or default risk of the issuer (or guarantor where applicable), contain
an exposure to an underlying asset, opportunity or risk that is usually unrelated to
the issuer or the guarantor. There are other Lehman investment products in the retail
market, issued or guaranteed by the Lehman group of companies, which are subject
to the credit risk of the issuer or guarantor and which have therefore been adversely
affected by the Lehman collapse. However, these products are generally regarded as
less complex for investors to comprehend than the structured products which have
generated most of the concern in the aftermath of the Lehman collapse. See, HKMA
(31 December 2008), Report of the Hong Kong Monetary Authority on Issues Concerning the Distribution of Structured Products connected to Lehman Group
Companies.

98 Interview No. 7.

99 Xiaoguo Wang (18 March 2009), 'Investor Protection is Facing the Challenge of Systemic Upgrading (Touzizhe Quanyi Baohu Mianlin Zhidu Shengji Tiaozhan)', *Shanghai Securities News (Shanghai Zhengquan Bao)*, http://cnstock.xinhuanet.com/
paper_new/html/2009–03/18/content_67647226.htm, last accessed 14 September
2009.

100 Yisheng Gao, 'A Brief Discussion of the Function of Investor Protection Legislation', http://old.csrc.gov.cn/n575458/n2470788/n2470973/n2475246/2951121.html,
last accessed: 14 September 2009.

101 Gongyan Chen, Suyi Liu, Mingwei Wang (April 2007), 'The Characters of the FSCS
and its Impact on China (Yingguo Touzizhe Baohu Jiuji Zhidu Tedian ji dui Women
de Qishi)', p. 51, www.sipf.com.cn/en/index.shtml, last accessed: 30 December
2009.

Conclusion

The Chinese securities market has made remarkable achievements in the past few years. Although the Chinese securities market was born with certain unique features, including strong political influence and administrative intervention, it has made significant positive improvements over the years, as illustrated in this book. The information disclosure system, as the fundamental basis for the healthy growth of the securities market, has attracted a great deal of attention in China. With the development of the Chinese economy, this regime has been improved substantially. The book concludes, however, that further reforms are necessary for the future development of the Chinese securities market. This conclusion is based on both the general and the specific findings of this research. The following concluding remarks, followed by a summary of the general and the specific findings of the book, suggest the necessary reforms in these areas.

General findings

The general findings of this book focus on the structure of law and regulations, the relationship between the law and national policy, administrative intervention, the self-adjustment ability of the Chinese securities market, the Chinese approach 'from the points to the entire surface' and the current Chinese regulatory approach.

Law and regulations

The structure of relevant laws and regulations concerning the securities market, particularly on the information disclosure regime, has been illustrated in the preceding chapters. Clearly, continuing reform and development constitutes the most significant feature. In fact, at the initial stage of the establishment of a modern Chinese securities market, what a Chinese securities market should be was a major issue. Efforts were made by the Chinese government and financial regulators to establish a modern, open and fair market. Currently, how to establish an efficient securities market is one of the fundamental concerns, and how to regulate the market economically and effectively is one of the major tasks.

Moreover, from a legal perspective, different laws, regulations and rules concerning the securities market, particularly on information disclosure, have been enacted in China. At the emerging stage, there were inconsistencies between different legal documents. With the enactment and revision of the laws and regulations, particularly the Securities Law, Company Law and Criminal Law, the regulatory gaps and vacuums have been filled in significantly, and the problem of inconsistency has been addressed. The question to consider is: what are the driving forces and causes of such an improvement? Furthermore, what led to the improvements of the securities market in China, a country without a comprehensive and complete financial regulation regime?

One of the Chinese approaches, the so-called 'from the points to the entire surface', helped to improve the regulatory regime. This approach is, in essence, to establish an experimental field first, then to promote successful experiences. Typical examples can be found in the acceptance of the mixed operation system in China. A formal legal recognition of this operational method requires further legislation to follow it up. Nevertheless, this method can minimize the market risk and systemic risk; by starting with a pilot experience, the potential financial tsunami can be restrained to a local area to avoid a further national financial disaster.

The revision and amendment of law and regulation reflect the relationship between rigidity and flexibility. The dynamic balance between rigidity and flexibility of law needs to be examined carefully. On one hand, the rigidity of law requires that the implementation and enforcement shall be carried out strictly according to the law once it has come into force. On the other hand, there should be some space prearranged for future development. There is nothing to prevent the revision and amendment of law and regulation. This is commonly recognized and practiced in most countries. For instance, the Berne Convention has stated that there shall be amendments for improving the system of the Berne Union, and a group of countries signed this Convention in order to protect art and literature in 1886.[1] And recently, the global financial system has seen a more enhanced regulatory regime. As illustrated in this book, the UK Financial Services Authority (FSA) has been replaced by the Financial Conduct Authority (FCA) and Prudential Regulation Authority (PRA). The regulations on Credit Rating Agencies (CRAs) in the UK, Hong Kong and the US have experienced the journey from nil to emerging, and to tightening from time to time. In the context of China, as an emerging and transitional country, the revision and amendments of law and regulation is quite necessary. The central point is that basic and fundamental laws shall maintain stability. Meanwhile, the detailed rules and implications may reflect flexibility according to the latest economic situation.

Government policies

Considering the complexities of the above issues, the overall response to the securities market must be based on a comprehensive understanding of China.

The combination of law and national policy has illustrated the necessity for control from the macro level. According to the current situation, the central policy of the State Council will have significant impacts on securities regulations. For instance, in the case of 'development', the policy could be announced with different emphasis: it may be 'to put great effort into development', it may be a 'comprehensive development', it may be a 'scientific development', or it may be a 'steady development'. These national policies will lead to the adjustments of the securities market in a different level. The adjustments are usually made when the national or international economic situation has changed significantly.

Administrative intervention

It may be too radical to conclude that administrative intervention is excessive in the regulation of the Chinese securities market. However, administrative intervention has a unique function indeed. This function in the Chinese securities market is a delicate issue. On one hand, it is necessary to have such a function at the current stage. The emerging and transitional nature of the Chinese securities market requires a continuing revision of the law and regulation. Hence, it is crucially important for the government and securities regulators at national and local levels to oversee, manage or intervene in the market where necessary, in order to maintain market confidence and financial stability. On the other hand, excessive intervention may lead to certain negative results. Among different issues, the administrative intervention should not hold back financial innovation. Being a developing country, innovation is essentially important to advance the whole financial system. Radical and random steps should be avoided for reasons of systemic safety, while an over-conservative attitude may not help the further development of the securities market.

Development and securities regulation

It can be seen from the earlier analysis that securities regulation aims to provide and facilitate stability and development in the market. From an international perspective, stability and development of securities market are a global concern. There are numerous international standards that focus on this area; for instance, IOSCO, the World Bank and the Basel Committee as discussed earlier.

The policies, laws and regulations of China are adjusting. This has been illustrated in different chapters of this book. In fact compared with other jurisdictions, China has made rapid progress in establishing its own regulatory system. Aiming to reach a higher level to be in line with international standards, China is putting efforts into promoting an open, fair and transparent financial market. This research has found, however, that the securities regulation, particularly the information disclosure regime formed in the earlier periods of the Chinese securities market, had a number of problems: the administrative measure was strong, but the legal supervision was relatively weak; the policy control was strong, but the legal control was relatively weak; the legal framework building was strong, but the enforcement and implementation was relatively weak. Today this situation has improved. More specifically, concerning the information disclosures regime, a numbers of cases and scandals have been examined in the previous chapters, which mirror the lack of transparency, false and misleading disclosure, major omissions in financial reports, insider dealing and market manipulation. Although these negative impacts were caused directly by some unique Chinese problems, nevertheless, as in other jurisdictions, one of the fundamental troubles is the imbalance and conflict between greed, continuity and stability. This has been very evident in the 2008 financial crisis.

Realising these potential risks, besides the explicit system or method, there must be a careful overview of the safety and reform of the financial supervisory network. How can securities regulation help? As a consequence of the inability of regulators to reach the systemic stability on their own, the UK's FSA has been replaced. Similarly the securities regulators in other jurisdictions have to be reformed. In terms of China, although it has experienced reforms and changes, overly dramatic changes from the regulators can result in significant negative impacts. Instead, the viability and integrity as the entire philosophy of an open market must be sufficiently addressed. Therefore, the Chinese securities regulator has to focus on the responsibility of the economy. Recalling the statement of US President Roosevelt who emphasized this in the 1930s:

> Many undertakings have been organized and forwarded during the past year to meet the new and changing emergencies which have constantly confronted us ... to cushion the violence of liquidation in industry and commerce, thus giving time for orderly readjustment of costs, inventories, and credits without panic and widespread bankruptcies.[2]

Though in different context, the idea of responsible capitalism and a responsible market is useful.

The emergence of the Chinese securities market and its subsequent reform has emphasized that the establishment of a vigorous market cannot be achieved without a sound legal system. In particular under a transnational market economy, transformed from a planned economy, law and regulation has been expected to take on more responsibilities. When looking back at the development history of the Chinese securities market, there are different stages to be examined: soon after China started economic reform in late 1978, the government and enterprises began to issue government and enterprise bonds; starting from 1984, joint stock companies were established and shares were issued to the public; in 1990, the Shanghai and Shenzhen Stock Exchanges were established, which marked an important stage of the establishment of China's emerging securities market; in 1998, China's first securities law was enacted; since the late 1990s, the securities investment fund market has had sustainable growth.[3] From its early emergence to the formal establishment and systematization of the Chinese financial market, changes and evolution are continuing.

Securities market reform is a part of the comprehensive reform of China. Facing globalization is even more challenging now, since these changes not only concern economic restructuring but are also, indeed, a reform of the political, social and legal system. Notably, this is only from a domestic level. Beyond the territory of China, surviving from the two recent financial crises does not mean that the Chinese securities market, or the regulatory structure, has already achieved a highly developed stage. In contrast, from a micro-level, taking the information disclosure system as an example, the deeply rooted problems illustrated in different chapters of this book have not been fully resolved. China is moving towards a greater emerging power status; although the deficiency issue has been broadly noticed, the neglect of potential threats to long-term stability may eventually lead to increased risks. Therefore, the greater concern of responsible capitalism and a responsible market must be raised.

China has recognized that not only is development essential, but the quality of development is also important. In the 5th Plenum of the 17th Communist Party of China Central Committee, 'more comprehensive, coordinated and sustainable growth' and 'sound and fast economic and social development' have been emphasized.[4] Similarly, financial and securities regulation should be developed to address this need.

Specific findings and suggested reforms

The specific findings of this book focus on the efficiency of regulation of the securities market, in particular using the information disclosure system as an example: the role performed by the securities companies, the financial intermediaries, the securities lawyers, the promotion of innovation and competition and the balance between innovation and supervision, and finally information disclosure for the protection of investors. Moreover, this book addresses the significance of disclosure as a means of providing the retail investor with the opportunity to make a sensible and rational investment decision. Therefore the core issues of concern, in looking at Chinese securities law and regulation, are the following: the reliability of the disclosure, historic problems and the current situation; the dissemination of financial information by the firms; the processing of information by the financial intermediaries; and the overseeing of the disclosure regime by the financial regulators. This leads to the following questions: what are the consequences of information asymmetry? And in particular, how can we improve investor protection? Overall, the book examines the development and effectiveness of the law and regulation concerning disclosure, and in the light of promoting a modern securities market, how China can improve the quality and value of financial information, and how China can enhance the quality and reliability of financial development. Based on these observations, and the issues illustrated in different chapters, the specific findings are as follows.

The function of information

In brief, there are three main issues of disclosure: the primary disclosure, continuing disclosure and major event disclosure, and the key contents are the financial information itself. However, one of the issues faced by China is whether traditional financial disclosure is meaningful.

Even in mature markets, these issues are of primary importance. Homer Kripke raised several issues as to the relevance of traditional accounting information for the market.[5] He argued that even in sophisticated economies, traditional financial information is less relevant. First, accounting principles are historic, based on the past not the future. Second, accounting information is lawyer-dominated: lawyers tend to be concerned about whether information is right or wrong. Finally, investors are not concerned about the quality of information, but the predictability for the future. On highlighting the importance of factual information, Kripke argued that investors are really concerned about simplified information and emphasized historic information. As a consequence, in the Chinese context, the important issue is to ensure the information is relevant to those who process it, i.e. the financial intermediaries and professionals.

China should take this on board, and be far more concerned about projecting, forecasting and soft information, in particular, management information. Moreover, apart from the general investors, disclosure should also be oriented in terms of context and dissemination to the intermediaries. However, this is a problem in China. To start with, the lack of professional standards needs to be addressed. The financial intermediaries are competing with, not pleasing, investors. Investors, especially retail investors, have not relied on financial intermediaries. Until using intermediaries can be better regulated, and unless the intermediaries are requested to comply, they cannot easily and fully develop in the market. Further suggestions are to recommend and emphasize the importance of the independence of intermediaries, who must be economically viable, and pass legislation to give them their required status and professional control and, most importantly, control the integrity and competence of these professionals.

Improvement in efficiency

In the last few years, the task of improving the efficiency of regulating the disclosure system has become more important. How to ensure the real time and accurate dissemination of the latest information of listed companies is a central issue. Accurate and efficient information disclosure can ultimately benefit the financial system. With financial innovation, the disclosure requirements are becoming increasingly complicated. In fact, it can be seen from the study that there are no material differences between the disclosure requirements in China, UK and Hong Kong. Mainland China is continuously improving its regime, for its own needs, and also taking into account the international best practices. However, the legislative technique is only the first step. The regulatory issue cannot be ignored. Besides the government regulatory bodies, the stock exchanges, through their daily functions, have the ability to continuously monitor the listed companies' information disclosure. As the front line market regulators, they are crucially important to the comprehensive and effective supervisory system. Integrated monitoring measures should be enhanced. In order to use the resources in the most efficient and economic way, the stock exchanges should be given a proper and clearly structured regulating power.

It will be interesting to further examine the self-adjustment ability of the Chinese securities market. Compared with other mature markets, the self-regulatory function cannot perform compatibly. As discussed in Chapter 1, the Chinese securities market still remains in a formative state with weak efficiency. Therefore, it would be dangerous to leave the problems to be resolved only by the market itself. The securities market is crucially important to the national economy. Consequently, there must be rules and regulations in force.

Based on these considerations, the current regulatory approach may last for a certain period of time. The next step for regulatory development should focus on the efficiency issue as well as the integrity issue. As can be seen from different chapters, there is a steady and gradual evolutionary process. The first step was standardization of the law and regulation. The second step was foundational reform carried out on the operational structure of the securities market. The third step was the strengthening of integrated management of the securities businesses, which facilitated the establishment of a fair market. Finally, effective long term investor protection was promoted which occupies a central point of this evolutionary process.

Securities companies

The securities companies are crucial components in the Chinese securities market. Their fast growth will definitely have a very positive impact on the economy. However, due to their business nature, the securities companies control more information, and sources of information, than the general public. Therefore, they may take advantage of this and further abuse the information obtained. Information disclosure of the securities companies is an important and necessary mechanism to prevent market malpractices. It can enhance the market transparency, improve the efficiency of supervision and regulation, and promote the healthy and steady growth of the securities companies. As for mixed operations, it can be seen from earlier analysis that insufficient system supply is the chief hidden danger. The initial target is to establish a complete and effective regulatory regime. Supervisory cooperation is vitally important with this background. At the same time, corporate governance and internal control can perform unique roles. As can be seen from the comparative study on the director disqualification system, a more complete regime is needed in China. Moreover, corporate disclosure is another approach which puts the financial institutions in front of the public, for the whole of society to monitor.

Financial intermediaries

Regulating the market professionals is a big issue in China. Chinese investors also tend to ignore financial advice; evidence can be found in Chapters 1, 4 and 6. However, the role of financial intermediaries is fundamental; therefore government must develop a major campaign in investment literacy. In particular, the campaign should distinguish between different categories of investors: specific concerns should be given to the institutional and individual investors and ensure a whole governance structure.

Information symmetry cannot be reached. There will always be an information imbalance. However, law and regulation should aim to reduce these defects, in particular discouraging the abuse of privileged information. One of the problems is that the more intermediaries are created, the more likely this will lead to different levels of understanding. Moreover, in creating a fair market, a particular jurisdiction has to balance the advantages of market efficiency, through intermediaries, with access to the market. It must be admitted, that increasing financial intermediaries can also increase costs, but the quality of investment advice is better. In this circumstance, it is crucially important to have sufficient intermediaries who would be independent and ensure integrity.

Credit rating agencies

The role played by credit rating agencies should also be strengthened. Financial intermediaries are playing an important role in information disclosure in the securities market. The regulation of CRAs is an ongoing issue. With the development of unsecured corporate bonds, the demand for credit ratings will increase significantly in China. Hence, on one hand, the law and regulation will provide a regulatory and supervisory system. On the other hand, the future of CRAs will also be decided by their own performance. Comparing with the newly developed regulatory structure for CRAs in the UK, EU and Hong Kong, technical concerns need to be further enhanced in China. However, it must be noted that given the various economic structures and individual needs for different countries, there is no 'one size fits all' model for financial development. Therefore, the process of emerging, repairing and developing the Chinese CRAs must focus primarily on the state's need.

Securities lawyers

The regulatory regime for securities lawyers is moving towards a more open and fair future. Equal access is just the first step, while continuing training is an efficient way to ensure the quality of securities lawyers. Moreover, considering the special nature of securities legal services, the following issues should be taken into account for a comprehensive, coherent and updated training plan: liberalization of capital markets, policy issues; foreign investment risk firms involved in the domestic market; Chinese companies' overseas listing; Chinese companies' cross listing issues; new technology relating securities crime; and Chinese securities firms' abilities to address changes.

Financial innovation and supervision

To facilitate innovation and competition is one of the tasks for the financial regulators. However, to achieve a balance between financial innovation and supervision is also crucially important. Traditionally, the supervisory bodies in an emerging market prefer a strict regulatory framework. But it should be noted that over regulation may constrain the development of the capital market. It may also create some 'side effects', for instance, the abuse of regulatory power, the increase of regulatory cost and the reduction of market efficiency. On the other hand, there are some regulatory actions that need to be improved for the CSRC. Suggestions have been made in the early parts of this book. Also, the regulatory philosophy of the CSRC should be adjusted according to the changing situation. From this point of view, it is very important to promote a rational attitude for all financial regulators. An overly cautious approach to financial liberalization may slow down financial development as well. The policy between relaxed and intensive vigilance should be balanced.

Real time disclosure

Problems in China are revealed in the lack of transparency, misleading disclosure or non-disclosure in the securities market. Most significantly, the problem is with regard to the provision of real time and accurate information by listed companies. This is a central concern. Based on the comparative analysis with the UK and Hong Kong, important issues need to be addressed in the future reforms of the Chinese information disclosure system: firstly, to develop a comprehensive, and effective electronic disclosure system along with the traditional paper-based discourse model; secondly, to improve the corporate disclosure of securities companies, in both areas of risk disclosure and innovative disclosure.

In order to establish a modern market, the reformed information disclosure system should be taken into account in China. A newly effective platform, for instance, the internet, needs to be involved more actively than before. The website disclosure system for ChiNext can be seen as a significant improvement. Notwithstanding, this reform should be conducted with a steady approach. Compared with other developed markets, retail consumers are significant consumers of disclosed information. However, retail consumers are not yet mature enough. Moreover, the disclosure system should be backed up by fast and safe internet services.

Overall, from the experiences of the London Stock Exchange and HKEx, electronic dissemination through the stock exchanges' website, a single, official, centralized location that can be easily accessed by both local and overseas investors, will ensure that information disclosure and securities investment are more efficient and secure than before. It may bring Mainland China's information dissemination system into line with other leading international financial markets. China can put efforts into this approach, although this must be in a steady and reasonable manner.

Role of the China Securities Regulatory Commission

In addressing this issue, besides the strict regulatory regime, the CSRC may also need to adopt a more open and modern attitude. The regulatory philosophy, for example, could slightly move towards the 'partnership' approach. The promotion of the best market practice should be an important task along with an improvement of regulatory behaviour.

As for improvement of the efficiency of the CSRC, one aspect to consider is the financial regulators in the UK, have been endowed with the power to bring criminal prosecutions. However, in some other jurisdictions, for example, Italy, the securities regulators must refer a criminal prosecution to the public prosecutor's office, a similar approach to China. Under the contexts analysed in this book, it can be imagined that empowered with this function, the CSRC could fulfil its responsibilities more efficiently. Because of the nature of its work, the CSRC has more resources than the other law enforcement departments relating to securities crimes. Therefore, the reaction time at an early stage of an offence will be reduced. On the other hand, if given this function, it must be conducted in a reasonable and rational manner. Cases in China cannot be separated from the whole regulatory regime. Consideration must be given to the fact that it may increase costs, since the CSRC has to reorganize its human resources and management structure. At the least, basic training in criminal prosecution for the relevant staff must be provided. Moreover, under the current regulatory framework, the financial regulators in China, not only the CSRC, but also the China Banking Regulatory Commission and China Insurance Regulatory Commission, have their respective roles. The necessary balance should therefore be maintained between the regulators. Transparency will enable the whole of society to act as a quasi supervisor.

Another solution for efficient dealing with illicit and illegal securities transactions could be a joint task force or working group of competent departments. Organized by the relevant agencies, for instance, the Ministry of Finance, the CSRC and the Public Security Bureau, this group could use resources and staff in an economic and effective way, to handle particular cases. Under the current legal structure of China, the latest situation could be addressed in real time.

Investor protection

The primary regime for investor protection regarding information disclosure has been established in Mainland China. Currently, the law and regulations in China tend to, in general terms, providing a basic regulatory framework; more detailed rules, with detailed implementation, in particular for the compensation regime are required. Enhancing information disclosure has substantial positive impacts for investor protection. Compared with securities companies, investors, especially retail investors, are in a weak position. They may require more corporate information in order to protect themselves. From the early stages, Chinese law and regulation have given a great deal of attention to promoting an open, fair and just information disclosure regime. The continuing improvements will be beneficial to all investors.

Litigation is now a common way for investors to achieve protection. Mediation or arbitration may be a fast and effective settlement mechanism. For the courts, it may reduce the amounts of litigation; for the investors, it may reduce the cost of litigation; for the defendant, it may reduce negative impacts, which is crucially important for the listed companies. Therefore, mediation or arbitration can be seen as a 'win-win-win' approach. Furthermore, in this context, taking a broader view, mediation will promote a fair market culture in China. The market will recognize the importance of investors, particularly retail investors. Laws and regulations have empowered investors with more tools and weapons, but there is still a long way to go. The protection of investors must be based on enhanced legal remedies. In particular, civil compensation should be available to cover losses resulting from insider dealing and other malpractices relating to the misuse of information. Compared with UK and Hong Kong, the usage of securities investor protection fund in China can be further enhanced. The improvement of market transparency should be the most important target of all the reforms.

Function of the criminal law

An issue that arises at various points in the book is the role of the criminal law, although the research mainly focuses on civil law and commercial law. Should greater use of criminal law be encouraged? Should insider dealing, the issuing of false information, market manipulation be punishable with stricter criminal penalties?

Currently, to regulate insider dealing and market manipulation, the three channels, civil, administrative and criminal law, are working together as a whole to protect investors, depending on individual circumstances. However, it has been argued that securities crimes bear a low cost for the offender in China: although Amendment VI and VII to the Criminal Law of the People's Republic of China has enhanced the range of sentences available, even in the case of market manipulation, fixed-term imprisonment of not less than five years but not more than ten years is still not strict enough. Compared with the numerous victims, and considering the amounts involved in the securities crimes, further enhanced punishments should be imposed in order to protect the victims and provide greater prevention and deterrence of similar crimes and misconduct.

The road ahead

It can be seen from the study that the information disclosure regime in China has experienced reforms, which promotes it towards a healthy, just and transparent regime. However, given the new challenges from both external and internal aspects, as well as national and international aspects, how the regulatory regime can perform its full function should be examined carefully. At the same time, certain aspects of the regulatory regimes of the UK and Hong Kong can be taken as helpful examples. The evolution of these regulatory regimes may give some useful inspiration to Mainland China. Moreover, addressing international standards will be another effective approach for China.

The differences in the securities regulation, particularly the information disclosure systems in Mainland China, the UK and Hong Kong, have been illustrated in the individual chapters. The regulatory structure of China's transitional securities market has its own features and because of the differences between jurisdictions, the models of the UK and Hong Kong cannot be transplanted entirely, directly into Mainland China. The Mainland Chinese market and the UK and Hong Kong markets are rooted in different political and economic backgrounds, which lead them in different directions. The UK has a free market culture, coupled with a comprehensive common-law system; Hong Kong being a common law jurisdiction has therefore adopted a similar legal infrastructure. In contrast, the Mainland Chinese securities market evolved from a socialist market economy and socialist legal system. It has experienced a range of problems, such as ownership-related problems and reform, weak legal enforcement, and so on. These special problems mean that China still has a long way to go before it can fully develop a mature stock market of its own.

The regulatory regimes in the UK and Hong Kong have demonstrated that they are, to a certain extent, helpful models for Mainland China. One of the significant features in the UK and Hong Kong markets is an integrated and complete regulatory environment. Chinese financial regulators could learn from the efficiency of the UK and Hong Kong financial regulatory and supervisory bodies. Their highly international approach may be a helpful reference for the future development of the market in China. With the development of a market structure, the information required in Mainland China may tend to be in line with international standards. China is becoming more of a global economic power house: in particular, Shanghai is aiming to perform as an international financial centre, so corporate regulations will need to take greater account of international issues. As one of the initial steps, an internationalized financial regulatory regime could facilitate these achievements.

Suggested future research

Prevention and an early warning system should be significantly improved. Currently, the regulation and supervision of information disclosure regime is mainly established under legal controls. In fact, technical measures should be further improved in China. Monitoring, prevention and an alert system must all have strong scientific support. Introducing more suitable models on trading prices can be helpful for the stock exchanges to establish and maintain effective monitoring on the information disclosure regime. Electronic backup must be enhanced, efficient, accurate, and fast-reacting monitoring and control systems are needed.

As stated in this book, one of the major issues in the Chinese securities market is the difficulty in obtaining civil compensation. Although continuing revision of the law and regulation paid attention to this problem and many victims have been compensated, the question remains whether their losses have been compensated in full. Further, who will pay the price for market failure? It has always been argued that securities crimes are low cost in China, so what is the appropriate standard for compensation? Compared with the reimbursement of the senior managers of listed companies, what is a suitable standard for the prosecution of economic crime? All these points call for further research. Such research should be conducted in a manner that combines the special characteristics of the Chinese securities market, taking into consideration, together, the legal, financial and economic elements.

In conclusion, the way towards future efficient securities market regulation in the Chinese securities market requires cooperation from all the participants.

Notes

1 Berne Convention for the Protection of Literacy and Art Works, Article 27 (1): This Convention shall be submitted to revision with a view to the introduction of amendments designed to improve the system of the Union. Promulgation date: 9 September 1886.
2 Murray N. Rothbard (2000), America's Great Depression (5th edition), Auburn, Ala.: Ludwig von Mises Institute, p. 285.
3 Sanzhu Zhu (2009), The Role of Law and Governance in Financial market: The Case of Emerging Chinese Securities Market, working paper.
4 Communique of the Fifth Plenum of the 17th Central Committee of the Communist Party of China, 18 October 2010.
5 Homer Kripke (1970), 'The SEC, The Accountants, Some Myths and Some Realities', *New York University Law Review*, 45.

List of interviews[*]

Interview 1: May 2008, China, official
This interview focused on quantifying law-breaching behaviours in the Chinese securities market; for details, see Chapter 5.

Interview 2: May 2008, China, prosecutor 1
This interview focused on the reasons for difficulties in prosecuting securities crimes; for details, see Chapter 5.

Interview 3: May 2008, China, prosecutor 2
This interview focused on the difficulties in proving that the consequences of securities crimes are serious; for details, see Chapter 5.

Interview 4: May 2008, China, official
This interview focused on the permission system under the CSRC; for details, see Chapter 5.

Interview 5: May 2008, China, legal scholar 1
This interview focused on the power of the CSRC; for details, see Chapter 5.

Interview 6: May 2008, China, legal scholar 2
This interview focused on the standard starting point for the prosecution of securities crimes; for details, see Chapter 5.

Interview 7: September 2009, UK, official (Hong Kong)
This interview focused on how to protect investors when they suffered losses from cross-border transaction; for details, see Chapter 6.

Interview 8: January 2010, China, Chinese lawyer
This interview focused on the reason for difficulties in prosecuting perpetrators of securities crimes; for details, see Chapter 6.

Interview 9: August 2010, UK, Chinese lawyer
This interview focused on the function of financial intermediaries; for details, see Chapter 4.

Interview 10 (informal talks and discussion): during my work and fieldwork for research. The talks and discussions are not directly cited in the book due to the requirements of confidentiality and also for disciplinary reasons. However, they have enhanced my understanding on securities regulation, which is reflected in this book.

Note

* The actual names of the interviewees cannot be disclosed because the interviews were conducted on condition of anonymity.

Bibliography

Books, articles and media

Akerlof, George A., 'The Market for "Lemons": Quality Uncertainty and the Market Mechanism', (1970) *The Quarterly Journal of Economics*, 84 (3), p. 488.

Ba, Shusong, 'Ba Shusong: To Broaden the Financing Channels for Securities Companies-Understanding of "Yijian" (Ba Shusong: Tuozhan Zhengquan Gongsi Rongzi Qúdao de Zhongda Tupo- Jiedu 'Yijian' Zhiyi)', (2004) www.macrochina.com.cn/zhtg/200405250 64608.shtml, last accessed: 17 September 2012.

Bailey, Andrew, The Prudential Regulation Authority, 2012.

Bettelheim, E., Parry, H. and Rees, W., Swaps and Off-Exchange Derivatives Trading: Law and Regulation, (1996) London: FT Law & Tax.

Bhalla, A.S., 'Collapse of Barings Bank: Case of Market Failure', (1995) *Economic and Political Weekly*, 30 (13), p. 658.

Chan, E., Hui, George W.L. and Lau, Wai-kee, Listed Companies: Balance Sheet Data 1968–1988, working paper.

Chen, Gongmeng, Firth, Michael, Gao, Daniel N. and Rui, Oliver M., 'Is China's Securities Regulatory Agency a Toothless Tiger? Evidence from Enforcement Actions', (2005) *Journal of Accounting and Public Policy*, 24, pp. 451–488.

Chen, Suyi and Wang, Mingwei, 'The Characters of the FSCS and its Impact on China (Yingguo Touzizhe Baohu Jiuji Zhidu Tedian ji dui Women de Qishi)', (2007) www.sipf.com.cn/en/index.shtml, last accessed: 30 December 2009.

Cheng, Hongming, Insider Trading in China: the Case for the Chinese Securities Regulatory, (2008) *Journal of Financial Crime*, 15 (2), p. 165.

Clarke, Donald C., 'Corporate Governance in China: an Overview', (2003) working paper, http://papers.ssrn.com/sol3/papers.cfm?abstract_id=424885, last accessed: 30 December 2012.

Clarke, Donald. C., 'Legislating for a Market Economy in China', (2007) *China Quarterly*, 101, p. 567.

'Credit Ratings in China Can Be Mere Guesswork', (2004) *Wall Street Journal – Eastern Edition*, 243 (2), p. C1.

Drinkhall, Jim, 'Internet Fraud', (1997) *Journal of Financial Crime*, 4 (3), p. 242.

Fama, Eugene, 'Efficient Capital Markets: A Review of Theory and Empirical Work'. (1970), *Journal of Finance*, 25 (2), p. 383.

Fang, Liufang, Jiang, Peng and Cheng, Haixia, 'Securities Lawyers and Informstion Disclsoure of the Listed Companies (Zhengquan Lüshi yu Shangshi Gongsi Xinxi Pilu)', (2002) http://news3.xinhuanet.com/fortune/2002–08/05/content_510364.htm, last accessed: 20 May 2012.

Fu, Guangyun and Huang, Hua, 'Closure of the Mediation of Hangxiao Steel Structure Case (Hangxiao Ganggou An Tiaojie zhong Poju)', (2009) *International Finance News (Guoji Jinrong Bao)*, http://paper.people.com.cn/gjjrb/html/2009–05/21/content_257767.htm, last accessed: 14 September 2012.

Gao, Yisheng 'A Brief Discussion of the Function of Investor Protection Legislation', http://old.csrc.gov.cn/n575458/n2470788/n2470973/n2475246/2951121.html, last accessed: 14 September 2012.

Goodhart, C., Hartmann, P., Llewellyn, D., Rojas-Suarez, L. and Steven, W., Financial Regulation: Why, how and where now? (1998) Routledge: London and New York.

Hannigan, Brenda, Insider dealing (2nd edition), (1994) London: Longman.

Hawkins, David F., Brown, Barbara A. and Campbell, Walter J., Rating Industrial Bond, (1983) Financial Executives Research Foundation.

He, Junguang, 'Establishing the Information Disclosure System for the Securities Companies (Jianli Zhengquan Gongsi Xinxi Pilu Zhidu)', (2005) *Productivity Research*, 12, p. 76.

Howson, Nicholas C., 'Regulation of Companies with Publicly Listed Share Capital in the People's Republic of China', (2005) *Cornell International Law Journal*, 38 (2005), p. 242.

Hsu, Berry Fong-Chung, Arner, Douglas W., Tse, Maurice, Kwok-Sang and Johnstone, Syren, Financial Markets in Hong Kong – Law and Practice, (2006) Oxford: Oxford University Press.

Hu, Wenwei, Mai, Deguang, Lu, Wenying, Kong,Guangwen and Shao, Zhe, 'The Comparison and Analysis between the Information Disclosure System for the Listed Companies in the SSE and HKEx (Hu Gang Shangshi Gongsi Xinxi Pilu Zhidu de Bijiao Yanjiu yu Fenxi)', (2007).

Hu, Yuping, Zhu, Wenke and Yan, Jing, 'The Closure of Hangxiao Steel Structure Case, 118 Claimants will Receive about 4,000,000 RMB Compensation (HangXiao Ganggou Xujia Chenshu An Jiben Jie'an, 118 Wei Touzizhe Gonghuopei yue 400 Wanyuan)', (2009) http://hzdaily.hangzhou.com.cn/dskb/page/3/2009–05/21/34/2009052134_pdf.pdf, last accessed: 15 September 2012.

Huang, Yanjun, 'An Empirical Study on the Influencing Factors of Listed Companies of China Disobeying Information Disseminating Regulation (Zhongguo Shangshi Gongsi Xinxi Pilu Weigui Yingxiang Yinsu de Shizheng Yanjiu)', (2005) *Journal Of Shanghai Finance College*, 2, p. 53.

Jiang, Bixin, 'Multi-measures shall be Applied to Resolving the High Cost Problem of Right-defending (Pojie Gaochengben Weiquan xuyao Duoguan Qixia)', (2006) *People's Tribunal*, 10, p. 36.

Jones, William C., (ed.), Basic Principles of Civil Law in China, (1989) Armonk, New York; London: M.E. Sharpe.

Keller, Thomas, 'The Role and Function of Rating Agencies', (2005) Speech on BIS/Seminar on Developing Corporate Bond Markets in Asia.

Kennedy, Scott, 'China's Emerging Credit Rating Industry: The Official Foundations of Private Authority', (2008) *The China Quarterly*, 193, p. 65.

Kong, Qingjiang, 'International Regulation of Finance: is regionalism a preferred option to multilateralism for East Asia?' in The Regulation of International Financial Markets-Perspectives for Reform, edited by Grote, Rainer and Marauhn, Thilo, (2006) Cambridge: Cambridge University Press.

Lawyers Association of Beijing, 'Notice of Training for Lawyers', (2005) www.bmla.org.cn/bjlawyers2/news/bulletinmore.jsp, last accessed: 19 May 2012.

Lewis, Robert, 'Shareholders in Action – Causes of Action are Many but the Action are Few', (2007) *International Financial Law Review*, 53, p. 52.

Li, Lei, 'Examining the Original Sins of Chinese Capital Market from 'Huang Guangyu' Case (You 'Huang Guangyu Shijian' Kan Zhongguo Ziben Shichang Yuanzui)', (2009) *Social Outlook*, 1, p. 59.

Li, Qiguang, 'An Analysis of the Liability System of Illegal Disclosure by the Chinese Listed Companies (Woguo Shangshi Gongsi Xinxi Piu Weigui zhi Falv Zeren Tixi Yanjiu)', (2006) *Market Modernization*, 12, p. 321.

Li, Xia, 'Gang Yao: The Information Disclosure Rules for the GEB will be Adjusted and Complemented (Yao Gang: Chuangyeban Xinxi Pilu Guize jiang Jinxing Tiaozheng he Buchong)', (2009) *Financial News (Jinrong Shibao)*, www.financialnews.com.cn/zq/txt/2009–11/07/content_240089.htm, last accessed: 8 January 2013.

Li, Yuqing, 'The Strange Phenomenon of High Cost Right-defending (Gaochengben Weiquan zhi Guai Xianxiang)', (2006) *People's Tribunal*, 10, p. 33.

Liu, Baoqiang, 'Weixing Zhang: The Association of Chinese Investors is a Weapon (Zhang Weixiang: Zhengquan Touzizhe Xiehui shi Gumin Weiquan de Gongqi)', (2004) http://finance.sina.com.cn/t/20040819/1345960936.shtml, last accessed: 15 September 2012.

Liu, Chang, Zhou, Nan, Wang, Na and Bao, Wenjuan, '80 Old Photos Showing the Storms in Chinese Securities Market (80zhang Laozhaopian Zaixian Xinzhongguo Zhengquan Fengyun)', (2007) *Guangzhou Daily (Guangzhou Ribao)*, http://gzdaily.dayoo.com/html/2007–08/18/content_29455.htm, last accessed: 9 January 2013.

Liu, Mingkang, 'Basic Rules Helped China sidestep Bank Crisis', (2009) *Financial Times*.

Liu, Zhihua, 'The Problems and Possible Improvements for the Self-regulation of the Chinese Stock Exchanges (Zhongguo Zhengquan Jiaoyisuo Zilü Jianguan Tizhi de Wenti ji qi Gaijin)', (2008) *Theory Front*, 11, p. 41.

Longman Dictionary of Contemporary English (2003 edition), Harlow: Longman.

Lü, Ruhan, Securities Market (Gu Piao Shi Chang), (1994) Hong Kong: Shangwu Yin-shuguan.

Lu, Yuan, 'Yinguangxia Ear became History, Legislative and Judicial Environment of Securities Right-defending has been Improved ('Yinguangxia' Shidai cheng Lishi, Zhengquan Weiquan Lifa Sifa Huanjing Dada Gaishan)', (2009) *First Finance Daily Newspaper (Diyi Caijing Ribao)*, www.china-cbn.com/s/n/001002000/20090714/000000120523.shtml, last accessed: 15 September 2012.

Ma, Chengguang (23 October 1998), 'Securities Law to regulate the Booming Sector', *China Daily (Zhongguo Ribao)*.

Ma, Shiguang, The Efficient of China's Stock Market, (2004) Aldershot, Hants; Burlington, VT: Ashgate.

Mao, Xiaomei, Zhao, Xiaohui and Wang, Yu, 'Beware of the Foreign Company in Charge of Chinese Credit Rating Business (Jingti Jingrong Huayuquan Pangluo)', (2009) http://news.xinhuanet.com/mrdx/2009–03/04/content_10940789.htm, last accessed: 20 May 2013.

Miao, Yan, 'Central Bank: Maintaining Financial Stabilities shall Establish the Unified Supervisory Information Platform (Yanghang: Weihu Jinrong Wending ying Jianli Tongyi Jianguan Xinxi Pingtai)', (2009) www.cnstock.com/08index/2009–09/02/content_4555553.htm, last accessed: 8 January 2010.

Nan, Yan, 'In front of the Stage and behind of the Scene – the Birth of the CSRC (Zhengjianhui Dansheng de Taiqian Muhou)', (2009) *China Economic Weekly*

(Zhongguo Jingji Zhoukan), www.ceweekly.cn/Html/magazine/200992741671604345. html, last accessed: 9 January 2013.

Newman, Peter, Milgate, Murray and Eatwell, John (eds), The New Palgrave Dictionary of Money and Finance (1992) London: Macmillan Press Ltd; New York: Stockton Press.

Ng, Lilian and Wu, Fei, 'The Trading Behavior of Institutions and Individuals in Chinese Equity Markets', (2007) *Journal of Banking and Finance*, 31 (9), p. 2695.

Noyer, Christian, 'Possible Ways of Improving the Process of Rating', (2007) Speech at the Symposium on Financial Rating, organized by the Cercle France-Amériques, Paris.

Omoyele, Olu, 'Disclosure, Financial Misconduct and Listed Companies: A Critical Analysis of the UKLA's Continuing Obligation Regime', (2005) *Journal of Financial Crime*, 12 (4), p. 310.

Pang, Jiemin and Wang, Qingren, 'The Risk Management of Chinese Securities Firms during the New Emerging and Transitional Period (Xinxing jia Zhuanggui Tiaojian xia Zhongguo Zhengquan Gongsi de Fengxian Chengyin ji Jiankong)', (2003) *Economic Research Journal*, 12, p. 60.

Pennington, Robert. R., The Law of the Investment Markets, (1990) Blackwell Law.

Peston, Robert 'BBC News – Greek credit status downgraded to "junk" ', (2010) http://news.bbc.co.uk/2/hi/business/8647903.stm, last accessed: 2 September 2012.

Poon, Winnie P.H. and Chan, Kam C., 'An Empirical Examination of the Informational Content of Credit Ratings in China', (2008) *Journal of Business Research, Elsevier*, 61 (7), p. 790.

Qin, Zhonglu, 'Amendments to Criminal Law of PRC (No. 6) and Reflection on Financial Crimes Legislation (Xingfa Xiuzhengan (Liu) yu Woguo Jinrong Fanzui Lifa de Sikao)', (2007) *Journal of Jinan University(Philosophy and Social Science Edition)*, 1, p. 79.

Rider, B.A.K. and French, H.L., The Regulation of Insider Trading, (1979) London: Macmillan.

Shang, Fulin, Preface of 'Report on China's Capital Market Development', (2008) Beijing: China Financial Publishing House.

Shao, Daosheng, 'The Chinese Anti Corruption Battle in 2009 (2009 Nian de Zhongguo Fanfubai Douzheng)', (2010) *Guangming Observation (Guangming Guancha)*, http://guancha.gmw.cn/content/2010–01/06/content_1033500.htm, last accessed: 6 January 2013.

Shi, Chenxia, 'Protecting Investors in China through Multiple Regulatory Mechanisms and Effective Enforcement', (2007) *Arizona Journal of International and Comparative Law*, 24 (2), p. 477.

Sina Finance, 'Focusing on the Human Flesh Search Engine and Listed Companies (Jujiao Shangshi Gongsi Renrou Sousuo)', (2009) http://finance.sina.com.cn/stock/gsrrss/index.shtml, last accessed: 15 September 2012.

Sina Finance, 'Whether the MOS is better than F10 (Example Attached)? (Renrou Sousuo shifou Zhenbi F10 Guanyong, fu Moban)', (2009) http://finance.sina.com.cn/stock/stockaritcle/20090319/23236000288.shtml, last accessed: 15 September 2012.

Sinclair, Timothy J., 'The Infrastructure of Global Governance: Quasi-Regulatory mechanisms and the New Global Finance', (2001) *Global Governance*, 7 (4), p. 441.

Tang, Libin, 'Experimental Analysis of the Characteristics of Listed Companies Disobeying Information Dissemination Regulation (Xinxi Pilu Weigui Shangshi Gongsi Tezheng de Shizheng Fenxi)', (2004) *Statistical Research*, 5, p. 30.

Tang, Xian, 'Some Thoughts on Establishing the Information Disclosure System of

Securities Companies in China(Goujian Woguo Zhengquan Gongsi Xinxi Pilu Zhidu de Sikao)', (2006) *Reform of Economic System*, 4, p. 39.

Tian, Junrong (22 July 1998), 'Building the Bridge, Crossing the Mountain – The First Stock Company Beijing Tianqiao Department Store Company (Feijia Tiaoqiao Du Guanshan – Diyijia GufenZhi Qiye Beijing Tiaoqiao Gufen Baihuo Youxian Gongsi Xunzong)', *People's Daily (Renmin Ribao).*

Thomann, Tim, presentation in FCIB International Credit Executive's Conference, 16–18 April 2008, from 'Credit Management Best Practices and Resources for Business Success in China', (2008) *Managing Imports and Exports*, 7, p. 1.

Tian, Hongwei and Zhang, Jun, 'The Analysis of the Qaulity of the Information Disclosed by the Listed Companies (Shangshi Gongsi Xinxi Pilu Zhiliang Diaocha Fenxi)', (2010) www.cnstock.com/ssnews/2001-9-20/shiban/200109200181.htm, last accessed: 11 August 2012.

Tian, Jianying and Hu, Jianfeng, 'An Analysis of the Illegal Behaviors of the Chinese Listed Companies (Woguo Shangshi Gongsi Weigui Weifa Xianxiang Tanxi)', (2003) *China Zhejiang Academic Journal*, 4, p. 179.

Tong, Xiaohu, Financial Services in China, (2005) Singapore: China Knowledge Press Private Limited.

'Vice-president of SPN Li Guoguang's Answers about the The Notice of the Supreme People's Court on Relevant Issues of Filing of Civil Tort Dispute Cases Arising From False Statement on the Securities Market (Zuigao Renmin Fayuan Fuyuanzhang Li Guoguang jiu Zuigao Renmin Fayuan guanyu Shouli Zhengquan Shichang yin Xujia Chenshu Yinfa de Minshi Qingquan Jiufen Anjian youguan Wenti de Tongzhi)', (2002).

Walter, Carl E. and Howie, Fraser J.T., Privatizing China: The Stock Markets and Their Role in Corporate Reform, (2003) Singapore: John Wiley and Sons, IX.

Wang, Junwei, 'Analysis of Chinese Listed Companies' Violations based on Incomplete and Non-cooperate Game (Jiyu bu Wangquan Feihezuo Boyi de Shangshi Gongsi Weigui Xingwei Fenxi)', (2006) *Finance and Trade Research*, 6, p. 94.

Wang, Liming, 'The Impacts of the Property Law on the Chinese Securities Market (Lun Wuqunfa dui Woguo Zhengquan Shichang de Yingxiang)', (2009) www.yadian.cc/paper/63734/, last visited: 21 March 2013.

Wang, Lu, 'SSE Takes Seven Measures to Crack down on Insider Dealing (Shangjiaosuo Caiqu Qixiang Cuoshi Yanda Neimu Jiaoyi)', (2010) *Shanghai Securities News* (Shanghai Zhengquan Bao), English version is available at: www.sse.com.cn/sseportal/en/home/home.shtml, last accessed: 27 August 2012.

Wang, Xiaoguo, 'Investor Protection is Facing the Challenge of Systemic Upgrading (Touzizhe Quanyi Baohu Mianlin Zhidu Shengji Tiaozhan)', (2009) *Shanghai Securities News (Shanghai Zhengquan Bao)*, http://cnstock.xinhuanet.com/paper_new/html/2009–03/18/content_67647226.htm, last accessed 14 September 2012.

Wang, Yue, 'Officials' Sword of Damocles (Guanyuan de Damokelisi Jian)', (2009) *Southern Motropolis Weekly (Nandu Zhoukan)*, 334, http://nbweekly.oeeee.com/Print/Article/8221_0.shtml, last accessed: 16 September 2012.

Wei, Xianzhou, 'Who Can be a Securities Lawyer? (Shuineng Shenren Zhengquan Falü Yewu)', (2003) *The Journal of Chinese Lawyer*, 6, p. 20.

White, Lawrence J, 'The Credit Rating Industry: An Industrial Organization Analysis', paper presented at the Conference on 'The Role of Credit Reporting Systems in the International Economy', The World Bank, Washington, D.C., 1–2 March 2001.

Wu, Jie, 'Listed Companies shall be more able to Stand up for the Human Flesh Search

Engine (Shangshi Gongsi Gengying Jingdeqi Renrou Sousuo)', (2009) http://finance.
sina.com.cn/stock/stocktalk/20090323/07246009494.shtml, last accessed: 15 September 2012.

www.secutimes.com (Zhengquan Shibao, Shibao Zaixian), Transcript from the Video: Investor Protection Series (5), (2009) www.secutimes.com/generalSubject.do? method=getShow&subjectId=61, last accessed: 15 September 2012.

Xie, Wenlin, 'Zhou Zhengqin: the Whole Story of 5 19 (Zhou Zhengqin: 5 19 Hangqing Shimo)', (2008) *Chinese Securities Journal (Zhongguo Zhengquanbao)*.

Xinhua, 'South China tiger photos are fake: provincial Authorities', (2008) *China Daily*, www.chinadaily.com.cn/china/2008–06/29/content_6803353.htm, last accessed: 15 September 2012.

Xu, Jian, 'The Significant Issues in the Revising of Chinese Securities Law (Woguo Zhengquanfa Xiugai de Ruogan Zhongda Wenti)', in *The Legal Frontier of the Chinese Capital Market (Zhongguo Ziben Shichang Qianyan)*, ed. Guo, Feng, (2007) Beijing: China Intellectual Property Publishing House.

Yeung, Wai Ho, 'Non-tradable Share Reform in China: A Review of Progress', (2009) *Company Lawyer*, 30 (11), pp. 340–346.

You, Wenli, Luo, Yinglin, 'A Research on the Supervisory Law System over Information Disclosure of Listed Companies in Chinese Stock Exchanges (Woguo Zhengquan Jiaoyisuo dui Shangshi Gongsi Xinxi Pilu Jianguan de Falü Zhidu Yanjiu)', (2009) *Humanities and Social Sciences Journal of Hainan University*, 27 (5), p. 509.

Yu, Ning, 'The Arrest of Kan Zhidong, Liu Dong and Guo Yuanxian (Kan Zhidong, Liu Dong, Guo Yuanxian Beibu)', (2006) *Caijing*, 5.

Yu, Ning,' Nanfang Securities Case: the Tiger's Head but a Snake's Tail (Nanfang Zhengquan Hutou Shewei)', (2007) *Caijing*, 10.

Yu, Weibin, 'The Bankruptcy of The NewChina Securities Co., Ltd (Jiekai Xinhua Zhengquan Cusi de Neimu)', (2004) *The Banker*, 2, p. 126.

Zhan, Zhongle and Li, Fengying, 'Securities Supervision and Judicial Review (in China)', (2004) 13 Pacific Rim Law and Policy Journal 329, translated by Inseon Paik.

Zhang, Lishang, Information Disclosure and Analysis of the Listed Companies (Shangshi Gongsi Xinxi Pilu yu Fenxi), (2005) Chengdu: Southwestern University of Finance and Economic Press.

Zhang, Yuanyuan, 'Investors Support Human Flesh Search Engine, Institutions Call on Regulation (Gumin Liting Renrou Sousuo, Jigou Huyu Guifan)', (2009) *www. secutimes. com (Zhengquan Shibao)*, www.p5w.net/today/200903/t2226140.htm, last accessed: 15 September 2012.

Zhang, Guojun, 'Establishing and Improving the Information Disclosure of Securities Companies (Zhengquan Gongsi Xinxi Pilu Zhidu de Jianli yu Wanshan)', (2006) *Financial Accounting*, 4, p. 52.

Zhao, Wanyi, Securities Law (Zhengquan Fa), (2006) Beijing: Legal Publishing House.

Zhou, Chong, 'Six Shortages of Rating System in the Chinese Bond Market (Woguo Zhaiquan Xinyong Pingji Zhidu Cunzai Liuda Buzu)', (2007) *Shang Hai Securities News* www.cnstock.com/paper_new/html/2007–03/20/content_52402983.htm, last accessed: 20 May 2013.

Zhou, Xiaochuan, 'China's Corporate Bond Market Development: Lessons Learned', based on the remarks made at the BIS/PBC seminar on 'Developing Corporate Bond Markets in Asia' held in Kunming, China, 17–18 November 2005. www.bis.org/publ/bppdf/bispap26b.pdf, last accessed: 20 May 2013.

Zhou, Zhengqing, Securities Knowledge Handbook (Zhengquan Zhishi Duben), www.

csrc.gov.cn/n575458/n870586/n1335340/n8200134/10644047.html, last accessed: 17 September 2012.

Zhu, Sanzhu, Securities Resolution in China, (2007) Aldershot, Hants: Ashgate.

Zhu, Sanzhu, The Role of Law and Governance in Financial market: The Case of Emerging Chinese Securities Market, (2009) working paper.

Reports and articles of government agencies, financial regulators, companies and international organizations

Allen and Overy Global Survey, The Future Direction of Global Financial Regulation, 2008.

Bond Information Department of China Government Securities Deposit and Trust Corporation, Annual Review of China's Bond Market, 2008.

Bond Information Department of China Government Securities Deposit and Trust Corporation, Annual Review of China's Bond Market, 2011.

Central Committee of Communist Party of China, Decision of Central Committee of CPC on Several Issues Concerning the Establishing the Socialist Market Economy Structure, 1993.

City of London, The Global Financial Centres Index, 2009.

City of London, The Global Financial Centres Index, 2012.

China Securities Association and China Securities Investor Protection Fund Companies Limited, Survey of Investors of Chinese Securities Market – Analysis Report, 2007.

China Securities Depository and Clearing Corporation Limited, China Securities Registration and Settlement Statistical Yearbook 2011.

China Securities Investor Protection Fund Companies Limited, Investors Confidence Index, 2009.

China Securities Investor Protection Fund Companies Limited, 'Mr. Chen Gongyan: Securities Investor Protection in the Context of Financial Crisis', (2009) www.sipf.com.cn/en/newsupdate/updates/11/4954.shtml, last accessed: 27 December 2012.

China Securities Investor Protection Fund Companies Limited, Monthly Statistical Report of China Securities Investor Protection Fund (November 2012).

China Securities Regulatory Commission, 'Why Need to Establish an Information Sharing System between Financial Regulators', http://hubei.csrc.gov.cn/n575458/n870586/n1335340/n8200134/10642077.html, last accessed: 25 August 2012.

China Securities Regulatory Commission, The CSRC Held the 2nd Conference of the Securities and Futures Regulatory System on Petition Method, (2007) http://old.csrc.gov.cn/n575458/n575667/n818795/4217682.html, last accessed: 15 September 2012.

China Securities Regulatory Commission, 'Q&A by CSRC Spokesman on Hot Issue', 2008.

China Securities Regulatory Commission, China Capital Markets Development Report, (2008) Beijing: China Financial Publishing House.

China Securities Regulatory Commission, 'The Challenges Facing China's Capital Markets', in China Capital Markets Development Report, (2008) Beijing: China Financial Publishing House.

China Securities Regulatory Commission, 'CSRC is Investigating ST Weida's Four Law-breaking Behaviours (Zhengjianhui Li'an Checha STWeida Sizong Zui)', (2008) www.csrc.gov.cn/n575458/n870654/n4243666/10104653.html, last accessed: 24 August 2012.

China Securities Regulatory Commission, 'CSRC News Spokesman Answers Reporters' Questions on promulgating the 'Interim Provisions on Appropriate Management of Investors on the Growth Enterprise Board Market (Draft for Comment)' and Relevant Supporting Documents', (2009) www.csrc.gov.cn/pub/csrc_en/newsfacts/release/200908/t20090822_121166.htm, last accessed: 9 January 2013.

China Securities Regulatory Commission, 'International Conference of 'The Reforming of Securities Administrative Punishment System and Investor Protection' has been held in Beijing ('Zhengquan Xingzheng Chufa Tizhi Gaige he Touzizhe Baohu' Guoji Yantanhui zai Jing Zhaokai)', (2010) www.csrc.gov.cn/pub/newsite/bgt/xwdd/201005/t20100519_180696.htm, last accessed: 10 June 2013.

China Securities Regulatory Commission, China Securities and Future Statics 2012.

China Securities Regulatory Commission, 'The Detective Ability for the Securities Crime has been Enhanced', (20 December 2012).

China Securities Regulatory Commission, 'The CSRC Reduced the Ratio for SIPF Payment Requirement', (19 April 2013).

European Commission (2 June 2010), 'Commission Proposes Improved EU Supervision of Credit Rating Agencies and Launches Debate on Corporate Governance in Financial Institutions', http://europa.eu/rapid/press-release_IP-10-656_en.htm?locale=en, last accessed: 20 May 2013.

European Parliament News (16 January 2013), 'Tougher Credit Rating Rules Confirmed by Parliament's Vote', www.europarl.europa.eu/news/en/pressroom/content/20130114 IPR05310/html/Tougher-credit-rating-rules-confirmed-by-Parliament%27s-vote, last accessed: 20 may 2013.

FCA, Business Plan 2013/14.

Financial Services Authority, Building the New Regulator: Progress Report 1, 2000.

Financial Services Authority, The FSA's Risk-Based Approach – A Guide for Non-executive Directors, 2006.

Financial Services Authority, Good and Poor Practices in Key Features Documents, 2007.

Fitch, Inside the Rating-What Credit Ratings Mean, 2007.

G20, Declaration on Summit on Financial Markets and the World Economy, 2008.

Government Report in 10th National People's Congress, 2003.

Hong Kong Exchanges and Clearing Limited, 'Exposure Paper on the Abolition of Requirement for Main Board Issuers to Publish Paid Announcements in Newspapers and Related Matters', 2005.

Hong Kong Exchanges and Clearing Limited, 'Exposure Conclusion – Abolition of Requirement for Main Board Issuers to Publish Paid Announcements in Newspapers and Related Matters', 2006.

Hong Kong Exchanges and Clearing Limited, 'Submitting a Document for Publication through e-Submission – Quick Reference Guide', Version 1.1.

Hong Kong Monetary Authority, Report of the Hong Kong Monetary Authority on Issues Concerning the Distribution of Structured Products connected to Lehman Group Companies, 2008.

International Monetary Fund, People's Republic of China – Hong Kong Special Administrative Region: 2007 Article IV Consultation – Staff Report; and Public Information Notice on the Executive Board Discussion, IMF Country Report No. 08/44, 2008.

International Organization of Securities Commissions, Final Report From the Co-Chairman of the May 1995 Windsor Meeting to the Technical Committee of IOSCO, 1995.

SAC, 'SAC Released Operating Statistics of Securities Companies of the Year 2012', www.sac.net.cn/en/update/201302/t20130206_61584.html, last accessed: 30 May 2013.

Securities and Futures Commission, Introducing the SFC, 2000.

Securities and Futures Commission, Retail Investor Survey 2003.

Securities and Futures Commission, 2011–2012 Annual Report.

Shanghai Stock Exchange, Guidance on the Block Trading of Stock Trading without Sales Limit, 2008.

Shenzhen Stock Exchange, 'Taking Multi-measures, the SZSE Controls the Illegal Shares Reducing', (2008) www.szse.cn/main/aboutus/bsyw/2008050912487.shtml, last accessed: 24 August 2012.

Shenzhen Stock Exchange, 'Clear Realizing the Risks of Human Flesh Search Engine (Qingxing Renshi Renrou Sousuo de Juda Fengxian)', (2009) www.szse.cn/main/aboutus/bsyw/2009032039739454.shtml, last accessed: 15 September 2012.

Shenzhen Stock Exchange Self-regulation Working Report 2009 (Shenzhen Zhengquan Jiaoyisuo 2009 Zilü Jianguan Gongzuo Baogao).

Shenzhen Stock Exchange, 'About ChiNext', www.szse.cn/main/en/ChiNext/aboutchinext/, last accessed: 5 January 2013.

Technical Committee of the International Organization of Securities Commissions: Final Report of International Disclosure Principles for Cross-border Offerings and Listings of Debt Securities by Foreign Issuers, 2007.

Xinhua Finance and Shanghai Far East Credit Ratings Co., Ltd, Xinhua Far East China Ratings – Pioneering Undertaking to Rank Credit Risks of Enterprises in China, 2003.

United States Securities and Exchange Commission, SEC Examinations Find Shortcomings in Credit Rating Agencies' Practices and Disclosure to Investors, (2008) www.sec.gov/news/press/2008/2008-135.htm, last accessed 20 May 2013.

Websites

China

Beida Lawinfochina, www.lawinfochina.com/
China Banking Regulatory Commission, www.cbrc.gov.cn/english/home/jsp/index.jsp/
China Government Securities Depository Trust Clearing Co., Ltd, www.chinabond.com.cn/Site/cb/en/
China Securities Depository and Clearing Corporation Limited, www.chinaclear.cn/
China Securities Regulatory Commission, www.csrc.gov.cn/pub/newsite/
iSinoLaw, www.isinolaw.com/
Lawyers Association of Beijing, www.bmla.org.cn/
Lawyers Association of China, www.acla.org.cn/
Ministry of Finance, www.mof.gov.cn/
National Bureau of Statistic of China, www.stats.gov.cn/
National Development and Reform Commission, http://en.ndrc.gov.cn/
People's Bank of China, www.pbc.gov.cn/
Securities Investors Protection Fund Corporation, www.sipf.com.cn/index.shtml/
Shanghai Feilo Acoustics Co., Ltd www.facs.com.cn/index.php
Shanghai Stock Exchange, www.sse.com.cn/sseportal/en/home/home.shtml/
Shenzhen Stock Exchange, www.szse.cn/
State Administration of Foreign Exchange, www.safe.gov.cn/model_safe/index.html/

EU

European Commission, http://ec.europa.eu/

UK

Bank of England, www.bankofengland.co.uk/Pages/home.aspx
Financial Conduct Authority, www.fca.org.uk/
Financial Services Authority, www.fsa.gov.uk/
Financial Services Compensation Scheme, www.fscs.org.uk/
London Stock Exchange, www.londonstockexchange.com/home/homepage.htm/

Hong Kong

Hong Kong Exchanges and Clearing Limited, www.hkex.com.hk/eng/index.htm/
Hong Kong Monetary Authority, www.info.gov.hk/hkma/
Investor Compensation Company Limited, www.hkicc.org.hk/
Securities and Futures Commission Hong Kong, www.sfc.hk/sfc/html/EN/

US

Securities and Exchange Commission, www.sec.gov/

International

G20, www.g20.org/index.aspx/
International Accounting Standards Board, www.ifrs.org/Home.htm/
International Organization on Securities Commissions, www.iosco.org/
Organization for Economic Cooperation and Development, www.oecd.org/home/0,2987,
   en_2649_201185_1_1_1_1_1,00.html/
United Nations Conference on Trade and Development, www.unctad.org/Templates/
   Startpage.asp?intItemID=2531

Companies

BOC International (China) Ltd, www.bocichina.com/boci/pagestatic/index/index.html
China Chen Xin International, www.ccxi.com.cn/
CITIC Group, www.citic.com/wps/portal/encitic
Fitch, www.fitchratings.com/index_fitchratings.cfm
Haier Group, www.haier.cn/
Hongta Group, www.hongta.com/model_ht/index.jsp
Ping An Group, www.pingan.com/homepage/index.jsp
ShenZhen Development Bank, www.sdb.com.cn/website/page
State Development and Investment Corporation, www.sdic.com.cn/cn/index.htm

Index